T3-BNW-606

PROCEDURES FOR INSTRUCTIONAL SYSTEMS DEVELOPMENT

THE EDUCATIONAL TECHNOLOGY SERIES

Edited by

Harold F. O'Neil, Jr.

U.S. Army Research Institute for
the Behavioral and Social Sciences
Alexandria, Virginia

Harold F. O'Neil, Jr. (Ed.) Learning Strategies

Harold F. O'Neil, Jr. (Ed.) Issues in Instructional Systems Development

Harold F. O'Neil, Jr. (Ed.) Procedures for Instructional Systems
Development

In preparation

Harold F. O'Neil, Jr. and Charles D. Spielberger (Eds.) Learning
Strategies: Issues and Procedures

PROCEDURES FOR INSTRUCTIONAL SYSTEMS DEVELOPMENT

Edited by

HAROLD F. O'NEIL, JR.

U.S. Army Research Institute
for the Behavioral and Social Sciences
Alexandria, Virginia

ACADEMIC PRESS   New York   San Francisco   London   1979

A Subsidiary of Harcourt Brace Jovanovich, Publishers

105117

COPYRIGHT © 1979, BY ACADEMIC PRESS, INC.
ALL RIGHTS RESERVED.
NO PART OF THIS PUBLICATION MAY BE REPRODUCED OR
TRANSMITTED IN ANY FORM OR BY ANY MEANS, ELECTRONIC
OR MECHANICAL, INCLUDING PHOTOCOPY, RECORDING, OR ANY
INFORMATION STORAGE AND RETRIEVAL SYSTEM, WITHOUT
PERMISSION IN WRITING FROM THE PUBLISHER.

ACADEMIC PRESS, INC.
111 Fifth Avenue, New York, New York 10003

United Kingdom Edition published by
ACADEMIC PRESS, INC. (LONDON) LTD.
24/28 Oval Road, London NW1 7DX

Library of Congress Cataloging in Publication Data
Main entry under title:

Procedures for instructional systems development.

(The Educational Technology series)
Includes bibliographies.
  1. Educational tests and measurements––Data
processing––Addresses, essays, lectures. 2. Computer–assisted instruction––Addresses, essays,
lectures. I. O'Neil, Harold F.
LB3051.P64   371.2'6   79–12002
ISBN 0–12–526660–X

PRINTED IN THE UNITED STATES OF AMERICA

79 80 81 82   9 8 7 6 5 4 3 2 1

Contents

v

105117

List of Contributors

Numbers in parentheses indicate the pages on which the authors' contributions begin.

GARY D. BORICH (205), Instructional Systems Laboratory, College of Education, University of Texas at Austin, Austin, Texas 78712

JOHN SEELY BROWN (273), Xerox Parc, 3333 Coyote Hill Road, Palo Alto, California 94304

RICHARD R. BURTON (273), Xerox Parc, 3333 Coyote Hill Road, Palo Alto, California 94304

JANE CLOSE CONOLEY (95), Psychology Department, Syracuse University, Syracuse, New York 13210

GERALD W. FAUST (1, 165), Courseware, Inc., 10075 Carroll Canyon Road, San Diego, California 92131

DONALD R. GENTNER (253), Center for Human Information Processing, University of California, San Diego, La Jolla, California 92093

M. DAVID MERRILL* (165), Instructional Science Department, Brigham Young University, Provo, Utah 84602

A. F. O'NEAL (1), Courseware, Inc., 10075 Carroll Canyon Road, San Diego, California 92131

H. L. O'NEAL (1), Courseware, Inc., 10075 Carroll Canyon Road, San Diego, California 92131

HAROLD F. O'NEIL, JR. (95), U.S. Army Research Institute for the Behavioral and Social Sciences, 5001 Eisenhower Avenue, Alexandria, Virginia 22333

* Present address: Research Division, Courseware, Inc., Brigham Young University, Provo, Utah 84602.

CHARLES M. REIGELUTH† (165), David O. McKay Institute, Brigham Young University, Provo, Utah 84602

GALE ROID (67), Teaching Research Division, Oregon State System of Higher Education, Monmouth, Oregon 97361

ROBERT J. SEIDEL (233), Human Resources Research Organization, 300 North Washington Street, Alexandria, Virginia 22314

RUSSEL E. SCHULZ (39), Human Resources Research Organization, 300 North Washington Street, Alexandria, Virginia 22314

HAROLD WAGNER (233), Human Resources Research Organization, 300 North Washington Street, Alexandria, Virginia 22314

DAVID J. WEISS (129), Department of Psychology, University of Minnesota, Minneapolis, Minnesota 55455

† Present address: Instructional Technology, Syracuse University, Syracuse, New York 13210.

Preface[1]

It is difficult to bring individuals who design and develop systems employing individualized instruction to the level of competence needed to produce good curriculum materials in a reasonable time at an acceptable cost. Similar difficulties have been especially noted for systems employing computer-based instruction. This problem is especially acute in any environment characterized by high turnover of personnel.

The field of instructional systems development provides a promising means for improvement in this domain. As in other emerging fields, the instructional systems development literature reveals little agreement on basic terms. Our model consists of five phases: analysis, design, development, implementation, and control. Details of these phases can be found in Chapter 2.

This book builds on the intellectual foundation of instructional systems development and provides some empirical data regarding the effectiveness of various procedures to accomplish selected aspects of our model. The various chapters have been grouped to indicate their primary focus with respect to instructional systems development. Thus, Chapters 1–4 focus on procedures for developing tests and instruction; Chapters 5–8 focus on procedures for evaluation; and Chapters 9–10 focus on procedures for intelligent computer-assisted instruction systems. These last two chapters

[1] The views and conclusions contained in this preface and the rest of the volume are those of the respective authors and should not be interpreted as necessarily representing the official policies, either expressed or implied by the Defense Advanced Research Projects Agency, the U.S. Army Research Institute for the Behavioral and Social Sciences, or the U.S. government.

reflect seminal ideas and thus tend to have less empirical support. However, both chapters reflect procedures in a domain that is a technological alternative to traditional instructional systems development.

This book summarizes our research to date and presents our collective ideas of where research in instructional systems development should be directed. It is both a preliminary progress report on the procedures we have developed and a means of sharing our ideas concerning ways of accomplishing our goals. We feel that our intellectual community consists of advanced students and professionals in the fields represented by the chapters. We feel that our work will be of interest and use not only to our colleagues in these disciplines but also to developers of instructional systems in education, industry, and the military.

This book could not have come into existence without the help and encouragement of many people. In particular, the intellectual and administrative support of Robert Young and Dawn Parnell formerly of the Defense Advanced Research Projects Agency; Robert Seidel, Harold Wagner, and Carol Hargan of the Human Resources Research Organization; and Joseph Zeidner of the U.S. Army Research Institute for the Behavioral and Social Sciences. Finally, I acknowledge my appreciation for the help and moral support I have received from the staff of Academic Press.

Harold F. O'Neil, Jr.

1

An Author Training Course[1]

H. L. O'NEAL, G. W. FAUST, and
A. F. O'NEAL

Historically, instructional development has tended to be an artistic endeavor carried out in a cottage industry setting (Molnar, 1971). All aspects of development responsibility including analysis, design, development, revision, and in many cases production and evaluation were concentrated in the individual instructional developer. The developer's approach to each instructional problem tended to be ad hoc and idiosyncratic. The developer himself, more often than not, had little if any formal preparation in instructional science.

This model of the Renaissance man as instructional artist, solving each instructional problem as it arose with combination of experience, intuition, and insight, began to be suspect as instructional development activities grew larger and more complex and as the consequences of inadequate training grew more and more expensive. As people searched for better and more systematic ways to handle instructional problems, several important tools, including task analysis, behavioral objectives, and measurement and evaluation methods, began to emerge. To protect against the consequences of poor training, more reliance was placed on empirical methods, which involved repeated tryout and revision of materials (Mer-

[1] The work reported in this chapter was supported in part by the Defense Advanced Research Projects Agency, contract number MDA 903-76-C-0216. Views and conclusions contained in this document are those of the authors and should not be interpreted as necessarily representing the official policies, either expressed or implied, of the Defense Advanced Research Projects Agency or of the United States Government.

PROCEDURES FOR INSTRUCTIONAL
SYSTEMS DEVELOPMENT

1

Copyright © 1979 by Academic Press, Inc.
All rights of reproduction in any form reserved.
ISBN 0-12-526660-X

rill & Boutwell, 1973). Although these methods were expensive and time-consuming, they did at least help pinpoint inadequate instructional segments and make possible the improvements of instructional effectiveness. However, once inadequate segments were identified, the job of revision of instructional materials was generally still left to the Renaissance man. His activities were still basically artistic in nature, his solutions to instructional problems were still idiosyncratic, and the procedures that he might apply tended to be based on his own experience and were not generalizable to other developers.

There is currently a growing trend in military, industrial, and academic circles away from this artistic approach to development, and toward the rigorous application of theory- and research-based models in an instructional engineering approach to development of instructional programs. This class of procedures has been variously known as instructional systems design or development (ISD), as a systems approach to training (SAT), or by other such designations. In general, the procedures are characterized by well-defined analysis, design, implementation, and evaluation activities. Unfortunately, they are better defined in terms of general outcomes than in terms of specific methods, and with very few exceptions, they are even less well defined in terms of the "authoring" activities that take place during the development phase.

Given the broad base of ISD applications now ongoing and the range of experience of personnel involved in these applications, there is a critical need for effective, individualized training on how to develop instructional materials. Although broadly documented, existing ISD models tend to be general and broad-based in their approach to design considerations and they tend to dwell primarily on format and technical aspects of development at the expense of specific instructional concerns. In very few cases do these models comprise the type of specific prescriptive "how to" guide needed in many development activities. This chapter describes an effort funded under a Defense Advanced Research Projects Agency (DARPA) contract to develop an author training course (ATC) to address these perceived needs.

In the spring of 1976 under this contract, a needs analysis of a range of Department of Defense ISD efforts was undertaken to establish more clearly the specific areas of concern identified by ISD practitioners (Bunderson, 1977). In general, the findings of this study verified the perceptions of a growing number of ISD observers and practitioners. Briefly, there is a need for (a) more prescriptive and detailed ISD procedures; (b) more efficient and effective author training; and (c) more consistency, accountability, and quality control in the ISD process.

THE NEED FOR WELL-DEFINED,
PRESCRIPTIVE ISD PROCEDURES

There is increasing recognition of the fact that current ISD models are deficient in their level of specificity in terms of well-defined procedures for performing ISD tasks. That is, the models tend to be descriptive rather than prescriptive. They tell what activities should be done but do not adequately specify the exact procedures for carrying out the activities. For this reason, Bunderson (1977) found that many so-called systematic approaches to training development were somewhat superficial in the degree of systematization that was employed. That is, though the general sequence and nature of ISD activities that were undertaken reflected generally accepted ISD practice, the specific procedures and techniques utilized to carry out those activities were still essentially ad hoc, idiosyncratic, and undefined. In other words, beneath the thin veneer of a systematic approach the careful observer finds that much ISD activity exhibits the unfortunate characteristics of Molnar's (1971) "cottage industry" and is indeed more properly described as an "artistic" rather than instructional engineering activity (Bunderson & Faust, 1976; Faust & O'Neal, 1977b).

One obvious effect of this lack of specificity is that the resulting instructional output often requires far too long to produce and is prohibitively expensive. Rather than continuing to approach each instructional development requirement as a new and unique problem in instructional design for which specialized ad hoc solutions must be created, instructional developers need to adopt well-defined, detailed, and prescriptive procedures for instructional design and development that would apply to broad classes of instructional design and development that could be consistently implemented by a wide range of ISD practitioners (Aagard & Braby, 1976; Bunderson, 1972; Faust & O'Neal, 1977a; Lipson, 1973; Logan, 1976; O'Neal, 1977a; O'Neal, 1977; Simonsen & Renshaw, 1974; Van Pelt & Rich, 1975).

THE NEED FOR MORE EFFICIENT AND
COST-EFFECTIVE AUTHOR TRAINING

There is a critical need within the Department of Defense and other instructional development environments to provide efficient, effective author training. Montmerlo (1975) found that existing ISD models did not allow the layperson to be as successful as the expert. Though on the surface this is hardly a startling finding, Montmerlo's investigations do show that there is a little positive effect of the guidance given by existing documentation. Therefore, there would seem to be a need for considerable training of ISD personnel to achieve more effective results. Bunderson (1977) found that in typical ISD environments a major portion of the training given to authors of instructional materials consisted of a sort of apprenticeship program. Typically, new people introduced to the ISD activity would receive a few weeks' training from available programmed instruction courses and would then serve an average of 6 months in apprenticeships, after which they were considered productive when under the supervision of a more experienced team member. When these persons had been on the job for at least a year they in turn would be used to supervise others' training. This is a very expensive type of apprenticeship and requires an incredibly long time to generate a productive staff.

The apprenticeship approach to ISD training has been widely adopted within the Department of Defense (DOD), primarily because specific ISD procedures are poorly detailed and because it is difficult and time-consuming to transfer (or encourage the development of) "artistic" skills. The problems of such an approach are compounded by two other problems:

1. Most ISD programs involve large, complex instructional development efforts that produce materials for a variety of instructional formats and delivery systems.
2. There is generally a high rate of turnover among Defense ISD personnel.

Development of materials for each format and delivery system requires its own type of expertise and therefore puts an additional load on an apprenticeship system. This load results in an extension of the apprenticeship period or a reduction in the flexibility of use for a given individual. That is, either we teach each person to handle all media or we allow individuals to work with only one medium. Unfortunately, the development of format- or media-specific staffs is generally an impractical alternative, since many of the people used on such projects are chosen for their subject matter expertise and each subject matter area is likely to be taught best using a variety of media. Most ISD within DOD is currently taking place in conjunction with large-scale development activities involving multimedia presentation formats and often involving differentiated staffs where apprenticeship-type training becomes even more difficult.

Now combine the use of a long apprenticeship program with another common facet of Defense organizations—a high rate of turnover—and the development and maintenance of an effective ISD staff is even more unlikely. Rickertson, Schulz, and Wright (1970) noted that within some curriculum development groups high rates of personnel turnover have resulted in a general reduction of systems engineering program productivity. Theirs is not an isolated finding. The rapid turnover of personnel in Department of Defense training development activities is more the rule than the exception. In extreme cases effects such as those reported by O'Neal (1975) on the S-3A ISD activity are observed in which some ISD personnel may be available for as short a total time period as one day, and where for long periods of time (6 months) the average duration of personnel assignments even on a part-time basis lasted only 3 weeks from introduction of the personnel to the activity to the time when they were reassigned. It should be obvious that in this type of environment the ISD program manager may find himself in a constant training mode resulting in extremely low productivity and a consequent high cost for training materials.

It seems clear that it would be very useful to have an ISD training program that would provide a procedural, prescriptive, and detailed "how to do it" model and would provide rapid access of usable skills for newly assigned ISD personnel.

THE NEED FOR BETTER CONSISTENCY, ACCOUNTABILITY, AND QUALITY CONTROL

There is a need to provide procedures and techniques within the Department of Defense that will provide more consistency in quality and effectiveness of instructional materials across authors and authoring sites.

At present there is very little consistency in instructional approach, the amount of time or money it takes to develop instructional materials (even within a given medium), or the general quality or effectiveness of the final product. This lack of consistency makes it extremely difficult to plan or budget adequately for ISD programs. It makes it difficult to interchange staff members, and the loss of a productive member of the staff can have even more disastrous consequences than might normally be expected. The inconsistencies in approach and quality are apparent to both the student and to persons in high places. They readily notice differences and seem to be indelibly imprinted with the scars of poor lessons or programs. Even if the lessons in a given program are effective, if they vary greatly in approach, format, and other design factors, the unevenness of the overall program can have a distracting effect on the students. The negative effects of this distraction can be compounded when students have to pore over several pages of new and different instructions before each lesson.

The degree of artistry or inconsistency of approach used in an ISD project is also directly related to the difficulty of implementing an effective quality-control system and therefore inversely related to the accountability of members of the instructional development team. Quality-control systems must be artistic, idiosyncratic, and heavily subjective if the approach to instructional development contains these same characteristics. The less systematic the authoring approach, the more dependent the evaluator is upon "looking at the final masterpiece before making any judgments." There are few intermediate products, few checkpoints within the design and development phases of a poorly structured ISD program. There may be both objectives and finished materials, but there are generally few intermediate, observable, and readily evaluated elements between them. In such cases it is easy to focus on flashy or extremely salient characteristics of the materials and in the process overlook critical errors. As quality control becomes more subjective and more focused on one document (e.g., the final product), there is generally more room for argument concerning any evaluation, and the accountability of the instructional developer is reduced.

The need for more systematic, objective, and proceduralized approaches to ISD and the potential benefits in terms of consistency, quality control, and accountability have been well documented (Aagard & Braby, 1976; Bunderson, 1977; Lipson, 1973; Van Pelt & Rich, 1975). With a carefully defined set of procedures for completing and integrating each step of the ISD process, we could achieve several much-needed advantages. First, instructional materials would become more consistent in structure and quality. Second, there would be identifiable intermediate products designed to have observable, readily evaluated characteristics. This would in turn make it possible to employ a quality-control system that is more objective and more responsive to the author (e.g., it would provide more immediate feedback on his work and be able to identify problems earlier). Finally, it would also produce more accountability. Authors would have more specific guidance as to what is expected of them. The system itself would allow for more precise data collection (e.g., time and cost factors related to the development of intermediate products). The collection of such data would itself be likely to increase accountability. It would allow the program manager to maintain a clear audit trail with respect to persons applied to tasks, time and cost per task, etc. In general, it would provide a basis from which a better accounting could be made of both product output and process used. It would also allow program managers to pinpoint specific staff members needing help on specific tasks, thus allowing a more advantageous use of training and supervisory time.

The clear implication of the perceived needs outlined previously is that for ISD, there is a strong rationale for defining and managing procedures and techniques at a much finer level of detail. There is also a strong rationale for developing an efficient training program and set of practical job aids for ISD team members that will teach the much-needed procedures and techniques. The author training course described in this chapter and its companion, the author management system (see O'Neal & O'Neal, 1979), were developed in an attempt to fill at least part of these needs.

THE AUTHOR TRAINING COURSE

In April of 1976, Courseware, Inc. under contract to the Defense Advanced Research Projects Agency began the development of an author training course that would teach a previously developed set of detailed and prescriptive procedures and specifications for ISD activities. This same project also involved the production of a computerized author management system that could be used by ISD program managers and their staff to manage and collect data on ISD activities. The author management system is described in O'Neal and O'Neal (1979).

The Limitations of the Course

The author training course was developed from a base of experience gathered in a wide variety of ISD projects. It should be pointed out, however, that the author training course did not attempt to teach the full range of ISD activities. Rather, it was developed with the assumption that many Defense Department ISD authors are given the results of a completed front-end analysis that includes training objectives and media selection. Within the context of the Interservice Training Review Organization's ISD model, which is currently well known within Department of Defense circles, the author training course deals primarily with the major activities III.1, entitled "Specify Learning Activities," II.2, "Develop Tests," and III.4, "Develop Instructional Materials". As was previously mentioned, it is within the area of these "authoring" steps that the least specific guidance is generally given to Department of Defense personnel. In addition, these activities are the most broadly needed no matter what general ISD approach is taken, and are the ones commonly undertaken by DOD personnel.

The course is intended for use in a variety of settings, but would seem to have particular application to resident school environments where large-scale, ongoing training development efforts are undertaken. The course is intended to be used by educational specialists, instructional designers, and subject matter experts with instructional design or development responsibilities. Although it presents an integrated approach to ISD, the course was developed in modular fashion so that parts of the course could be used to develop a team of specialists (e.g., test-item writers) who could be combined into a team with differentiated areas of responsibility. This approach makes it possible to get a new person to a high level of proficiency in the development of one element of an instructional sequence very rapidly. Once this is done, the individual can be made a productive member of an ISD team, and the team manager has the option of then expanding training to produce proficiency in developing other elements of instruction or simply using the person as a productive member of the "instructional assembly line."

In general, the philosophical approach taken in the development of the author training course is performance- and product-based rather than theory- or rationale-based. The emphasis is on what to produce, how to produce it, and the criteria to be met by each intermediate and end product of the authoring process. The materials do not deal extensively with the research or theory base behind ISD or the instructional strategies being developed. This more direct production-oriented approach was chosen because it was felt a large portion of the intended audience for this course did not need or want to spend time on theory or rationale and because the goal of the project was to develop a course that would get people to a usable level of productivity as soon as possible.

Because of the practical "how to" philosophy adopted by the course developers and the limitations of project time and budget, some restrictions had to be placed on the scope and content of the course. The course was restricted to include instruction for a broad yet less-than-complete range of classes of instructional objectives and instructional strategies. The course does not attempt to define or teach strategies for the development of instruction directed at complex psychomotor objectives (Gagné & Briggs, 1974). Rather, the course focuses on the development of instruction directed at cognitive objectives.

These objectives include those which are directed at the development of bodies of knowledge (e.g., memory tasks), and the application of concepts, principles (rules), and procedures. In reviewing their work over the past several years, the developers of the author training course surveyed over 20,000 objectives for military and industrial training programs. It was found that the classes of objectives covered in the author training course account for the vast majority of objectives (over 80%) in formal training courses. It was felt that by focusing on these—the most common objective types—the greatest impact could be achieved.

Certainly there are a variety of instructional strategies that can be used to teach the range of objectives covered in the author training course. However, in order to keep the course relatively uncomplicated and straightforward, a limited set of instructional strategies that research has proven to be most effective for teaching each class of objective was selected for inclusion in the course. Generally speaking, the author training course assumes that complex hierarchies or groupings of instructional objectives have been broken down into individual objectives, that these objectives can be classified into a limited set of objective types, and that a single instructional strategy model that is most effective for teaching each type of objective can be identified and taught.

The strategies taught are essentially *media-independent*. It is understood that the method or medium chosen for delivery of instruction can have a significant effect on the development and production of instructional materials. However, this course does not include media-selection models and focuses on the elements of instructional strategy that are necessary no matter what instructional medium is used. The course teaches the learner to produce critical instructional components that may be used directly in the production of written instructional materials or can be the basis (i.e., major elements) of instruction in another medium. Should a medium other than printed text be selected, the technology and rules of thumb associated with that other medium could be applied to the developed components to produce the materials.

Within the constraints of content and strategy imposed by the author training course there remains considerable room for individual creative overlays that take full advantage of media characteristics. It is felt that the aspects of instructional design and development addressed by the author training course are basic and important to the success of instruction in any medium, and experience has shown that the procedure of developing instructional components and then using them as the base element in instruction employing a variety of different media can be very effective.

The format of the author training course lends itself to either a self-paced workshop or an on-the-job training application. In either case an observer–evaluator or course manager is extremely helpful. The success of the training program is in some degree dependent upon the effectiveness of the training of this individual. In terms of actual interaction with the materials, the author training course can be given in a group or individualized setting. Therefore, it can be useful to start off an ISD project or for that individual who joins a project in midstream. In either case, one important advantage of the detailed procedural approach taken and the particular management model utilized in the author training course is that persons taking the course become productive on the first or second day. The primary implementation model used is one that involves learning by doing under the direction of a very specific set of detailed job aids supported by a rich set of instructional materials that can be used as needed.

Description of the Author Training Course

The self-imposed limits in scope and purpose of the author training course (ATC) have been described. These limits help define what the author training course is **not**. Let us now proceed to a description of what the author training course **is.** The author training course consists of seven workbooks: The *User Manual, Classifying Instructional Objectives, Designing Segments for Rules, Designing Segments for Concepts, Designing Segments for Procedures, Designing Segments for Memory Level Instruction,* and *Identifying Technically Correct Test Items* (Courseware, Inc., 1977). In addition, there is a slide–tape program on classifying instructional objectives and annotated job aids that accompany each of the content workbooks.

The *User Manual* provides a basic introduction to the entire course. Functionally, it is divided into two parts. The first part is an introduction to the course structure. It describes the course, its history, purpose, design, how to use the books, what is expected of the learner, and the role of the course manager. It explains to the learner that the course is self-paced, and that it is not expected that all learners will use all components of all workbooks (i.e., the course is designed to be individualized with some learner control of strategy provided). The learner-control options are explained and instruction is given as to where to find help in making decisions for wise use of these options. Part 2 of the *User Manual* introduces the learners to the content to be taught in the author training course. Learners are familiarized with the concept of instructional components and strategies and given some of the rationale behind the model of instructional development to be used. *Components* are defined as the basic pieces of instruction. The components defined by the model used are generalities (the core information the learner acquires), helps (additional, supporting information), examples, practice items, feedback, and wraparound materials (introductions and summaries). These instructional components were chosen because they have been found to be the most effective for the subset of objectives considered in the author training course (Faust, 1977). They can be put together in different ways to form different strategies.

Strategies are defined as prescriptions for the use of specific components in specific sequences. A strategy can be imposed by an instructor or course developer if a specific sequence of components is put together, or it can in some measure be determined by the learner if he is given a set of components and allowed to use whichever he chooses in whichever order he chooses. Generally, the ATC itself uses a modified learner control system that presents a series of components organized in a logical sequence that has been proven effective. However, the components are identified and students are advised that they need not use them all and that they are free to refer back to previous components or skip ahead to others as they feel their own learning needs dictate. The identification of components has several benefits in both the development and use of instructional materials. The identification of components and prescription of strategies allows the instructional developer to make rapid decisions about what to work on next and when he has done enough on an instructional sequence. This has been shown to increase the efficiency of the instructional development effort. In addition, the components used can be easily identified in the instructional materials themselves, thus allowing easy review of key points or tailoring of instruction to the individual needs of students. This tailoring can be done by the instructor through the use of prescriptions, or it can be done by the student if some form of learner control is allowed.

The discussion of instructional components and strategies is supported in the *Users Manual* by two sample lessons that illustrate all of the components and two diverse strategies appropriate to the content of those examples.

The workbook entitled *Classifying Instructional Objectives* is supported by a slide–tape presentation. This portion of the course teaches students to classify objectives according to the behavior specified in the objective and the content being taught. An objective may be classified on the behavior dimensions into two categories, depending on whether the student needs simply to **remember** what he is told or whether he must **use** what he has learned in making decisions or applying rules in new situations. An objective can also be classified based on whether the content being taught consists of facts, concepts, rules, or procedures.

This classification system results in a 2 × 4 matrix (see Figure 1.1).

There is an appropriate instructional strategy for teaching objectives that can be classified into each cell of this matrix (with the exception of the use fact cell). For this reason, the classification of objectives is the first step in the selection of instructional strategies.

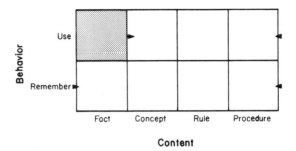

Figure 1.1 Content–behavior matrix.

Students using the author training course are tested on their ability to classify objectives by behavior and content by being asked to classify objectives from their own content area. Certain of these objectives will be used during design and development activities in later parts of the course.

Given this base line of instruction (familiarization with components and strategies and the ability to classify instructional objectives), students using the course proceed to produce instructional components for four or five selected objectives from their own content area. Students are led through the development effort by the annotated job aids that are supported by the remaining workbooks. There are five job aids relating to the five basic instructional strategies being taught: for use–rule objectives, for use–concept objectives, for use–procedure objectives, for remember–fact objectives, and for remember–rule, concept, or procedure objectives. Each annotated job aid defines each product and intermediate product to be produced. It also provides a procedure to be followed for how to produce that product. The job aid provides criteria for evaluating each product or intermediate product and for diagnosing deficiencies. It is expected that students will begin to design and develop instructional components and strategies for the objectives identified earlier, using the job aids as guides.[2] If the student finds that a job aid is not adequately self-explanatory or that the component produced does not meet criteria, the job aid directs the students to specific instruction found in an appropriate content workbook. There are five of these workbooks; *Designing Segments for Rules, Designing Segments for Concepts, Designing Segments for Procedures, Designing Segments for Memory Level Instruction,* and *Identifying Technically Correct Test Items.*

The workbooks dealing with design and development of instructional segments for rules, concepts, procedures, and memory-level material all follow the same format. They define appropriate components and instruc-

[2] An example of the use–procedure job aid can be found in the appendix.

tional strategies to be used with the various classes of objectives. In other words, *Designing Segments for Rules* presents appropriate components and strategies for objectives that have been classified on the behavior dimension as *use* and on the content dimension as *rule*. *Designing Instruction for Concepts* presents appropriate components and strategies for developing instructional materials for objectives that are put in the *use* category on the behavior dimension and the *concept* category on the content dimension. Likewise, the procedure manual deals with use–procedure objectives. The workbook on designing instruction for memory-level materials deals with strategies for remember–fact objectives and the strategy used for all the other content types when the objective requires the student to behave on a memory level only.

Each of these workbooks is divided into many segments. Each segment deals with a process or an instructional component encountered on the annotated job aid. The workbook begins with a statement of the process, definition of a component, or criteria for evaluation of a component as presented on the annotated job aid, and goes on to expand the learner's information by providing instructional helps, examples, contrasting examples and nonexamples, and practice and feedback. The instructional helps provide supporting information to further clarify material presented in the annotated job aid. This includes definitions of terms that may not have been clear before, some partial examples, and rationale behind the process or components discussed.

Two or three complete and adequate examples of each of the components being taught are presented. Each of these examples is as different from the others as possible. They deal with a wide variety of content and present a range of possible techniques and styles. Some deal with content that is highly technical, others with content that is more commmplace and simple (e.g., correctly filling out a check). Some content is highly visual in nature, and some is more abstract. There are also series of contrasting examples and nonexamples of well-devloped components, and, again, these use a wide variety of content and presentation.

The nonexamples presented include components with some inadequacy or deficiency. Each is paired with an example of the same component with the deficiencies corrected. If students or the course manager feels that it is necessary, there are still further supporting materials provided in the form of optional (extra) practice and feedback. In these optional materials learners are presented with a set of instructional components and are asked to determine whether they are adequate or inadequate. If they are determined to be inadequate, the learners are asked to identify specific deficiencies.

The final workbook in the series, *Identifying Technically Correct Test*

Items, gives the criteria for determining the validity and reliability of test items in a variety of formats (e.g., multiple choice, true–false, short answer, and fill-in-the-blank). It presents examples of the various types of test items and allows students to practice identifying adequate and inadequate test items of the various types. This workbook is referenced from the annotated job aid at the point where students begin writing practice and test items for the instructional segments that they are developing.

While taking the course, students normally produce a minimum of five segments of instruction involving different types of objectives. This means that the time spent progressing through the author training course results in development of complete and, it is hoped, usable instructional materials. This has two advantages: Ideally the time spent for training is not totally lost, as far as any ongoing ISD production schedule is concerned; and it has been found that early application of skills in what they perceive as practical everyday work promotes learning and is very rewarding to the learners.

Implementing the Author Training Course

Although the author training course is self-paced and highly individualized, it is not entirely self-instructional. There is a need for a strong experienced course manager. The role of the course manager is multifaceted. He acts as a guidance counselor or director. Experience has shown that some students are unfamiliar with, and therefore uncomfortable with, self-paced, individualized instruction with learner-control options. In such cases, the course manager can provide the guidance necessary to encourage students to make correct use of the options, to prevent students from becoming distracted or sidetracked, and to keep them on task without their becoming bogged down or discouraged. The course manager also acts as a liaison between the author training course and its goals for training and the needs of the specific ISD project in which the learners will eventually work. In other words, he must help students see how they can use the author training course, use the procedures, components, and strategies in the ISD project they are currently working on or will be working on. He should help students adapt the author training course instructional model to the demands of their particular environment. He should also aid students in using the model creatively so that the procedures, components, and strategies are looked upon as beneficial aids to making their instructional efforts more efficient and effective, and not as restrictions limiting their originality or creativity. He must help them select instructional objectives for use in the design and development activities. These objectives should be chosen so that they provide adequate learning experiences, but they should if at all possible also be taken from the learner's job environment.

Finally, the course manager is the final judge as to the adequacy of the products and the success or failure of students attending the author training course. The manager must review all the instructional materials developed and help guide students to the appropriate training materials when deficiencies are noted. The role of the course manager in the author training course is not a trivial one, and his training and experience play an important part in determining its success.

As an ISD project progresses, there is inevitably turnover of authoring personnel or the need to increase the authoring staff. This necessitates some on-the-job training. The author training course was designed with this need in mind. There are logical breaking points in several places in the course, most obviously after the design and development activity for each different instructional strategy. As new authors need training, they can access the related job aid and workbooks and use them in developing the instructional materials for which they are responsible.

The author training course can easily be used to train a large, differentiated staff to produce effective instruction with each person on the instructional staff responsible for different components or intermediate products leading to the development of final components. For instance, the staff of subject matter experts might be divided into senior (those with a great deal of experience or training in the content to be taught) and junior subject matter experts (those with less training and experience). For efficiency, and in order to provide the most valid content, the senior SME might be required to write generalities, to do analyses such as common-error analysis, and to define the range of example and practice items to be produced. The junior subject matter expert would develop instructional helps and develop the examples, practice items, and feedback. The instructional model used in the ATC lends itself readily to such division of labor, and the individualization provided by the design makes it possible for persons filling each of these roles to select easily the specific portions of the course that best meet their needs. Its well-defined job aids also help to ensure that the output of a staff with each member producing different instructional components can still be integrated smoothly into the final instructional product.

The author training course has been through both formative evaluation and a test workshop of the materials that were revised on the basis of the formative evaluation. The formative evaluation was carried out using such diverse groups as 34 instructional designers and subject matter experts at Johnson Space Center at Clear Lake, Texas; 10 instructional developers, administrators, and instructional systems vendor personnel at the Model Secondary School for the Deaf in Washington, D.C.; 3 Chief Petty Officers from the Company Commanders School at the Naval Training Center, San Diego; 6 Marine instructors from the Infantry Training School, Camp Pendleton, California; 6 instructional design personnel and subject matter experts at Northern Virginia Community College, Alexandria, Virginia; and several new instructional design trainees at Courseware, Inc., in San Diego. Based on the diverse inputs of this group, and upon extensive internal reviews, the materials were extensively revised in terms of presentation and implementation format and organization.

A final evaluation workshop was then held at Lowry Air Force Base to obtain data on the effectiveness of the revised materials and to provide inputs to the final modifications to the course before delivery. As before, the requested test population was personnel with current instructional design and development responsibilities. The group of subjects provided only approximated those characteristics requested. Thirty-one instructional packages were produced and then evaluated against the detailed author training course job-aid criteria and 12 of the 31 products were analyzed using an Instructional Quality Inventory instrument developed under funding by the Naval Personnel Research and Development Center (NPRDC) (Ellis, Wulfeck, Merrill, Richards, Schmidt, & Wood, 1978).

Important findings of a needs analysis study conducted as the first major task of the contract, and the formative and final evaluations include the following:

1. It was typically reported across the six Department of Defense ISD sites studied that under the prevailing "apprenticeship" model followed at these sites, instructional and training designer–developers take 6 months to obtain a good level of supervised productivity and 1 year to become productive without close supervision (Bunderson, 1977).

2. Typically, similar personnel using the author training course materials become productive under little supervision within a week (some within hours).

3. The great majority of initial products turned out by new learners meet criteria with very minor revision. Almost all meet criteria by the second revision with an elapsed time of 1–2 days per product. Criteria used were detailed criteria from the job aids that form the basis for the author training course design and development procedures. Where appropriate, based on the instructional content and strategy involved (approximately 40% of segments produced), output of the final evaluation group was validated against the Courseware–NPRDC developed-

Instructional Quality Inventory instrument. These additional, externally validated criteria were met within the same revision parameters.

4. User affect seemed to be a function of two major factors: (*a*) whether the user indeed was currently faced with the problem and responsibility of designing and developing training materials (i.e., if you have a problem the course looks good); and (*b*) whether or not the user was severely constrained in terms of institutional limitations on "how training and instruction materials should look." The author training course instructs in formats and strategies that are completely compatible with the general direction given by the interservice model, but it is very detailed and specific in its detail. Although this has been shown to lead to early and consistent productivity, it is perceived as unsettlingly unique by those with real or perceived instructional format and strategy constraints.

In summary, then, it would seem that initial data from the implementation of the author training course indicates that it will be an efficient and effective tool for consistently producing effective instruction with short gear-up time, and that it can be a valuable tool for the manager of an ISD program, since its detailed and well-specified criteria offer an excellent basis for unifying development approach and quality-control philosophy across large staffs.

APPENDIX: USE/PROCEDURE JOB AID

The appendix for this chapter follows on pages 18–35.

NOTES	STEPS	FOR HELP, SEE:
	Here is a list of steps to follow when designing a procedure segment.	
1. Existing resources are relevant manuals, previous instruction, etc., to be used in determining the content of the procedure.	1. Assemble lesson objectives and existing resources or background material. Choose one use/procedure segment to work on.	Course Manager
2. Clearly identified segments allow easier tracking through production and easier use by students.	2. Check to make sure that the segment is clearly identified by number and topic or title.	Course Manager
	OBJECTIVE	
	3. Review the segment objective to ensure that it:	
	a. Requires use/procedure behavior	
	b. Describes desired learner behavior (not instructor behavior).	Classifying instructional Objectives, pp. 1-12
	c. Is expressed with an action verb.	
	d. States conditions and standards, as appropriate.	Course Manager
	These steps help you focus on what the learner needs to know to perform the procedure. The steps you write should be complete enough for the learner to perform them from the generality alone.	

18

GENERALITY

In preparation for writing the generality, make sure you understand exactly what is required by the objective and familiarize yourself with the resource material needed to meet that requirement.

4. Write the name or outcome of the procedure as a lead-in to the steps.

Designing Segments for Procedures, pp. 1.1-1.2

5. Using resources as necessary, think through the procedure as it should be performed and write a rough draft of it by using the guidelines below:

   a. If start cues or preliminary steps are used to begin the procedure, write them down.

   b. Write the first step of the procedure.

Designing Segments for Procedures, pp. 1.1-1.2

---

4. The outcome of the procedure is the result of performing it (e.g., in the lead-in "The procedure for cleaning an ACME Meat Slicer," the outcome is underlined).

A lead-in is a brief phrase which describes the procedure steps which follow it (e.g., "The steps for assembling an M-16 rifle are..." or "To perform the Dewey Rain Gauge procedure...").

5a. Start cues let you know when to use the procedure.

5a. Preliminary steps include checking to see that the necessary conditions for using the procedure exist (all necessary materials are available, start cues are present, etc.). When preliminary steps are self-evident, they need not be included.

19

Appendix (*continued*)

NOTES	STEPS	FOR HELP, SEE:
5c. Show complex decision steps as separate steps so they won't be overlooked.	c. Determine if the step involves any important or complex decisions, and if so, state those decisions as separate steps.	p. 1.2
5d. Signals might be a variety of cues like a light eg. changing color, bleeding stopping, etc.	d. Determine if there are any important signals that indicate when the first step is over and the next should begin. If there are any signals, add them to the step.	p. 1.3
5e. Writing steps in list form makes the steps easier to read and shows each step distinctly.	e. Write the next step. Steps should be parallel and written in list form, whenever possible.	
	f. Repeat steps c, d, and e until all steps have been written.	
	g. Consider whether there are any signals that tell you when the whole procedure has been completed. If there are, add them to the last step.	p. 1.3
5h. Keep it simple and clean, so it is clear what needs to be learned.	h. Ensure that you haven't included any nonessential information or specific examples.	p. 1.3
	i. Check that you have included all necessary steps and that they are accurately stated.	Course Manager

20

and determine if any of the steps:

a. Contain more than one action or an embedded decision. If so, break the step(s) into single-action steps.

b. Are made up of several smaller steps which have not been learned previously. If so, add the component steps to the generality.

c. Are substeps for a larger step which is not stated. If so, state the larger step with the substeps below it.

Course Manager

Course Manager

Course Manager

6a. Steps should not require more than one action, unless the combined step is known by most students. For example, using a soldering iron is a step in the procedure of making copper enamel lapel pins. Although soldering involves several steps of its own, those steps should not be included in the copper enameling procedure unless they have not been previously learned.

6c. For example, showing the following substeps for "determining if the victim is breathing" without stating the major step:

Substeps—Look for chest movement. Listen for heartbeat, feel pulse, etc.

21

Appendix (continued)

NOTES	STEPS	FOR HELP, SEE:
	7. Consider the students' previous learning (from earlier segments and other sources) and any student performance data (when available) to help you determine if:	Course Manager
	a. The generality contains unknown or difficult terms. If so, either simplify them in the generality, teach them in an earlier segment, define them in the introduction, or make a list of the terms to redefine later in the generality help.	
7a. Terms should be taught in an earlier segment when the learner must be able to recall the definitions. If he or she only needs to be familiar with them, then they can be defined in the introduction to the segment.	b. Students are likely to make common errors in performance. If so, make a list of the common errors to use later in the generality help, demonstration, and practice.	Course Manager
7b. If most students misperform a particular step or set of steps, have trouble recognizing particular cues, or have other problems, note them here and refer to this information when designing the generality help and demonstration.	8. Check the generality against existing resources and ensure that it is complete and accurate. Ensure also that it:	
IMPORTANT		
8. This step is your final check for adequacy of the generality. These criteria are the same as those used in the procedure manual.		

22

the procedure or states the outcome.

2. Contains all steps necessary to perform the objective.

3. Lists steps in order, when appropriate.

4. States steps as single or simultaneous actions.

5. Indicates important or complex decisions, when present, as separate steps.

6. Indicates start cues, preliminary steps, and/or end points, when appropriate.

7. Is concise and well organized.

8. Avoids unfamiliar terms or symbols, where possible.

9. Excludes nonessential information.

10. Excludes specific examples or illustrations.

11. Includes complete and accurate information.

9. Have another subject matter expert review the generality for completeness and accuracy.

10. Revise the generality, as necessary.

NOTES	STEPS	FOR HELP, SEE:
These steps teach you to develop several types of helps. You can choose to develop one or more of these types of helps.	GENERALITY HELP	Designing Segments for Procedures, p. 2.1
Remember, however, that the helps are only supposed to include relevant, helpful information. They are not a license for adding lots of nonessential information. Remember, too, that no help is needed if the step is self-explanatory or easy for most students to understand. As you write the helps, you'll probably also revise the generality as new points come to mind.	11. Examine the procedure to see if it, or portions of it, relate to what the learner already knows. If the learner already knows something about the procedure, point this out in your help.	
	12. Examine the procedure to see whether the learner might question why the procedure includes certain steps or why it is performed the way it is, etc. If questions are likely, explain the reasoning behind all questionable steps.	p. 2.2
13. It's important to keep these common errors in mind.	13. Look at each step and consider whether any additional explanation or description of the step would be helpful to learners in understanding how to do it. Be sure to explain those steps which you identified earlier as the source of common errors (Step 7b).	p. 2.2
14. Illustrations often say it best and most succinctly	14. Consider whether a graphic illustration would help the learner recognize a cue or step when encountered in the real world. Describe or roughly sketch the illustrations to be included.	p. 2.2

you listed earlier that need to be explained. If so, explain those terms. If they have been defined previously, but you feel review might be helpful, either restate the definition or give a reference as to where the definition can be found.

16. If no helps are required for a particular step, simply restate that step.

17. Repeat 13-15 for each step in the procedure.

18. Look over your helps, and group those for each step together.

19. Check to see that the helps you have written are clearly linked to the information in the generality.

20. Check the generality help to be sure it does NOT introduce essential information for the first time. If it does, go back and revise the generality to include that information.

Course Manager

p. 2.3

16. Remember, don't write a help if it's not needed.

18. By grouping the helps by steps, you make the context of the information clear.

20. This is very important! All the information the student must know to do the procedure must be included in the generality. For example, a help should not add new safety precaution information for a particular step since that information is critical and might cause injury or damage if misperformed.

Appendix (*continued*)

NOTES	STEPS	FOR HELP, SEE:

It's easy to omit critical information from your generality and then catch it when you write the help. That's why it's important to be continually checking between components and making necessary revisions.	21. Check the generality help and ensure that it:
	
	1. Makes the generality easier to use and overcomes expected problems or common mistakes. The help section uses one or more of the following techniques. It
	
	   a. Relates all or part of the procedure to the learner's prior general knowledge or previous learning of specific steps.
	
	   b. Gives the reasoning behind all or part of the procedure.
	
	   c. Explains common errors, expands, or restates each of the steps as needed.
	
	   d. Redefines or explains terms which were previously introduced but may need to be reviewed.
	
	   e. Uses graphics or illustrations for emphasis or clarification.
	
	2. Is clearly related to the generality information in form and content.
		Designing Segments for Procedures, Segment 2

23. Show the generality help section to a colleague to ensure that it is accurate, complete, helpful, and easy to understand.

DEMONSTRATION

24. Decide whether the demonstration should be written, mediated, or live. Use the following information to help you decide:

Situation	Appropriate Medium:
Characteristics:	
Motion or sound required	Live or mediated
Color	Live, mediated, or written (if color printing available)
Limited instructor time, or limited or very expensive materials to be used during demonstration.	Mediated (videotape or slide/tape)

Write down your choice.

Designing Segments for Procedures, pp. 3.1-3.2

These steps teach you to either write out the complete demonstration as it would appear (written demonstration) or to write directions to the person performing the demonstration (if live) or producing it (if mediated).

27

105117

Appendix (*continued*)

NOTES	STEPS	FOR HELP, SEE:
25. Remember, you won't be there, so make your directions clear and explicit.	25. Set up a format that will allow you to communicate what should be done during the demonstration. Be sure that it allows for easy coordination of verbal narrative and visual or action aspects of the demonstration.	Course Manager
	26. Using your generality, think through the procedure or watch it being performed to determine what needs to be shown and explained.	Designing Segments for Procedures, p. 3.2
	27. Create an introductory statement that describes the specific situation in which the procedure is demonstrated. Include a description of tools, equipment, and anything else provided.	Examples, pp. 3.7, 3.10
	28. If preparing a live demonstration, give step-by-step directions of what the demonstrator needs to do to begin the procedure (preliminary steps) and what he or she should do, say, use, point out, and explain as he or she performs each step. Be sure to include decision steps with the alternate actions shown, and point out common errors.	pp. 3.3, 3.7-3.13

28. ...rawings, sketches, etc., are valuable for helping an unfamiliar artist create the desired demonstration. Don't assume the artist knows any more than what you tell him or her. It's important to show the decision steps and how it might look if different decision alternatives are taken.

29. In preparing a mediated demonstration (slide/tape or videotape) give detailed descriptions and rough sketches --when possible--of required visuals illustrating each step. Detail the motion, special actions, or sound effects required, and the verbal explanation which must accompany each step. Be sure to include decision steps with the alternate actions shown, and point out common errors.   p. 3.3

30. If preparing a written demonstration, outline the explanation and visuals which must accompany each step, including preliminary steps. Be sure to include decision steps with the alternate actions shown, and point out common errors.   p. 3.3

31. As with the other components, the demonstration should not confuse the student with unnecessary information.

31. Check over the demonstration you've outlined, and eliminate any nonessential information you might have included.   p. 3.3

32. Using a rough draft of the demonstration and the generality, think through the procedure or watch it being performed again to ensure that it: Designing Segments for Procedures, Segment 3

29

Appendix (*continued*)

NOTES	STEPS	FOR HELP, SEE:
	1. Indicates the medium or media to be used for the presentation (live, video, slide/tape, written, or other).	
	2. Begins with a description of the specific situation in which the procedure will be demonstrated, including all necessary tools, equipment, etc.	
	3. Covers all steps in the generality in the order presented, including start cues, preliminary steps, and end points.	
	4. Indicates all steps requiring decisions and shows or describes responses for each decision and the basis for making them.	
	5. Contains descriptions of all audiovisual requirements and explanatory narrative (including common errors and other helpful information) necessary for each step to be performed or produced.	
	6. Is clearly and simply worded.	
	7. Excludes nonessential information.	

33. Give the draft of the demonstration directions to a colleague to review for accuracy, completeness, and ease of understanding.

34. Revise the demonstration directions, as necessary.

35. Write the smooth version of the demonstration directions with all visuals and verbal information on the appropriate sheet.

PRACTICE

36. Consider what the instructor might need to set up an adequate practice situation. Design a set of directions to the instructor to enable him or her to do that, specifying:

    1. Conditions for performance as stated in the objective--the materials, equipment, and information--and the arrangements needed to set up those conditions.

Designing Segments for Procedures, p. 4.2

Segment 4

Note that these materials are designed to be used by the instructor.

36. Remember that practice for procedures usually involves some psychomotor performance by the student which the instructor eventually observes and evaluates. Your directions need to help him or her set up that practice situation.

31

Appendix (*continued*)

NOTES	STEPS	FOR HELP, SEE:
	2. Learner directions on what to do in the practice situation (including provisions for self-checks and number of possible trials).	
	3. Criteria (as stated in the objective) for scoring overall performance which enables the instructor to evaluate the student on the whole procedure.	
37. You must decide which aspects (critical evaluation points) of the performance need to be measured to convince you that the procedure has been performed satisfactorily.	37. Examine the generality to identify which steps are critical evaluation points and those which are desirable but not critical.	Designing Segments for Procedures, p. 4.2
38. For some sample checklist formats, see the Examples.	38. Develop a rough-draft checklist or grade sheet to be used by the instructor for evaluating practice performance. The checklist should:	Examples, pp. 4.4–4.7 Segment 4
	a. Measure performance on the critical evaluation points (each step of the procedure, critical aspects of the procedure, or the procedure's outcome, as appropriate).	
	b. Specify criteria for adequate performance of each behavior.	

c. Exclude irrelevant behaviors or those which cannot
be measured.

d. Permit the instructor to easily record performance
and feedback comments.

e. Contain student, course, and segment identification
information.

39. Look over your rough-draft checklist to be sure it can
be easily used by the instructor (that it contains
enough room for recording responses, comments, and
all necessary identifying information).

40. To ensure the adequacy and completeness of the checklist,
either mentally review the procedure or observe its
performance by using the checklist.

41. Revise the instructor directions and checklists, as
necessary.

p. 4.2

33

Appendix (*continued*)

NOTES	STEPS	FOR HELP, SEE:
	FEEDBACK	
42. The criteria for the behaviors may be numbers of times they can be performed, acceptable margin of error, amount of time taken, etc.	42. Ensure that the checklist gives complete criteria for each behavior, to be used as the basis for pinpointing inadequate performance.	Course Manager
43. If you know about certain steps students are likely to misperform or certain cues they might miss, etc., your directions to the instructor should include the likely errors and how to point them out or respond to students when they occur.	43. Look over the typical performance errors you listed in Step 7b, and think about the responses you might suggest that an instructor make to each error. Write the responses next to the errors.	Course Manager
44. The student can use the reference for refreshing his or her knowledge before the next practice session.	44. For each of the errors listed, give a reference to the materials that would help the student correct the error.	Designing Segments for Procedures, p. 5.1
45. When you have the instructor give feedback depends on how much self-learning you want the student to do. Generally, it's a good idea in the beginning to give feedback after each step to correct early errors and then to fade feedback as practice continues.	45. Suggest a strategy to the instructor for giving feedback which tells him or her to watch the student perform, measure performance with the checklist, and do one of the following: a. Give feedback as the student performs each step by pointing out errors and reinforcing correct responses, or	

b. Wait until the student completes entire performance and give feedback, or

c. Give no direct feedback, but reference where the student can find the corrections to his or her errors.

46. Review the feedback directions to make sure they include:

1. A list of commonly made mistakes for particular steps and suggested instructor responses to them.

2. A set of references, when appropriate, for correcting errors.

3. A strategy for giving feedback which tells when and how the feedback should be given.

Segment 5

REFERENCES

Aagard, James A., & Braby, Richard. *Learning guidelines and algorithms for types of learning objectives* (TAEG Report No. 23). Orlando, Fla.: Training Analysis and Evaluation Group, March 1976.

Bunderson, C. V. *Team production of learner–controller courseware: A progress report.* Provo, Utah: Brigham Young University, 1972.

Bunderson, C. V. *Analysis of needs and goals for author training and production management systems* (Tech. Rep. No. 1). San Diego, Calif.: Courseware, Inc., March 1977. (DOD Contract Number MDA-903-76-C-0216).

Bunderson, C. V., & Faust, G. W. Programmed and computer-assisted instruction. In N. L. Gage (Ed.), *The psychology of teaching methods.* Chicago: The University of Chicago Press, 1976.

Courseware, Inc. *Classifying instructional objectives.* San Diego, Calif.: Author, 1977.

Courseware, Inc. *Designing segments for concepts.* San Diego, Calif.: Author, 1977.

Courseware, Inc. *Designing segments for memory level instruction.* San Diego, Calif.: Author, 1977.

Courseware, Inc. *Designing segments for procedures.* San Diego, Calif.: Author, 1977.

Courseware, Inc. *Designing segments for rules.* San Diego, Calif.: Author, 1977.

Courseware, Inc. *Identifying technically correct test items.* San Diego, Calif.: Author, 1977.

Courseware, Inc. *User manual.* San Diego, Calif.: Author, 1977.

Ellis, J., Wulfeck, W., Merrill, M. D., Rchards, R., Schmidt, R., & Wood, N. *NPRDC Tech Note 78-5.* San Diego, Calif.: Naval Personnel Research and Development Center, 1978.

Faust, G. W. Selecting instructional strategies or once you've got an objective, what do you do with it? *Journal of Instructional Development,* 1977, *1*, 18–22.

Faust, G. W., & O'Neal, A. F. *Computer-based management of instructional development, or how to keep track of the players and pieces while you play a good game.* Paper presented at the meeting of the Association for Educational Communications and Technology, Miami, April 1977. (a)

Faust, G. W., & O'Neal, A. F. *Instructional science and the evolution of computer-assisted instruction systems.* Paper presented at the Institute of Electrical and Electronic Engineers (Electro 77), New York, April 1977. (b)

Gagné, R. M., & Briggs, L. J. *Principles of instructional design.* New York: Holt, Rinehart and Winston, 1974.

Lipson, Joseph I. Needed: A collaborative open university network. *Productivity in Higher Education,* proceedings of Educational Technologies Symposium, Stony Brook, New York, September 1973.

Logan, R. S. *An exploratory computer-based model for comparing instructional alternatives and a bibliography of aids for course material development: A two-part study* (Vol. 2). St. Louis: McDonnel Douglas Astronautics Company–East, September 1976.

Merrill, M. D., & Boutwell, R. C. Instructional development: Methodology and research. In F. N. Kerlinger (Ed.), *Review of research in education* (Vol. 1). Itasca, Ill.: F. E. Peacock Publishers, 1973.

Molnar, A. R. *The future of educational technology research and development.* Washington, D.C.: National Science Foundation, 1971. (ERIC Document Reproduction Service No. ED 054 642)

Montmerlo, Melvin D. *Instructional systems development state-of-the-art and directions for the future.* Paper presented at the Eighth Naval Training Equipment Center–Industry Conference, Orlando, Fla., Nov. 1975.

O'Neal, A. F. *Monthly report under contract MDA 903-77-C-0265.* San Diego, Calif.: Courseware, Incorporated, October 1975.

O'Neal, A. F. *Specification of computer aids to ISD.* Paper presented at the meeting of the American Educational Research Association, New York, 1977.

O'Neal, A. F., & O'Neal, H. L. Author management systems. In Harold F. O'Neil, Jr. (Ed.), *Issues in instructional systems development.* New York: Academic Press, 1979.

Rickertson, D., Schulz, R. E., & Wright, R. H. *Review of the CONARC systems engineering of training program and its implementation at the United States Army Aviation School* Alexandria, Va.: Human Resources Research Organization, April 1970.

Simonsen, R. H., & Renshaw, K. S. CAI—Boon or boondoggle. *Datamation,* March 1974, pp. 90–102.

Van Pelt, K. B., & Rich, J. J. *Effective writing for a computerized training system.* (TRADOC Interim Report CTS-TR-75-1). January 1975.

2

Computer Aids for Developing Tests and Instruction[1]

RUSSEL E. SCHULZ

BACKGROUND

This chapter describes computerized aids developed by the Human Resources Reseach Organization (HumRRO) for on-line development of tests and instruction. As a first step in developing these aids, HumRRO completed the development of an earlier generation of aids called MONIFORMS (Schulz, 1975a, 1975b). MONIFORMS represent a series of partially completed programs coded in TUTOR, the programming language of the PLATO IV computer-based instruction system (Ghesquiere, David, & Thompson, 1974; Stifle, 1973, 1974). MONIFORMS are used to create certain frequently used question types, such as multiple choice, constructed response, and matching questions. They require the author to provide only information relevant to the specific question, such as the text for the question, feedback messages for correct and incorrect responses, and instructions for analyzing the student's response. A user of MONIFORMS need not be skilled in the TUTOR programming language. The user need know only basic editing procedures for the PLATO system.

Though MONIFORMS were a valuable first step, there still existed a

[1] Preparation of this chapter was supported jointly by the Defense Advanced Research Projects Agency and the U.S. Army Research Institute for the Behavioral Sciences under contract DAHC 19-76-C-0041. Views and conclusions contained in this chapter are those of the author and should not be interpreted as necessarily representing the official policies, either expressed or implied, of the Defense Advanced ·Research Projects Agency, U.S. Army Research Institute for the Behavioral Sciences, or the United States Government.

Copyright © 1979 by Academic Press, Inc.
All rights of reproduction in any form reserved.
ISBN 0-12-526660-X

need for more advanced author aids. Preliminary study at HumRRO indicated the feasibility of developing author aids that through interrogation of the course author would **automatically** convert lesson content and structure into executable program code. Therefore, the author would require no previous programming experience and thus make the aids much easier to use. This concept formed the basis of the approach taken in the development of the computerized aids described in this chapter.

In spite of the fact that developmental support for the aids was obtained through Department of Defense channels, we feel that they have complete generalizability to the civilian sector as well.

The systems approach has been used to develop computerized aids. The systems approach is just what that name implies: a systematic process for specifying the desired products of training and selecting what will be taught, how it will be taught, and what the presentation mechanism will be, and for evaluating the effects of each phase of the process. It focuses upon the job that is ultimately to be performed and upon the individual who is to learn to perform that job. In the systems approach, it is feasible to engineer flexibility into the instruction, thereby adapting the instructional system to individual differences among the students. Special consideration is given to

- Evaluation of the needs of each individual student
- The nature of instructional content to be imparted
- The instructional decision rules that mediate between student needs and instructional content

Major efficiency is achieved by directing instruction *precisely* to the student and to what the student will do on the job, thereby assuring relevance and efficiency, precluding oversights, and adapting instruction to the individual.

During the past 20 years, many attempts have been made to codify a definitive technology for the systems approach to training. Early efforts in this area included those by HumRRO on behalf of the U.S. Army (Baker, 1958; MacCaslin, Woodruff, & Baker, 1959; Hammes, Kelly, McFann, & Ward, 1957; McFann, Hammes, & Taylor, 1955) and the development of the U.S. Air Force personnel subsystem (U.S. Air Force, 1970). The Air Force had undertaken a large activity to develop, define, and record a definitive technology for instructional systems development, and the Army had embarked on an ambitious 5-year program to systems-engineer all of its training courses (U.S. Army, 1968). Some of the development of the systems approach to training has gone on outside the services, particularly in industry (American Airlines, Inc., 1969; Smith, 1971; Wydra, 1975). In addition, Mager (1962) and others such as Ammerman and

Melching (1966), Bloom (1968), Bond and Rigney (1970), Butts (1970), Esbensen (1970), Gagné (1970), Glaser (1966), Krathwohl, Bloom, and Masia (1969), and Melching (1969), to mention only a few, have made significant contributions to systems approach models through their research in the development of behavioral objectives and sequencing of instruction. In the Navy, much of the work dealing with the systems approach has been carried out by the U.S. Naval Training Equipment Center with reference to simulation (Jeantheau, 1972; Micheli, 1972). In addition, the Navy has initiated several major efforts related to training systems design of a more general nature (Braby, Micheli, Morris, & Okraski, 1972; Rundquist, 1967; U.S. Navy, 1973).

One of the more notable of recent systems approach efforts is the Interservice Procedures for Instructional Systems Development (IPISD) Model (Interservice Procedures for Instructional Systems Development, 1975a, 1975b). This model was prepared by the Center for Educational Technology at Florida State University under contract with the Interservice Committee for Instructional Systems Development, involving the Army, Navy, Air Force, and Marine Corps. The IPISD contains standardized rationale, terminology, and basic concepts of instructional systems.

The IPISD model shows promise as a useful tool in instructional systems development activities and is presently undergoing preliminary field evaluation. The model consists of five major phases: analyze, design, develop, implement and control. Figure 2.1 is a breakdown of the five phases into more detailed activities (blocks) comprising each phase. This model has been adopted by our group as a framework for our effort.

Early applications of the systems approach to training were accomplished by expert training developers. In the 1960s, the possibility of having laypersons use these models to achieve the success of the experts, by imitating their actions, was explored. The use of an instructional systems development (ISD) manual by existing military personnel with little or no experience in training program design may be a fraction of the cost of hiring or contracting experts to do the development. Even so, the cost-effectiveness of the approach will still depend on the effectiveness of the model, or tools, in enabling laypersons to produce effective instruction.

In the past few years, problems with attempts at implementing ISD models by laypersons have surfaced. Though the "what to do" may remain relatively constant across training problems, the "how to do it" may vary enormously. Therefore, the instructional systems designer needs a wealth of aids to refer to in dealing with a specific training problem in a specific subject area. Though the IPISD manuals do provide

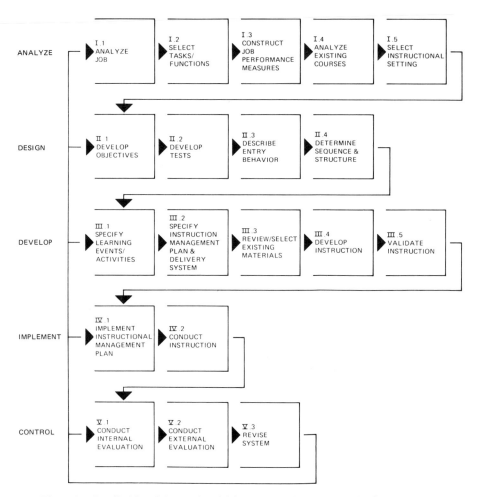

Figure 2.1 Detailed breakdown of activities to be performed in each phase. [TRADOC PAM 350-30, Executive Summary and Model, August 1975.]

far more references to the literature than previous manuals did, they do not provide specific how-to-do-it guidance for specific design and development tasks.

Another major problem area of ISD implementation in general is the management of the instructional development process. For example, when a change is made in the conditions of a particular test item, this has ramifications backward and forward in the ISD process. For example, task conditions may require change as a result of the change in the conditions for testing the task. Any instructional materials relevant to the task covered by the test item must also be reviewed and perhaps modified. The management of these changes, including the communication among various members of the IPISD team, is complex and usually requires some management aids.

Other problems of using IPISD or other ISD models relate to the background skills of the team leader and of the members of the development team. This is pointed out in the Interservice Procedures for Instructional Systems Development (1975a), in the Montmerlo study (1975), and in many other sources (Hartley, 1968; Koberg & Bagnall, 1972; Quade, 1968).

The IPISD model is advanced over other systems approach models in providing guidance to the training manager. However, the IPISD manuals are not presently intended to provide specific procedures for every instructional situation that can be encountered. Some situations are now covered only by the general principles underlying the model. If IPISD is to have a fair chance of being accepted by training managers, it is essential that tools or author aids be developed that will permit training personnel readily and effectively to translate recommended IPISD procedures into meaningful instructional products.

I view author aids as any products used in accomplishing one or more steps of the IPISD procedures. Under this definition, thousands of guidebooks, research studies, texts, professional articles, and technical reports could be considered as aids. The problem for the author (any member of the development team), is to know what aids to use when, to know they exist, to have access to them in a timely way, and to have some facility and judgment in their application.

In this chapter, author aids will be described for only two of the activities of the IPISD model: develop tests (Block II.2), and develop instruction (Block III.4). These activities were selected because many leading instructional technologists and designers (Aagard & Braby, 1976; Lipson, 1973; Simonsen & Renshaw, 1974; Van Pelt & Rich, 1975) have concluded from their experience that the development phase of instructional preparation is **the** significant component of the systematic approach to producing quality instruction. It is expensive, time-consuming, and critical, and requires specialized capabilities.

In developing tests (IPISD Block II.2), authors need help in performing such activities as the following:

• Developing test items that actually test the terminal learning objectives, learning objectives, and learning steps. (Terminal learning objectives are to be attained during training. They are broken down into their component parts, which are documented as learning objectives that may be further divided into learning steps. Each terminal learning objective contains actions, conditions, and standards.)

- Developing scoring procedures
- Writing test items that will assist in validating instructional materials
- Devising test items that will support remediation strategies
- Generating test items and alternative forms of items
- Managing the test development process—for example, asking whether all terminal learning objectives have been tested
- Obtaining reliability measures on test items
- Determining the validity of test items

In the development of instruction (IPISD Block III.4), a variety of aids are needed. Some of the activities and decisions that require support include the following:

- Ensuring reading level is appropriate to the audience
- Deciding what kind of drill and practice is needed, and how much, for a given task
- Deciding how the student will be able to obtain additional help
- Determining the nature, frequency, and type of feedback to provide to the student during the instruction

As an overriding concern, aids are needed to help reduce the time it takes to develop quality instruction and tests, and to make the development process as efficient as possible.

A wide variety of aids exist. Recently, Logan (1978) completed a survey of existing tools–procedures that could be used by instructional developers in conjunction with the IPISD. The results of this survey indicated that aids exist for a number of IPISD components. Unfortunately, a considerable technical background and level of expertise are required for their use. Thus, even when aids are available, there remains the problem of using them without imposing an undue burden on the author.

The majority of existing materials are more of the what-to-do than the how-to-do-it variety. Thus, to provide the most efficient aids to IPISD developers, the guidance found in some of these manuals and guidebooks needs to be translated and integrated into the IPISD framework and emphasize how-to-do-it guidance.

PURPOSE

The purpose of this research effort was to conduct a development and feasibility demonstration of on-line, query-based author aids. The use of computers in a variety of training situations is currently being evaluated. Results to date suggest that the computer can be a valuable additional resource for meeting the requirements of training but that the full potential of computer assistance still remains to be exploited. In addition, results also suggest that person–computer interactions should be designed to minimize the requirement for computer-experienced personnel. Query-based techniques are one means for increasing ease of use. The research was designed to include author aids for developing tests (Block II.2) and developing instruction (Block III.4) of the Interservice Procedures for Instructional Systems Development (IPISD). Specifically, the activities of the project were to result in author aids that

- Are suitable for creation of both on-line and off-line instruction
- Are generalizable for differing subject matter areas
- Are documented in a flowchart form to permit timely conversion as appropriate to other computer-based instructional systems

The utility of the author aids developed was to be evaluated and revised as necessary with military authors–instructors preparing relevant instructional material.

APPROACH

The goal of the project was to construct, implement, and provide a feasibility test of on-line authoring aids that can be integrated with the IPISD model. In order to attain the objectives of this project, the approach taken was

- User-oriented
- Guided by the IPISD model
- Multilevel in its parallel development–evaluation activities.

A cooperative working relationship was established with instructional and curriculum development personnel of the U.S. Army Engineer School, Ft. Belvoir, Virginia. Input from these personnel was an important influence in the selection of author aids that would help the instructional development team at Ft. Belvoir to implement the IPISD.

Author aids to be developed in this project were presented on the University of Illinois PLATO IV computer-based instruction system (Bitzer, Sherwood, & Tenczar, 1973). During the course of the project, four PLATO IV terminals were located in the HumRRO laboratory, Alexandria, Virginia. In addition, eight terminals located at Ft. Belvoir, Virginia, were also available during the project.

A 9-hour segment of the Engineer Noncommissioned Officer Advanced course was selected for this project in consultation with Ft. Belvoir curriculum development and training personnel and with the agreement of the Army Research Institute. The subject matter for this segment of the Engineer Noncommissioned Officer Advanced course includes content such as construction and emplacement of field fortifications (e.g., wire entanglements), and U.S.–foreign mine warfare doctrine. The content of this segment of the course includes computational problem solving (soft skills), as well as procedural tasks (hard skills). It was thought that if authoring aids were developed that would be useful for handling instruction and testing of hard skills as well as soft skills, the set of authoring aids would be more applicable to other courses and other schools than if just the hard skills were chosen for the targeted materials. Arrangements were made to permit participation in the project of three instructors who teach the Engineer Noncommissioned Officer Advanced Course (two noncommissioned officers and one officer).

Initially, a set of detailed flowcharts was constructed to describe information elements and features required by instructional developers in performing the steps of developing tests and instruction. The flow charts were designed to be sufficiently detailed and annotated for ready adaptation to any system (i.e., relatively hardware- or software-independent).

The multilevel nature of the research activities is demonstrated by the three levels of evaluation undertaken in the project. The first level was an informal evaluation of **existing** IPISD guidance, procedures, and author aids. HumRRO staff, as users of this guidance, were the primary source of evaluation data at this level.

Level 2 was directed toward a formative evaluation of **new** author aids and procedure developed specifically for on-line application for IPISD Blocks II.2 (develop tests) and III.4 (develop instruction).

Level 3 evaluation assessed the adequacy of the instructional materials created by the military authors. These materials were then administered to U.S. Army Engineer School trainees, who provided an additional data source.

Revision activities occurred continuously throughout the period of project performance. The purpose of these revisions was to assure maximum utility of the flow charts and author aids in implementing the IPISD process. The test items and lesson material were not revised as a basis of trainee data because of time limitations, but these data were incorporated as part of the research conclusion. The project activities were divided into four major tasks. These were

Task 1. Analysis and determination of required author aid elements
Task 2. Conversion of flow charts to interactive program

Task 3. Evaluation of the programmed materials
Task 4. Revisions

The activities and accomplishments in each of the tasks will now be described.

PROJECT ACTIVITIES AND ACCOMPLISHMENTS

Task 1: *Analysis and Determination of Required Author Aid Elements*

Activities during Task 1 were conducted in two research subtasks: (1) Task 1-1: Expansion of IPISD flow charts in order to provide greater detail about the specific activities required for each block (what to do), and (2) Task 1-2: Selecting, identifying, designing, and flow-charting of author aids to completing the activities (how to do).

Develop What-To-Do Flow Charts

Figures 2.2 and 2.3 are flow charts from the IPISD model for the development of tests block (II.2) and the development of instruction block (III.4). These flow charts provide a broad description and sequencing of necessary activities. However, because of their global nature, they provide only minimal assistance to the instructional systems designer. For example, in Figure 2.2 the IPISD element determine scoring procedure (element 2.6) provides no guidance on the specific steps required for determining scoring procedures for a test. The instructional systems designer must be made aware of these specific steps. Therefore, in this project we used the IPISD flow charts as the basic framework for expanding each IPISD element into detailed step-by-step subelements that must be performed (or considered) in completing the specific flow chart block. Figure 2.4 shows how the IPISD element determine scoring procedure (2.6) was expanded into subelements.

It was found that the activity descriptions shown in subelement blocks were not always sufficiently descriptive of the activities required by the block. Consequently, it was necessary to flow-chart several of these subelement blocks further. An example of further flow-charting of subelement Block 2.6.1 (determine qualitative scoring procedures) is shown in Figure 2.5. The narrative on the right of the flow chart further clarifies the block and lists any references to existing author aids.

The product that resulted from the Task 1-1 activities is itself a valuable author aid for instructional systems designers (Hibbits, Wagner, &

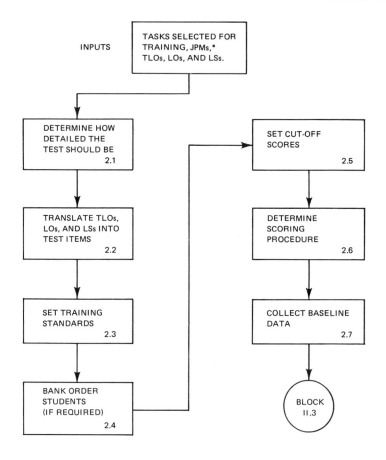

*JOB PERFORMANCE MEASURES
 TERMINAL LEARNING OBJECTIVES
 LEARNING OBJECTIVES
 LEARNING STEPS.

Figure 2.2 Flow chart of Block II.2: Develop tests. [TRADOC PAM 350-30, Executive Summary and Model, August 1975.]

Schulz, 1976). It provides a step-by-step enunciation of activities that must be performed. The revised and expanded flow charts were produced as off-line materials. As such, they can be converted to checklists and used as procedural guides by designers of instruction.

Identify and Reference How-to-Do-It Author Aids

In Task 1-1 the detailed activities (subelements) needed for developing tests and instruction were defined and arranged into sequential order. In

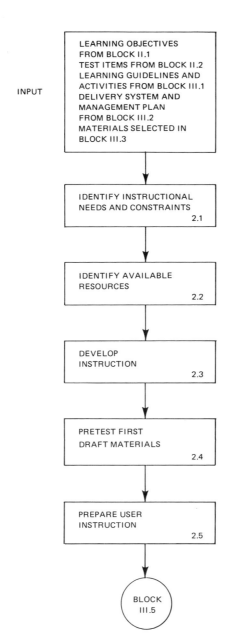

INPUT

LEARNING OBJECTIVES
FROM BLOCK II.1
TEST ITEMS FROM BLOCK II.2
LEARNING GUIDELINES AND
ACTIVITIES FROM BLOCK III.1
DELIVERY SYSTEM AND
MANAGEMENT PLAN
FROM BLOCK III.2
MATERIALS SELECTED IN
BLOCK III.3

IDENTIFY INSTRUCTIONAL
NEEDS AND CONSTRAINTS
2.1

IDENTIFY AVAILABLE
RESOURCES
2.2

DEVELOP
INSTRUCTION
2.3

PRETEST FIRST
DRAFT MATERIALS
2.4

PREPARE USER
INSTRUCTION
2.5

BLOCK
III.5

Figure 2.3 Flow chart of Block III.4: Develop instruction. [TRADOC PAM 350-30, Executive Summary and Model, August 1975.]

49

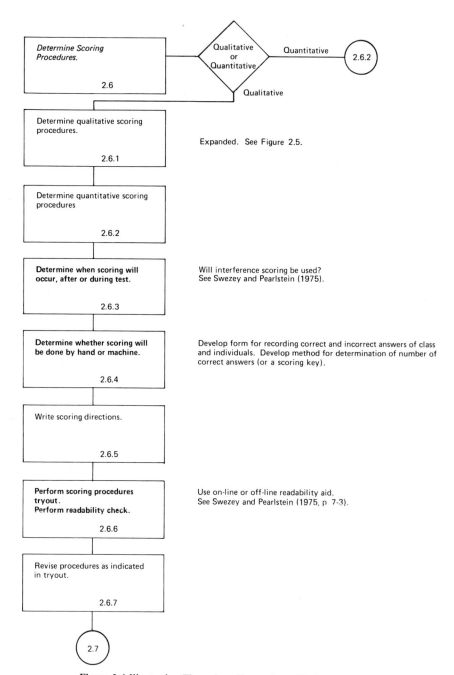

Figure 2.4 Illustrative Flow chart Expansion of IPSD Block 2.6.

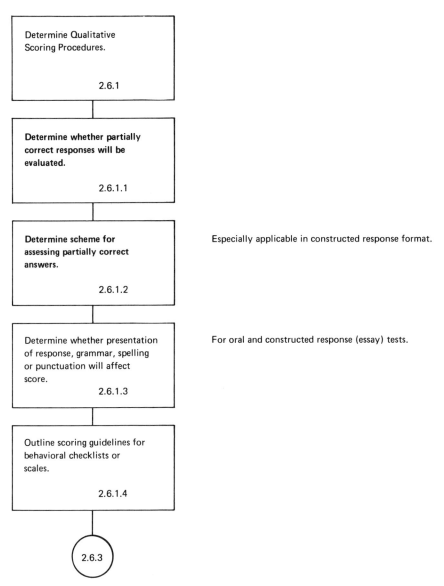

Figure 2.5 Illustrative Flow chart Expansion of Block 2.6.1.

Task 1-2, each subelement was examined to determine specific authoring aids desirable to accomplish the subelement. In other words, Task 1-1 **describes what must be done,** and Task 1-2 **defines author aids for doing it.** Time constraints did not permit the development or selection of author aids for every subelement. Therefore, aids were provided for those subelements that were identified as of highest priority for potential users. The selection was based on such factors as

1. Available HumRRO expertise gained from previous author aid development (Schulz, 1975a)
2. A review of the literature to identify aids already available for use
3. Opinions of instructional systems designers at the U.S. Army Engineering School concerning aids they considered would be helpful to them

Throughout Task 1-1 and Task 1-2, care was taken to assure that the flow charts were sufficiently detailed and annotated to be of practical use to instructional systems designers and would readily permit adaptation to any system (i.e., be hardware- or software-independent).

Task 1 activities resulted in an interim report and guide to the use of flow charts (Hibbits *et al.*, 1976). This report contains flow charts providing detailed guidance on the procedural steps necessary for developing tests and instruction and identifies the subelements of each for which author aids were developed. In addition, the interim report includes a guide to the use of flow charts, which was thought necessary since many authors may not be familiar with a flow chart format.

The flow charts prepared in Task 1 are of value from three standpoints:

1. They are useful as tools for instructional systems designers in the implementation of the IPISD process.
2. They may be used as a model for detailing the processes covered in other IPISD blocks in terms of level of detail, style, and format.
3. They may be used in the preparation of on-line author aids on any CAI system.

Task 2: *Conversion of Flow Charts to Interactive Program*

In Task 2, author aids identified in Task 1 were developed for presentation on the PLATO IV computer-based instruction system. Since the PLATO IV system was considered a research vehicle only, care was taken to ensure that the author aids developed could be readily modified to be hardware- or software-independent. Where possible, the author aids were also created so as to have application for off-line use.

Author aids were developed to assist authors in preparing instructional and test materials for both computer-based instruction and non-computer-based instruction. Computer-based instruction was the principal mode used in this research because the computer-based instruction mode provides opportunity for ease of gathering and analyzing data regarding both student and author activities.

Develop-Instruction Author Aids

Tutorial Author Aids. This series of author aids provides authors with guidance in the preparation of lesson materials. On-line the guidance is automatically presented at appropriate points during the lesson development process, but it may be reviewed at any time. The guidelines are available in both on-line and off-line versions. Specific guidelines included in this series of aids are

1. Instructional sequencing rules
2. Guidelines for the preparation of terminal learning objectives
3. Guidelines for reducing reading difficulty level
4. Guidelines for the preparation of text material
5. Guidelines for the use of practice question formats (general)
6. Guidelines for the preparation of multiple-choice practice questions
7. Guidelines for the preparation of true–false practice questions
8. Guidelines for the preparation of constructed response practice questions

After studying rules or guidelines, the author may interact with the following series of aids that provide direction during the development process:

Author Aid for the Sequencing of Instruction. Instructional content is, of course, based on terminal learning objectives, learning objectives, and learning steps. However, how these are sequenced in the instruction may very well determine whether an instructional module is effective or ineffective. (A module, as here defined, begins with a learning objective or learning step and is usually followed by 5–10 frames of text and practice questions that teach the learning objective or learning step.) To assist authors in the creation of modules and the sequencing of instruction, worksheets have been prepared for off-line creation of learning objectives, learning steps, text frames, and various types of practice questions.

Author Aid for the On-Line Management of Learning Objectives and Learning Steps. Learning objectives and learning steps are the backbone of the IPISD process. The instructional systems designer must attend to them carefully to ensure that they are represented in the instruction and test situation. As described earlier, each module of instruction begins with a learning objective or learning step. This aid, therefore, requires the author to input the learning objective or learning step prior to inputting instruction for the related module. During the preparation sf the instruction for the module, the associated learning objective or learning step is available to the author as a continual reminder of the instruction to be addressed. A byproduct in the computerized version that is available to students studying a particular module of instruction is the option to access the learning objective or learning step statement underlying the instructional module.

Author Aid for Computing Reading Difficulty. When preparing any instructional material, it is essential for the author to consider the intended audience for the material (Caylor, Sticht, Fox, & Ford, 1973; Flesch, 1948; Kincaid, 1972; Klare, 1963; Klare & Sinaiko, 1971; Sticht, 1975; Taylor, 1953). Therefore, this author aid was prepared for use on the PLATO system and automatically computes the reading difficulty of instructional material as the material is inputted into the system. In using the aid, authors specify the reading ability level of the intended audience and if this level is exceeded, the computer so informs the author, who can then revise the instructional material to a lower reading level.

Author Aid for Creation and Editing of Text Materials. This author aid permits authors to create CAI executable textual material without a knowledge of the programming language required by the system. The text may be placed at the author's option any place on the CAI screen and permits revision after initial creation.

Author Aids for Practice-Item Creation. These are a series of several author aids that allow creation of practice questions. They can be in either a multiple choice, a true–false, or a constructed-response format. The author aids do not require a knowledge by authors of a computer programming language. Detailed characteristics of the constructed-response author aid are shown in Table 2.1.

Author Aids Controlling Within-Lesson Branching. These are of two kinds:

1. *Author-directed branching.* Today in most forms of self-paced instruction students must demonstrate a mastery of current instruction before being allowed to go on to new instruction. That is, students are branched depending upon their particular needs. This process requires that student performance be continuously monitored. Author aids have been provided to assist authors in these efforts.

2. *Student-directed branching.* Students themselves frequently know when they need additional assistance and should have the opportunity of accessing this assistance whenever they desire. However, they must be

TABLE 2.1
Characteristics of Practice-question Author Aid (Constructed Response)

Question may be a maximum of six 50-character lines.
Author specifies number of attempts (one to three) student is permitted on question.
Student response analyzed for one to four correct or partially correct answers.
Student response analyzed for one to four anticipated incorrect answers.
Congratulatory messages (one to four) permitted depending upon number of correct or partially correct answers specified by author. Messages may be a maximum of five 40-character lines.
Wrong answer messages (one to four) permitted depending upon number of incorrect answers specified. Messages may be a maximum of five 40-character lines.
Author has option of permitting misspelling of answer, words in answer to be out of order, extra words in answer, and disregarding capitalization of answer.
Correct answer given student if number of permitted attempts reached without student's correctly answering question.
Reading difficulty of question and feedback messages automatically computed. If desired reading level exceeded, author has option to revise material.

able to identify what assistance is available and the means for accessing it. This series of author aids provides students the options of accessing auxiliary information, of returning to previously studied material, and, if permitted by the author, of branching to the end-of-lesson test from any place in the lesson.

Develop-Tests Author Aids

Tutorial Author Aids. This series of author aids is similar to those discussed in the tutorial author aids for lesson development. These aids, however, provide both on-line and off-line guidance in the various facets of test development. Like the lesson-development tutorial author aids, they are automatically presented to authors at appropriate points during the test-development process and are available for review at any time. Specific guidelines included in this series of aids are

1. Guidelines for writing test instructions
2. Guidelines for the preparation of multiple-choice test items
3. Guidelines for the preparation of true–false test items
4. Guidelines for the preparation of constructed-response test items
5. Guidelines for assigning scores to test items
6. Guidelines for posttest student review of test items and remediation strategies

The following aids provide more specific interactions with the author during the actual development activities.
Author Aids for the Off-Line Preparation of Test Instructions and Test

Items. Worksheets are provided to authors for off-line creation of test instructions and the various types of test items. These aids permit authors to organize and sequence their test items prior to input into the computer.

Author Aid for the Preparation and Sequencing of Terminal Learning Objectives, Learning Objectives, and Learning Steps. This author aid is somewhat different from the corresponding aid used for creating objectives in the lesson-development process. Using this aid prior to the input of any test items or test instructions, authors input all objectives into the computer in the sequence in which they wish to cover them in the test. The aid then maintains records of which objective has been addressed and "cues" the author as to the objective they should next address.

Author Aid for Creation of Test Instructions. This aid is identical to the aid for creation of text materials described earlier. Authors use this aid to create initial and within-test student instructions for taking the test.

Author Aids for Creation of Test Items. This series of author aids is used for creation of representative types of multiple-choice, constructed-response, and true–false test items.

Author Aid for Student Time Restrictions on Test. This aid permits authors to establish, if desired, a time limit for individual items in the test **or** a time limit for the entire test, which is then managed by the computer.

Author Aid for Test Item Scoring. This aid permits test developers to establish their own test scoring procedures. Included in the aid are such considerations as the setting of cutoff scores, differential weighting of various answers to a test item (e.g., correct, partially correct, and incorrect answers), and/or differential weighting of different test items.

Author Aid for Reporting of Test Results to the Student. Subsequent to test item scoring, authors establish the minimum passing score required. This aid then scores the test and automatically reports to students their obtained score and the minimum score required for passing the test.

Author Aids for Providing Posttest Review of Test Items Missed. These aids permit the test developer to select different student review options for test items missed. For example, if the student passes the test with less than a perfect score, the author may elect to show the student the correct answer to items missed. Or, in the case of students who fail the test, the author may elect to (*a*) show the students test items missed without providing the correct answers; (*b*) show test items missed and include the correct answers; or (*c*) not permit a review of items missed.

Author Aids for Providing Remediation Actions. These are a series of author aids that permit the test developer to select the type of action that will be taken if a student fails the test. The actions possible in these aids are as follows:

1. Readministration of instructional lesson followed by readministration of test items previously missed
2. Readministration of instructional lesson followed by readministration of **entire** test
3. Immediate readministration of test items previously missed (no readministration of instructional lesson)
4. Immediate readministration of **entire** test (no readministration of instructional lesson)
5. Readministration of test items missed. Give student option of reviewing instructional lesson first
6. Readministration of entire test. Give student option of reviewing instructional lesson first
7. No readministration of instructional lesson or test—student is finished with lesson or goes to new lesson

Task 3: *Evaluation*

Three levels of evaluation were undertaken in this project. The first level was an informal evaluation of **existing** IPISD guidance, procedures, and author aids. Project staff judged the ease and effectiveness with which selected IPISD procedures and guidelines could be used to develop instruction.

The second level of evaluation was a comprehensive formative evaluation of the **new** author aids and procedures for developing tests and instruction. Three instructors from the Engineer Noncommissioned Officer Advanced course (one officer and two noncommissioned officers) served as study participants and as a data source for Level 2 evaluation. A small group of authors was selected since the author aids were in their formative stage of development. The authors selected were representative of typical instructional developers at the U.S. Army Engineer School. These instructors used the aids to create test items and lesson material. Evaluation data were gathered as the authors developed their instructional material. Each of the instructors developed a lesson in his content specialty as part of a 2–3 hour block of different, but related, subject matter from the Engineer Noncommissioned Officer Advanced course. Table 2.2 lists the subject matter blocks selected for this project. Formative evaluation of the author aids was accomplished by examining author performance and acceptance of the aids. Data collection, to a large extent, resulted from direct observations of the authors creating and inputting their instruction and from structured interviews with the authors. We gathered user ac-

TABLE 2.2
Lessons Authored Using Aids

Lesson	Time to create lesson (in hours)	Completion time in current course (in hours)	Average completion time in CAI version (in hours)
Field fortification emplacement construction	48.5	4	1.57 ($N = 9$)
U.S.–foreign mine warfare doctrine	41.0	2	1.00 ($N = 11$)
Protective mining	35.0	3	.54 ($N = 9$)
Total	124.5	9	3.11

ceptance data and information on various areas of difficulty that the authors experienced while using the aids.

In the third evaluation level, the adequacy of the instruction created by the military authors was assessed. This instruction was administered to U.S. Army Engineer School trainees, who provided the data for evaluation. Prerequisites for students selected were that they be noncommissioned officers with entry qualifications for the Engineer Noncommissioned Officer Advanced course, but that they not have been exposed to the material covered in these lessons. All students received preliminary training on using PLATO. Since all the students could not go through all the instruction and testing within the time allotted by the U.S. Army Engineer School for this project, only two of the three lessons were presented on a random basis to each student. Table 2.2 shows the number of students ($N = 9$, 11, and 9) who received each block of instruction.

Presentation of lesson content occurred on-line, as did the administration of the posttests. Cognitive data regarding student performance were collected, and exit questionnaires were administered to obtain information regarding opinions of the clarity of the instructional material, problems encountered in the practice and test items, and attitudes toward the computer-based instruction experience.

Task 4: *Revisions*

Task 4 activities consisted of making revisions to the descriptive flow charts and author aids. The purpose of the revisions was to assure maximum utility of the flow charts and author aids in implementing the

IPISD process. Revisions constituted a series of activities that spanned almost the entire research period and paralleled all development and evaluation actions in the other tasks.

FINDINGS

Data for instructional development and test development author aids were combined because of the essential similarity of the aids used for lesson–test development.

Instruction and Test Development

The tutorial aids were presented to each author prior to inputting the relevant test–instructional material. In no instance did the authors seek to reread these aids, which presented guidance on test and lesson development. It appears that more emphasis in describing their applicability and value to the authors is required in order for them to pay attention to this guidance. This may involve a considerable change in their presentation format.

As a result of our initial formative evaluation (Evaluation Level 1), the authors were able to prepare their test and lesson material without the appearance of many problems. In developing almost 360 frames of instruction and testing, a total of 65 problems were experienced by the authors as recorded by the monitors. Over 25% (18) of these problems were trivial errors caused by the author's pushing the wrong key. Fourteen instances were due to unclear instructions in the aids, which were remedied as soon as possible after they were noted. Twenty-one problems were due to "bugs" in the aids, which were eliminated as soon as their diagnosis was confirmed. Six problems arose for miscellaneous reasons. Thus, most of the instructional and test development activity undertaken by the authors occurred smoothly and without undue difficulty.

Time

The blocks of instruction from the course that were put on-line are traditionally taught in 9 hours. The average completion time was under 3¼ hours for this instruction, including taking the associated tests (see Table 2.2).

The time to prepare and input into the computer the test items and lesson materials did not vary much from one author to another. It ranged from 41 hours (for the officer with 14.5 hours on-line), to 35 for one noncommissioned officer (15 hours on-line), and 48.5 for the other non-commissioned officer (18.5 hours on-line). However, no comparable data for developing traditional instruction was available.

Readability Index

This author aid provided information if the reading grade level established by the authors was surpassed for each text frame or test item. However, it was hardly ever used. That is, no matter what the index showed, the authors chose to ignore it. About 220 text frames of instruction were produced in this study. More than 50% (126) exceeded the prespecified reading levels. However, only 1 frame of instruction was revised by the author as a result of this information. This was due either to a lack of confidence in the measure's validity or to reluctance on the part of the author to change the text to conform with the prespecified reading level, or to a combination of both. In any event, no changes have yet been made to this aid. However, at least two possible changes are needed. First, authors should be given more instruction in the usefulness of this aid together with more practice. Second, the options available to override this aid should be removed entirely or severely constrained (i.e., within one grade level on either side of the prespecified one).

Multiple-Choice Items

As authors prepared multiple-choice practice and test items, an author aid assigned the correct answer alternative on a random basis. Authors were given the option to change the designation of the correct answer alternative, and approximately half the time exercised this option. Authors were thus indicating their preference for retaining control over the manner in which they created instruction.

Another author aid compared the lengths of answer alternatives and indicated when they were unequal. This aid was developed because of our belief that answer alternatives should be of approximately the same length in order that the length of the answer alternative itself would not be a cue to the correct answer. Answer alternatives of unequal length were written for about half the items. However, authors unanimously disregarded this information and left the alternatives as they were. It appears that more restrictions should be built into the author aid in order for this feature to be used.

Constructed-response Items

In constructed-response format, authors used the following aids:

• They used the aid that permitted them to define the rigor with which answers would be scored. They selected those options that permitted misspelling, allowed extra words, and did not count whether capitalization was correct or not. However, they did not permit the words in the answer to be out of order.

• They made full use of the various aids available for preparing response feedbacks. They varied in their choices of giving trainees specific as well as general feedbacks to both anticipated and unanticipated answers. The most positive reaction by students was to the explanatory feedbacks presented after each response to practice questions. The author aids for presenting response feedbacks were used frequently by the authors.

• They were able to use the aids to specify anticipated correct and incorrect answers. However, there appeared to be a problem with anticipating all the answers given by the trainees. The student questionnaire data collected showed a strong negative reaction to the constructed response questions provided by all the authors. In addition to their attitudes, the student performance data showed that these were the items that gave the students the most trouble during both learning and test taking. These results were traced to the problem that authors did not adequately anticipate all the alternate synonymous correct answers given by the trainees. As a result of this finding, it is recommended that the guidance for preparing constructed-response items be revised to emphasize those situations where authors should or should not use that type of question. That is, constructed-response formats should be used only in cases where the number of possible alternate correct answers is small.

Student Options

Of the student options, the ability to back up to a previous frame (BACK) was considered helpful by almost all of the trainees in all three lessons. The other three options were (a) HELP, in which the relevant learning objective was displayed; (b) LAB, in which the student could return to the beginning of the lesson; and (c) DATA, in which the student could go back to the beginning of module. All three options were rarely used, and so it was not surprising that students were divided in their opinions about their necessity.

RECOMMENDATIONS

The evaluation of the author aids has demonstrated the utility of the aids developed in implementing development of tests (IPISD Block II.2) and development of instruction (IPISD Block III.4). User acceptance of the aids is high and the time required for creation of test and lesson material was found to be less than 50 hours per student contact hour. Because of this, further developmental effort of on-line author aids seems warranted. A continued development effort should include five major areas. A discussion of each follows.

Modification of Current Author Aids

There was insufficient time during the project to make all of the modifications that were indicated during formative evaluation. These modifications should be made if the lesson and test development author aids are to be maximally effective. The specific author aids for which modification are recommended are as follows.

Reading Difficulty Index

As reported, our experimental authors **did not** revise lesson or test material when the material was written at a reading difficulty level in excess of that intended. We therefore recommend that the author aid be revised to force authors to revise material when the reading difficulty level of the material is more than one grade level above the desired reading level.

Author Aid for Creating
Constructed-Response Questions

Authors require additional guidance in determining how to use constructed-response questions appropriately. When constructed-response questions are used, guidance is needed in the selection of the correct answers and alternate forms of the correct answer (e.g., George Washington, Geo. Washington, President George Washington, etc.).

Editing of Text and Lesson Material

With the present author aids, all editing must occur only during the creation of text or questions. Once material has been completed, there is no provision for further editing. This is a severe weakness of present author aids. It is possible to revise the author aids so as to permit text and question revision after trial administration of the lesson. However, this is a major effort that requires much programming time.

Additional Author Aids for Instructional Development

Although we had planned to develop certain author aids, project time constraints did not permit us to complete this effort. We recommend that the following aids be developed.

- Author aid for creation of matching questions
- Author aid for creation of arithmetic manipulation questions
- Author aid for creation of multiple-choice questions with more than one correct answer

Author Characteristics

Authoring of CAI lessons requires a certain discipline and level of competence that may not be present in all instructors assigned to this task. Aids are thus needed that constrain the author much more than we have done in this project, in order that useful guidance and techniques can be applied in creating effective instruction. A research effort is needed to establish what are the minimal prerequisites for authoring both on- and off-line materials, and then to see whether author aids can be created to compensate for characteristics not present in such personnel. If such a study indicates that many individual proficiencies are lacking and cannot be overcome by author aids, then a selection and classification problem would have been uncovered, and a study assessing the needs of an "author" job–duty position should be undertaken.

REFERENCES

Aagard, J. A., & Braby, R. *Learning guidelines and algorithms for types of learning objectives* (TAEG Report No. 23). Orlando, Fla.: Training Analysis and Evaluation Group, March 1976.

American Airlines, Inc. *Optimized flight crew training, a step toward safer operations.* Fort Worth, Tex.: Flight Training Academy, 1969.

Ammerman, H. L., & Melching. W. H. *The derivation, analysis, and classification of instructional objectives* (HumRRO Tech. Rep. 66-4). Alexandria, Va.: Human Resources Research Organization, May 1966.

Baker, R. A. *The determination of job requirements for tank crew members* (HumRRO Tech. Rep. 47). Alexandria, Va.: Human Resources Research Organization, May 1958.

Bitzer, D. L., Sherwood, B. A., & Tenczar, P. *Computer-based science education* (CERL Report X-37). Urbana: University of Illinois, Computer Education Research Laboratory, May 1973.

Bloom, B. S. (Ed.). *Taxonomy of educational objectives—the classification of educational goals—Handbook I: Cognitive domain.* New York: David McKay, 1968.

Bond, N. A., & Rigney, J. W. *Measurement of training outcomes* (Tech. Rep. 66). Los Angeles: University of Southern California, Department of Psychology, June 1970.

Braby, R., Micheli, C. S., Morris, C. L., & Okraski, H. S. *Staff study on cost and training effectiveness of proposed training systems* (TAEG Report 1). Orlando, Fla.: Training and Evaluation Group, U.S. Naval Training Equipment Center, 1972.

Butts, D. P. *Stating instructional objectives. First experimental edition.* Austin: University of Texas, Research and Development Center for Teacher Education, 1970.

Caylor, J. A., Sticht, T. G., Fox, L. C., & Ford, J. P. *Methodologies for determining reading requirements of military occupational specialties* (HumRRO Tech. Rep. 73-5). Alexandria, Va.: Human Resources Research Organization, March 1973.

Esbensen, T. *Using performance objectives.* Tallahassee: Florida State University, Department of Education, April 1970.

Flesch, R. F. A new readability yardstick. *Journal of Applied Psychology,* 1948, *32*(3).

Gagné, R. M. *The conditions of learning.* New York: Holt, Rinehart and Winston, 1970.

Ghesquiere, J., Davis, C., & Thompson, C. *Introduction to TUTOR.* Urbana: University of Illinois, Computer Education Research Laboratory, 1974.

Glaser, R. Psychological bases for instructional design. *AV Communication Review,* 1966, *14*(4).

Hammes, J. A., Kelly, H. E., McFann, H. H., & Ward, J. S. *TRAINFIRE II: A new course in basic techniques of fire and squad tactics* (HumRRO Tech. Rep. 41). Alexandria, Va.: Human Resources Research Organization, July 1957.

Hartley, H. S. Twelve hurdles to clear before you take on systems analysis. *American School Board Journal,* July 1968.

Hibbits, N., Wagner, H., & Schulz, R. *Interim report and guide to the use of flowcharts* (IR-ED-76-48). Alexandria, Va.: Human Resources Research Organization, November 1976.

Interservice Procedures for Instructional Systems Development. Executive summary and model (TRADOC Pamphlet 350-30). Washington, D.C.: U.S. Army Training and Doctrine Command, August 1975. (a)

Interservice Procedures for Instructional Systems Development. Phases I, II, and III, Analyze, Design and Develop (3 vol); *Phases IV and V, Implement and Control* (1 vol) (TRADOC Pamphlets 350-30). Washington, D.C.: U.S. Army Training and Doctrine Command, August 1975. (b)

Jeantheau, G. G. *Handbook for training system evaluation* (NAVTRADEVCEN 66-C-0133-2). Orlando, Fla.: U.S. Naval Training Device Center, 1972.

Kincaid, J. P. Making technical writing readable (the Fog Count and an alternative). *Human Factors Society Bulletin,* 1972, *15*(5).

Klare, G. R. *The measurement of readability.* Ames: Iowa State University Press, 1963.

Klare, G. R., & Sinaiko, H. W. *The CLOZE procedure: A convenient readability test for training materials and translations.* Arlington, Va.: Institute for Defense Analysis, January 1971.

Koberg, D., & Bagnall, J. *The universal traveler.* Los Altos, Calif.: William Kaufman, Inc., 1972.

Krathwohl, D. R., Bloom, B. S., & Masia, B. B. *Taxonomy of educational objectives—The* classification of education goals—Handbook II: Affective domain. New York: David McKay 1969.

Lipson, J. I. Needed: A collaborative open university network. Productivity in Higher Education (Proceedings of Educational Technologies Symposium). Stony Brook, N.Y.: September 1973.

Logan, R. S. An instructional systems development approach for learning strategies. In H. F. O'Neil, Jr. (Ed.), Learning strategies. New York: Academic Press, 1978.

MacCaslin, E. F., Woodruff, A. B., & Baker, R. A. An improved advanced individual training program (HumRRO Tech. Rep. 59). Alexandria, Va.: Human Resources Research Organization, December 1959.

Mager, R. F. Preparing instructional objectives. Palo Alto, Calif.: Fearon Publishers, 1962.

McFann, H. H., Hammes, J. A., & Taylor, J. E. TRAINFIRE I: A new course in basic rifle marksmanship (HumRRO Tech. Rep. 22). Alexandria, Va.: Human Resources Research Organization, October 1955.

Melching, W. H. Behavioral objectives and individualization of instruction (Professional Paper 18-69). Alexandria, Va.: Human Resources Research Organization, May 1969.

Micheli, G. S. Analysis of the transfer of training, substitution and fidelity of simulation of training equipment (NAVTRAQUIPCEN TAEG Report 2). Orlando, Fla.: U.S. Naval Equipment Center, Training and Evaluation Group, 1972.

Montmerlo, M. D. Instructional systems development state-of-the-art and directions for the future. Paper presented at eighth NTEC–Industry Conference, Orlando, Fla.: U.S. Naval Training Equipment Center, 1975.

Quade, E. S. Systems analysis and policy planning: Applications in defense. New York: American Elsevier Publishing Company, 1968.

Rundquist, W. A. Course design and redesign manual for job training courses (Research Report SRR 66-17, revised, 1st ed.). San Diego, Calif.: U.S. Naval Personnel Research Activity, January 1967.

Schulz, R. E. Lesson MONIFORM: An authoring aid for the PLATO IV CAI system (RP-ED-75-6). Alexandria, Va.: Human Resources Research Organization, April 1975. (AD-A034 153 ED-127 926) (a)

Schulz, R. E. MONIFORMS as authoring aids for the PLATO IV CAI system (HumRRO Tech. Rep. 75-5). Alexandria, Va.: Human Resources Research Organization, May 1975. (AD-A102 674 ED-111 338) (b)

Simonsen, R. H., & Renshaw, K. S. CAI—Boon or boondoggle. Datamation, March 1974.

Smith, R. G., Jr. The engineering of educational and training systems. Lexington, Mass.: D. C. Heath, 1971.

Sticht, T. G. Readability of job materials. In T. G. Sticht (Ed.), Reading for working. Alexandria, Va.: Human Resources Research Organization, 1975.

Stifle, J. The PLATO IV architecture (CERL Report X-20). Urbana: University of Illinois, Computer Education Research Laboratory, 1973.

Stifle, J. The PLATO IV student terminal (CERL Report X-15). Urbana: University of Illinois, Computer Education Research Laboratory, 1974.

Swezey, R. W., & Pearlstein, R. B. Guidebook for developing criterion-referenced tests. Arlington, Va.: U.S. Army Institute for the Behavioral and Social Sciences, 1975.

Taylor, W. CLOZE procedure: A new tool for measuring readability. Journalism Quarterly, 1953, 30,

U.S. Air Force. Instructional System Development (AFM 50-2). Washington, D.C.: Department of the Air Force, December 1970.

U.S. Army. *Systems engineering of training* (CONARC Regulations 350-100-1). Washington, D.C.: Department of the Army, 1968.

U.S. Navy. *Design of training systems: Phase I report, volumes 1 and 2* (TAEG Report No. 12-1). Orlando, Fla.: U.S. Naval Training Equipment Center, Training and Evaluation Group, February 1973.

Van Pelt, K. B., & Rich, J. J. *Effective writing for a computerized training system* (TRADOC Interim Report CTS-TR-75-1). U.S. Army Training and Doctrine Command, January 1975.

Wydra, F. T. Learner controlled instruction: How allied supermarkets made it work. *Training,* August 1975.

3

The Technology of
Test-Item Writing[1]

GALE ROID

A radical but plausible argument could be made that tests and the items that compose them are the most important elements in an instructional system. The word *test* is used in a very general way to mean a series of cognitive or performance tasks requiring responses from students that are capable of being scored in a consistent manner. Tests used in instructional systems provide information to both instructors and students concerning learning achievement. Results from tests provide feedback to the developer of the system and are essential in the empirical revision and improvement of the instruction. Tests provide data to consumers of an instructional system to help them choose between competing instructional programs or to identify a valid program. Tests and the items that compose them are essential to student learning as indicated by research on prose learning, which has shown that questions promote learning and attention to text (Faw & Waller, 1976).

Many important decisions that have a bearing on the future education and employment of students and trainees are made by tests given as part of educational and training programs. The goal of test developers is to make such tests as precise and accurate as possible. Precise and accurate

[1] This work was supported by Contract No. MDA–903–77–C–0189, Defense Advanced Research Projects Agency, Washington, D.C. The Navy Personnel Research and Development Center, San Diego, provided technical monitoring of this contract. Contracting officer's technical representative was Pat-Anthony Federico. Opinions or recommendations in this chapter are those of the author and not necessarily those of the supporting agencies.

67

Copyright © 1979 by Academic Press, Inc.
All rights of reproduction in any form reserved.
ISBN 0-12-526660-X

tests are able to detect small differences in the achievement of students and are systematically related to educational experiences that the students have had prior to taking the tests.

In addition to helping make decisions about students, educational tests are increasingly used to evaluate the effectiveness of educational and training programs. Decisions about programs can be crucial in that they are frequently politically charged or involve allocations of money, resources, and people's jobs. Thus, tests must be precise and accurate in measuring the learning of students exposed to programs and other benefits and the costs of these programs.

In using tests to make educational decisions, educators need a criterion-referenced interpretation of test results where the performance of students is compared to an external criterion or performance standard, rather than compared to other students or a norm group. Using test results for comparisons between individuals and norm groups has been called *norm-referenced testing*; using test results to compare individual performance to a standard has been called *criterion-referenced testing*. Recent reviews of the literature on criterion-referenced testing (Hambleton, Swaminathan, Algina, & Coulson, 1978; Millman, 1974) have clarified the definition of criterion-referenced tests as those "used to ascertain an individual's status with respect to a well-defined behavior domain." The *domain of behavior* for a criterion-referenced test is defined by the universe of possible test items (Osburn, 1968) from which a sample of items is taken to form a test. The universe of items is defined by the purposes and specifications of an instructional system (Shoemaker, 1975) or by rules or algorithms for generating items (Hively, 1974; Osburn, 1968). This is in contrast to the writing of test items for each learning objective, which results in what could be called *objective-based tests*. For a full discussion of the differences between domain-based criterion-referenced tests and objective-based tests see Millman (1974), Popham (1975), and Hambleton *et al.* (1978).

Development of good-quality tests for instructional systems is a challenge, particularly for systems involving the mastery learning model (Bloom, 1968) or the personalized system of instruction (Sherman, 1974). These systems allow students to repeat tests until mastery of a unit of instruction is demonstrated. A large number of items is needed in order to provide multiple test forms for use by students who may be retested several times. Each of these test forms must be equivalent in terms of content coverage and difficulty. The challenge of providing a large number of equivalent tests has prompted considerable interest in a technology of test-item writing.

BACKGROUND

The Need for a Technology of Item Writing

Bormuth (1970) has convincingly argued that there is currently a crisis in education stemming from the fact that a scientific basis for writing achievement test items is not always employed. The most widely used methods of writing test questions, for both objective-based and norm-referenced tests, rely on the intuitive skills of the item writer or panels of experts who judge the merits of questions. Even when item writers are given learning objectives that describe what is to be learned in terms of expected student performance under specified conditions and standards, it has been shown (Roid & Haladyna, 1978a) that two writers will not generate the same items or items of similar quality. The Roid and Haladyna study showed that one of two item writers produced consistently more difficult test items from the same learning objectives. In addition, they have established that modified Bormuth procedures (Bormuth, 1970; Finn, 1975) in which sentences from prose passages were transformed into test items in only a partially operationally defined way were also equally susceptible to the influx of item-writer bias. This bias resulted in tests of different difficulty depending on the writer, which would have serious implication for the criterion-referenced uses of such tests (e.g., affecting decisions about who passes or fails such tests).

In assessing the precision and accuracy of commonly used norm-referenced and objective-based tests, several investigators such as Osburn (1968), Bormuth (1970), Anderson (1972), and Hively (1974) have been critical of conventional methods used to construct items for such tests. Bormuth has described conventional methods of test construction as "primitive" and "defined wholly in the private subjective life of the test writer [p. 3]," and he has contended that it is impossible to construct true criterion-referenced tests using conventional item-writing methods, such as those in which test writers compose items from their subjective interpretations of learning objectives:

1. Conventional methods cannot be taken as unbiased evidence upon which to base policy because the characteristics of the items are biased by the subjective standards of the item writer.

2. Conventional tests are difficult for persons other than the original developers to reproduce because of the vagueness of the item-writing methods used, so that studies based on them cannot be easily refuted or confirmed by other investigators.

3. Conventional item writing is based on the private intuition of the item writer rather than on a set of operations open to public inspection.

4. Conventional test development does not separate test design from item writing—that is, the item writer both selects content for inclusion in the test and writes items for the content chosen. In this process, there is no guarantee that the content has been systematically sampled in the most rigorous way possible. Systematic sampling of items representing important elements of a performance would be essential for criterion-referenced testing.

5. Conventional methods are not precise as to the relationship between the instruction and the test items, and the relationships that do exist are not open to public description or inspection. Criterion-referenced testing would require a precise relationship between the performance standards upon which instruction is based and the tests used to assess performance.

Bormuth (1970), Anderson (1972), and others have called for a technology of item writing to correct these deficiencies in conventional testing methods. Several item-writing methods capable of being computerized have been proposed, including a technology for transforming sentences from prose passages in instructional materials into test items (Bormuth, 1970) and the use of rules, or *item forms*, which specify an exact format for a set of items (Hively, 1974; Osburn, 1968). It is these newly proposed methods of item writing that are the focus of this chapter.

A Continuum of Item-Writing Methods

The great variety of approaches to writing questions for achievement tests can be represented by the levels of a hypothetical continuum from informal to formal item-generation methods as shown in Figure 3.1.

At the first level of this continuum is a heterogeneous mixture of informal methods that an individual might use in constructing a test. For example, items could be written to test learning from a textbook by leafing

1. Informal methods
⇓
2. Writing from learning objectives
⇓
3. Writing from detailed learning objectives
⇓
4. Writing from item-generation rules with writer's choice
⇓
5. Writing from item forms or computerized methods

Figure 3.1 Continuum of item-writing methods.

through the pages of the text and selecting important points that might catch the readers' attention. Questions could be written for each important point that happened to be seen.

At the second level of the continuum, items are constructed by item writers who read statements of learning objectives—descriptions of tasks the student is expected to perform under specified conditions to accepted standards. The choice of the exact wording of each item is left to the item writer.

At the third level, the item writer reads a more detailed statement of a learning objective, which provides delimiting specifications concerning testing situations, response alternatives, and criteria for the correctness of answers. Popham (1974) has called these statements *amplified objectives*, and he has provided examples of them. An item writer who uses these detailed learning objectives has more guidance than that provided by a standard learning objective, because the form and wording of possible test items are more completely described.

At the fourth level of the continuum are item-generation rules that allow some choice by a human item writer, such as those used in the study by Roid and Haladyna (1978a) or the more rigorous method of Finn (1975). These methods include the rigor of specifying a domain (e.g., the domain of all instructional sentences in a textbook), from which a random sample is taken for generating items. Also, the type of transformation to be made to a sentence is specified. At the same time, these methods are not fully automated in that the item writer retains some choice in such things as the wording of a sentence transformation or the choice of the wrong answer alternatives (the *foils*) in a multiple-choice version of a question.

At the fifth level of the item-writing continuum are the methods of generating items that can be exactly followed so that any two item writers will produce identical items—for example, by using the methods of Hively (1974). This level also includes methods in which items are generated by a computer program such as those described by Fremer and Anastasio (1969), Olympia (1975), or Millman and Outlaw (1977).

Thus, the continuum represented in Figure 3.1 emphasizes one dimension on which item-writing methods differ—the degree to which the human item writer has an influence on the wording or elements in each individual item. More importantly, however, the role of the human item writer changes as one moves toward the level of computerized methods. At the level of computerized methods all the human effort goes into defining the set, or *universe*, of items rather than each individual item. The challenge here is to create a meaningful item form that is related to the purposes of an instructional system and that produces a large number of high-quality items. The quality of items would be assessed by noting the number of flawed items (those with ambiguities, more than one correct answer, etc.) and the statistical characteristics of items generated by a particular method, algorithm, or set of rules.

To understand more fully the challenge of producing high-quality items, the methods of item forms, computerized techniques, and rule-based procedures will be described in more detail. Then an empirical study of the rule-based techniques will be reported.

ITEM-WRITING ALGORITHMS

Item Forms

Hively (1974) was the first to use the term *domain-referenced testing.* Millman (1974) has described domain-based tests as the purest form of criterion-referenced tests. A domain-based test is primarily distinguished from other tests in terms of the method of creating and selecting items. The selection or creation of items for an objective-based test is typically governed by the learning objective(s). Items for a domain-based test are constructed using a list of rules that specify the structure, format, and even some of the wording of the resulting items. These rules are called *item forms* (Hively, 1974), and the total set of items that an item form generates can be considered the *domain* to be measured. A domain-based criterion-referenced test is constructed by randomly sampling items from the pool of items representing the domain. A student's score on that sample of items is an unbiased estimate of his performance on the entire set of items.

An item form, as explained by Osburn (1968), "has the following characteristics: (a) it generates items with a fixed syntactical structure; (b) it contains one or more variable elements; and (c) it defines a class of item sentences by specifying the replacement sets for the variable elements [p. 97]." Most of the item forms developed by Osburn and Hively have been in computational or mathematically based areas. For example, the following is an item form for a basic mathematics concept:

Item Wording: Which number is second to the smallest of these numbers?

(a), (b), (c), (d), (e)

Elements to Complete the Item: Five numbers, (a)–(e), are provided and the student is required to check the one that is second to the smallest. These numbers must be three-digit integers, with at least two numbers created by rearranging digits in the answer number, and the

other numbers with the same "hundreds" digit as the answer number but with randomly generated remaining digits.
Sample Item: Which number is second to the smallest of these numbers?

> 628, 611, 862, 629, 682

Correct Answer: 628

Millman and Outlaw (1977) have recently applied the concepts of domain-based testing and item forms to tests used in several college courses. Using a small-computer system, they have developed a special programming language that allows an instructor to write an *item program*. An item program is a computer program that is capable of producing multiple questions algorithmically, as is done with an item form. The item program specifies a structure for each question. Some of the wording of the item can be fixed, and elements in the item can be variables that are replaced to form unique questions. Variable elements can be words or other strings of alphabetic characters, random numbers, or quantities computed from mathematical functions. An example of a very simple item form and an item program for an arithmetic problem are shown in Figure 3.2. The item program is processed by a control program written in BASIC and operates on a small computer. The major advantage of this system is that only the item program needs to be stored, not the individual items that it generates. A test can be assembled and printed by computer and given to the student at a later time.

Other Computer-Implemented Methods

Computers have been used as aids in assembling or administering tests for many years (e.g., Atkinson & Wilson, 1969). Many attempts centered on the use of item banks containing all of the actual items from which samples were drawn for testing. More sophisticated systems had the ability to compose items, as was done in the mid-1960s in the drill-and-practice exercises of the Stanford computer-assisted instruction project (Suppes, Jerman, & Groen, 1966). Systems with the capability of generat-

Item Form	*Item Program*
"How much is (X) plus (Y)?"	10 LET X = RANDOM (1, 10)
Where X and Y are integers from 1	20 LET Y = RANDOM (1, 10)
to 10.	30 QUESTION CONTENT "How much is", X, "plus", Y, "?"
	40 ANSWER CONTENT X + Y

Figure 3.2 Item form and item program from Millman and Outlaw (1977). [Reprinted by permission.]

ing items can be used to implement domain-based testing, and for that reason, they will be described in more detail in the section that follows.

Most of the major computer-assisted instruction (CAI) author languages have the capability of producing algorithms for domain-based test items. Several of the CAI languages discussed by Roid (1974), such as COURSEWRITER, PLANIT, and TUTOR, have functions that allow an item program to be written as described by Millman and Outlaw (1977). For example, Atkinson (Atkinson & Wilson, 1969, p. 153) used COURSE-WRITER to program reading exercises and criterion tests for the Stanford initial reading programs. A sample exercise is the sentence, *Dan saw the* ___ *hat*, for which the student is to choose one of a set of computer-assembled words such as *tan, fat, man,* or *run*. The fill-in answers are selected by rules from words previously presented in lessons to the student.

Another example is the work of Fremer and Anastasio (1969), who developed computer-generated items for testing spelling. They conducted an analysis of types of misspellings that are used by writers of spelling items. A set of error-generation rules was developed and programmed for a computer using the SNOBOL programming language. SNOBOL is a language developed at Bell Telephone Laboratories especially to handle strings of symbols or alphabetic characters. Error-generation rules included the inversion of letters within a word, omission of letters, and substitution or insertion of letters. An example for the word *preferable* would be *perferable* or *preforable* or *preferabal*. Fremer and Anastasio found that computer-generated lists of spelling items were judged highly useful by a panel of spelling test developers.

Beginning with the pioneering work of Hively, Patterson, and Page (1968), a great deal of work has been done on domain-based tests in mathematics. For example, Hsu and Carlson (1973) developed item-generation routines used to help construct tests for the elementary mathematics level of the individually prescribed instruction program at the University of Pittsburgh. They used the concept of item forms developed by Hively in programming item-generation routines in FORTRAN IV for a PDP-10 time-sharing computer system. Hsu and Carlson make the important suggestion that the difficulty level and discrimination of item forms be tested by collecting data from tryouts of each item form. Because individual test items are automatically produced, the only way to ensure the quality of test items is to improve the quality of the item forms. By field testing and keeping item statistics at the item-form level, it will be possible to develop higher-quality domain-based tests.

Beginning with the work of Osburn (1968), a number of university professors have developed computer-generated testing systems, particularly in the sciences. For example, Johnson (1973) has developed a system for computer-generated repeatable examinations in chemistry at the college level. His system includes control programs and subroutines written in FORTRAN IV. Each subroutine defines an item form. These item forms include numerical constants that are randomly generated by computer or variable wordings that might include different names of chemical compounds that are substituted into various versions of each individual item. An example of an item form and an individual item from Johnson's system are given in Figure 3.3.

A number of technological developments have recently improved the efficiency of computer-aided testing systems. For instance, McClain, Wessels, and Sando (1975) described the unique advantages of Iowa's "Item Pool System for Instructional Management." This system was written in PL/1 (Programming Language 1) for the IBM 360 and includes an item-generation capability. The prototype of an item is stored in a pool from which the system can retrieve it on demand. The prototype states the rules for creating the specific variable components in both the question and its multiple-choice foils. As a unique part of this system, the functions to be used in generating the numerical values or variable elements in the item form are coded in with the prototype item. When the prototype is retrieved from the pool, the computer program then processes the prototype and its imbedded rules in order to generate a specific item or items. This system has the unique advantage of having the item-generating algorithm somewhat independent from the control program.

Item Form
If ____ ml. of ____ molar ____ is mixed with ____ ml. of ____ molar ____, the final solution will be:
(A) ____ molar in ____
(B) ____ molar in ____
(C) ____ molar in ____
(D) ____ molar in ____
(E) ____ molar in ____

Sample Item
If 43.6 mls. of 1.50 molar NAOH is mixed with 38.5 mls. of 1.14 molar HNO3, the final solution will be:
(A) 1.33 molar in OH (−)
(B) 1.10 molar in H (+)
(C) .260 molar in H (+)
(D) 1.33 molar in H (+)
(E) .260 molar in OH (−)

Figure 3.3 Example of an item form and item from Johnson's Computer-Generated Repeatable Chemistry Exam System (Johnson, 1973). [Reprinted by permission.]

That is, instead of having specific subroutines for each algorithm, a coding system is developed for placing the algorithmic rules into the item form in a coded fashion. Then the control program simply needs to interpret those codes in order to implement the algorithm. This would seem to lead to less "overhead" in computer programming.

Other computer-based item-generation programs have been described by Olympia (1975) and Vickers (1973). The work of Vickers is interesting in that it involves the computer generation of questions useful in the teaching of FORTRAN programming. A series of subroutines that employ random number generators are used to compose FORTRAN-like statements or variables. Then the student might be asked to discriminate between correct and incorrect statements or to classify types of variables. This is an excellent example of a sophisticated item-writing method that produces a virtually unlimited number of items.

In summary, there is a wide variety of examples where computerized item-writing methods have been implemented. Many of these methods are used in college and university courses, particularly in the sciences. The capability to implement these methods is available on most of the major computer installations in the nation. Thus, the technology is available for creating domain-based criterion-referenced tests. The challenge that remains is in the definition of domains and the creation of item-writing algorithms in a wide variety of subject matter areas. Also, creativity is required to develop domains at the conceptual as well as factual levels of learning.

Domain-Based Testing of Concept Learning

The work of Tiemann and Markle on the teaching and testing of concepts is an excellent example of domain-based testing that goes beyond the factual level of learning (Markel, 1975; Markle & Tiemann, 1974; and Tiemann, Kroeker, & Markle, 1977). They have defined concepts as classes of objects, events, or relations that vary among themselves and yet are all grouped together and called by the same name. A student's understanding of a concept is tested by checking for generalization to new examples and discrimination of nonexamples. Examples and nonexamples are used in teaching a concept, and then a new set of examples and nonexamples is used to test the student's understanding of the concept. If we were teaching the concept *chair,* we might use the examples of a wooden chair and an upholstered chair and the nonexamples of a stool and a love seat in the teaching exercise. In testing for understanding of the concept of chair we might use the examples of a rocking chair and a rattan chair, and the nonexamples of a bench and a chaise longue.

Tiemann and Markle (1978b) provide guidelines and many practical examples of the analysis of concepts. The analysis of concepts involves listing the variable and critical attributes of the concept. A variable attribute is a property of any particular example that can be varied without changing an example to a nonexample. For instance, the number of legs is variable in the concept *chair*, because we can have a modernistic chair with a pedestal or a standard four-legged chair. Critical attributes are properties of every example of the concept, and if they are removed, the example becomes a nonexample. For instance, possession of a back, a rigid seat, and space for a single person are the critical attributes of *chair*. Variable attributes of *chair* are whether it has rockers or arms, the size of the back, etc. After the critical attributes and variable attributes have been listed and lists of examples and nonexamples have been generated, it then becomes possible to construct domain-based criterion-referenced tests for a given concept, a series of concepts, or a principle (a statement of relationship between concepts). Such a test would be constructed by choosing a random sample of examples and nonexamples and systematically varying critical attributes and variable attributes. An example of a concept analysis and a sample item for the concept *antonym* is given in Figure 3.4.

Tiemann and Markle recently extended their work to the case of multiple coordinate concepts (Tiemann, Kroeker, & Markle, 1977). An example of coordinate concepts is the four contingencies of positive and negative reinforcement and positive and negative punishment. In this case, the four concepts overlap to the point where an example of one concept is a nonexample of the other concept. Students need to learn to reject a nonexample in one case but accept it as an example of another concept that is related. The Tiemann, Kroeker, and Markle study provides an example of how a domain-based test is produced for the set of four coordinate concepts by systematically sampling examples of each of the concepts, varying them on their attribute dimensions.

Linguistic-Based Algorithms

Bormuth (1970) proposed operationally defined item-writing rules for achievement tests used to assess learning from prose material. These rules are a series of directions that tell an item writer how to rearrange segments of the instruction to obtain the items of that type. Bormuth described two general types of transformations that are possible on prose materials: (*a*) items derived from sentences; and (*b*) items derived from the relationships between sentences (pp. 39–55). An example of sentence-derived items that test recall of prose material are those pro-

Grammar Concept: Antonym

A word which:

Critical Attributes
1. has a meaning opposite to the meaning of some other (given) word
2. is the same part of speech as the given word
3. is a new word, not a variation of the given word

Variable Attributes
4. may be drawn from various parts of speech:
   (a) nouns   (c) pronouns   (e) adjectives
   (b) verbs   (d) adverbs   (f) prepositions
5. relative syllabic length of two words may be:
   (a) equal
   (b) unequal
6. opposition of meaning may exist:
   (a) across some continuum
   (b) in a dichotomous sense

Teaching Examples			*Teaching Nonexamples*	
1. bad; good	4e,5a,6a		1. vain; greedy	lacks only 1
2. danger; safety	4a,5a,6a		2. reason; motive	lacks only 1
3. live; die	4b,5a,6b		3. we; us	lacks only 1
4. he; she	4c,5a,6b		4. above; upon	lacks only 1
5. rapidly; slowly	4d,5b,6a		5. merrily; sad	lacks only 2
6. in; out	4f,5a,6b		6. happy; unhappy	lacks only 3
			7. capable; incapable	lacks only 3
			8. disputable; agree	lacks only 2

Testing Examples			*Testing Nonexamples*	
1. hot; cold	4e,5a,6a		1. imaginary; fanciful	lacks only 1
2. loss; gain	4a,5a,6a		2. chair; couch	lacks only 1
3. elevate; lower	4b,5b,6a		3. behind; next to	lacks only 1
4. you; me	4c,5a,6b		4. gloom; bright	lacks only 2
5. gaily; sadly	4d,5a,6a		5. violent; nonviolent	lacks only 3
6. over; under	4f,5a,6b		6. valid; invalid	lacks only 3
			7. weak; forcibly	lacks only 2

Sample Test Item

Which of the following pairs of words are antonyms?

    a. imaginary—fanciful
*b. elevate—lower
    c. valid—invalid
    d. weak—forcibly

*Correct answer: b

Figure 3.4 Example of a concept analysis used to develop domain-referenced tests of concept learning. [Adapted from P. W. Tiemann and Susan M. Markle. *Analyzing Instructional Content: A Guide to Instruction and Evaluation*. Champaign, Ill.: Stipes Publ., 1978, p. 257. By permission of the publisher and author.]

duced by the *wh-transformation*. Wh-transformation items would be written using a detailed rule summarized as follows: "Select sentences from the instructional materials, replacing a 'wh-pro' word such as *who, what,* or *where* for the appropriate part (e.g., subject) in each sentence." For instance, *The test specialist computes the reliability index* could be transformed to *Who computes the reliability index?* Wh-items are particularly useful because they can be written to question each separate part of a sentence, and can be made into either multiple-choice or fill-in format.

Sentence-derived items can also be written to test comprehension of prose material through the use of paraphrasing. Anderson (1972) has emphasized the importance of paraphrasing and has defined it as the case where (*a*) all substantive words in a sentence are replaced; and (*b*) the original and paraphrased sentences have equivalent meaning.

Items derived·from the relations between sentences can be produced, for example, by questioning the cause of an action or result described in prose passages. For instance, the sentences (*a*) *Jim hurt his foot*; (*b*) *He was cleaning his gun*; and (*c*) *His gun accidentally fired* can be examined for implied causation, resulting in the question, *What caused Jim's hurt foot?* (Bormuth, 1970, p. 54).

Finn (1975) and Roid and Haladyna (1978b) have extended the work of Bormuth by developing question-writing algorithms for prose learning. Finn's original work (1975) involved a rather lengthy and detailed algorithm that contained 82 steps. Finn (1978) and Roid and Haladyna (1978b) streamlined the original algorithm and proposed the following important steps in using the algorithm:

1. Analyzing the text
2. Identifying and classifying key words and their sentences
3. Transformation of sentences into questions
4. Generation of foils for the questions

Analyzing Text

To develop questions that measure important aspects of a prose passage requires an objective analysis of the text. One approach to this was proposed by Finn (1978), who used a computer analysis of the words in a prose passage. All the words in the passage are keypunched for input to a computer program that does two major tasks: (*a*) counts the number of times that each word appears in the passage; and (*b*) identifies the standard frequency index of each word. The standard frequency index of each word is a numerical estimate of how often the word occurs in a large corpus of American English (Carroll, Davies, & Richman, 1971). The Carroll, Davies, and Richman book or its computer-tape version can be used to get the standard frequency index of each word in the passage. The word *the* has the highest standard frequency index of any word, because the average American student is likely to encounter the word *the* once in every 10 words of his school book reading. The word *incarnation*, for example, has the lowest index because the average student is likely to encounter the word *incarnation* less often than once in every billion words of his school book reading.

Identifying High-Information Words

The goal of this analysis is to identify *high information* words—words that are relatively rare in American English and occur only a single time in the passage. The sentences in which these high information words occur can then become candidates for transformation into questions that tap important information in the passage. High information words are those that are difficult for students to guess if they are deleted from a prose passage such as is done in a CLOZE test (Culhane, 1970). CLOZE tests use segments of prose that are presented to a student, usually with every fifth word deleted. The task for the student, then, is to supply the missing words. The ease with which a word is guessed or filled in by a student on a CLOZE test is a measure of the amount of information it provides. The task in a CLOZE test is similar to the typical problem in information theory (Shannon & Weaver, 1949) in which a person is receiving a message, but because of noise on the channel, he is not always sure which message he hears (Finn, 1977). The information in a missing or garbled message is a function of the amount of doubt the receiver has about its identity and is related to the probability of occurrence of certain words or letters. A missing word that is highly predictable, or a common word in the English language, would present less information because students would have less doubt that it completes the prose segment.

Finn (1977) has done considerable research to show that the ease with which a word is guessed on a CLOZE test is predicted by the two important indexes derived from the computer analysis of a passage: (*a*) the standard frequency index and (*b*) text frequency. Words that have a low standard frequency index (infrequent in American school books) are typically high in information. However, there is one circumstance in which the information of these words is reduced in relation to a given passage. If the word is repeated frequently (i.e., it has a high text frequency), the information value of that word is diminished and students will supply it more often in a CLOZE test following reading of the passage. In other words, repetition of words, even if they are rare in American English, lowers their information value. Therefore, Finn (1978) has proposed that candidates for good question words are those which are rare in American English (have a low standard frequency index) and are singletons in a prose passage (i.e., have a text frequency of 1).

Not all parts of speech are equally good candidates for question words even though they may be high information words. Verbs and adverbs, in particular, are difficult words to remove from a sentence that is transformed into a question. For example, the sentence *Finn echoed the concern of Bormuth* when transformed to *What did Finn do to the concern of Bormuth?* seems clumsy and seems to be a less important question than the question *Who echoed the concern of Bormuth?* Finn (1978) has concluded that the most promising parts of speech are adjectives and nouns, or phrases that contain them.

Preparation and Analysis of Sentences

Once an important word has been identified for a possible question, the sentence it occurs in must be examined and prepared for transformation. Finn (1975) explains how text and sentences can be analyzed by examining the underlying structure of sentences rather than simply their surface structure. A schema is used to diagram each sentence to identify the important parts of a sentence such as the subject, the verb, and the object. As Finn has said (1975, p. 344), there are advantages to basing question-writing procedures on underlying structure analysis rather than on surface structure:

1. Explicatives, functional verbs, articles, and prepositions either appear as part of phrases or they do not appear at all.
2. The number of questions possible for a given sentence becomes independent of the number of words in the sentence and is a function of the number of case phrases and non-zero verbs in the underlying sentence.

These are important advantages, because prepositions, articles, and many verbs are not desirable as question words in most transformations.

The next step in processing the sentence is to eliminate the question word and to transform the sentence into a question. The question word, usually an adjective, a noun, or a phrase including an adjective or a noun, is removed and is replaced with a wh-word. Where several wordings are possible, an attempt is made to stay as close to the wording of the original sentence as possible. There are a number of further guidelines for preparing sentences for analysis, such as replacing pronouns with their appropriate nouns or replacing references to previous sentences by clauses or phrases from those references.

The algorithm does not produce 100% agreement among item writers in all cases because of such things as the replacement of phrases from previous sentences. Finn (1975, pp. 357–363) discusses some of the discrepancies among item writers.

Generating Foils

As is common knowledge among test developers, the writing of good foils for multiple-choice questions is challenging work. The first step in an algorithmic generation of foils is to classify the question words that are the correct answers to the question so that possible foils can be obtained from a list of words in the same classification. The most logical source of foil words would seem to be from the prose passage itself, but in some cases, there may be published lists of words, such as that of Carroll *et al.* (1971), that may be useful sources, if the words cover the same type of subject matter.

The Roid and Haladyna (1978b) study experimented with a foil-writing method based on the Carroll *et al.* (1971) list of words. The location of the question word from the prose passage was identified in the Carroll list and then semantically similar words in adjacent parts of the list were identified. These adjacent words, having similar standard frequency indexes, were used as foils. In this particular case, the Carroll list proved to be an unacceptable source, because it produced foils that were too obviously in the wrong subject matter area and were simply absurd in many cases. Therefore, Roid and Haladyna developed another method of algorithmic foil construction. The algorithm relies on extracting foils from the prose passage itself. Two variations of the algorithm were developed: one for nouns and one for adjectives.

In the case of nouns, all nouns with a standard frequency index of 60 or less were semantically classified using the method of Frederiksen (1975). For example, some nouns were classified as concrete animate nouns. For a given question word, a random sample of other nouns from the passage that were in the same semantic classification were drawn to create foils.

In the case of adjectives, research on semantic differential technique was used as a basis for constructing a classification of adjectives from the passage (Nunnally, 1967, pp. 536–538). In semantic differential research there are typically three factors that are descriptive of words: (*a*) *evaluation* (including words such as *good* or *bad*); (*b*) *potency* (*strong, weak,* etc.); and (*c*) *activity* (*fast, slow,* etc.). In addition, Nunnally (1967, p. 538) has defined a fourth factor, *familiarity,* including words such as *simple* or *complex*. These four factors were used to group the adjectives in the passage that had standard frequency indexes of less than 60. As a further check on these adjectives, they were subjected to an analysis of whether or not they were "familiar," as determined by the Dale–Chall list of 3000 familiar words (Dale & Chall, 1948). The adjective, to be a candidate for a foil, needed to be absent from that list. The rationale for this was that there are some extremely common adjectives that would be too easy as foils.

AN EXPLORATORY STUDY OF A
LINGUISTIC-BASED ALGORITHM

Roid and Haladyna (1978b) conducted an empirical study of Finn's (1978) extension of the Bormuth technology for deriving items from sentences. Cronbach (1970) had indicated that this technology needed to be more developed on a practical level to be useful to test developers. Bormuth and Cocks (1975) commented also that Bormuth's earlier work was a "crude version" of the theory that he would like to see extended. Procedures were needed for choosing words to delete in wh-transformations of instructional sentences and for developing foils for making these items into multiple-choice format. Such procedures would be widely applicable. Multiple-choice items are the most frequently used type in education and training, and the testing of recall of prose material remains a basic element in many instructional programs.

Specific research questions of the Roid and Haladyna (1978b) study were designed to contrast two methods of selecting sentences for transformation from prose passages: (a) selecting sentences that contain *keywords* versus (b) selecting sentences that contain *rare singletons*. Keywords and rare singletons are nouns or adjectives that have a low (less than 60) standard frequency index. The difference between the two types of words is that the keywords are high in text frequency, whereas the rare singletons appear only once in the passage. The Roid and Haladyna study also examined the differences among four item writers who used the sentence transformation methods of Finn (1978). Two types of multiple-choice foils were contrasted also: (a) those chosen by the item writers themselves and (b) those chosen by an algorithm from words in the passage.

Procedures

Roid and Haladyna (1978b) used a prose passage, at an approximately high school level of reading, on insect development (DeWaard, 1964, pp. 1–15). The passage was subjected to the computer analysis suggested by Finn (1978). Algorithms for producing sentence-derived wh-transformations, as described in the previous section of this report and in

Finn (1975), were applied to the passage. A set of eight parallel test forms of 20 items each was constructed. Tests were given to 24 college subjects and 249 high school students before and after they studied the prose passage. Subjects were randomly assigned test forms containing a mixture of item types. A total of 160 items were the objects of analysis for the study.

Five words and their sentences from the passage were selected for transformation into items in each of the following categories: (a) keyword adjectives; (b) keyword nouns; (c) rare singleton adjectives; and (d) rare singleton nouns. This represents a total of 20 sentences from the prose passage. The first sentence in which the keyword adjective or noun occurred was selected as the sentence to be transformed into a question. Each sentence was transformed by each of four item writers.

Results

Analysis of Item Difficulties

A repeated-measures analysis of variance was used to compare the item difficulties of items of each type. A $4 \times 2 \times 2 \times 2 \times 2$ factorial design was used to examine differences in item difficulties between (a) the four item writers; (b) keyword and rare singleton; (c) nouns and adjectives; (d) the two foil types (writer's choice and algorithmic); and (e) the two test occasions (pretest and posttest).

An important finding of the Roid and Haladyna experiment was the main effect for word type. Items based on keyword nouns were significantly easier (72.4%) on the pretest as compared to other items. The first occurrence of the keyword noun in the text was used to create the item. An examination of the sentences in which these keyword nouns appeared provided a possible explanation for the results. These sentences are typically introductory sentences that are very general and that address the main topics of the entire passage. For example, in the passage on insect development, the keyword noun *insects* appears in the very first sentence of the passage and is a very general statement—*The life of most insects is short but active.* Questions derived from this type of sentence seem to be invariably a common-knowledge type of item that students can answer without having read the prose passage. Also, keyword nouns were relatively easy for subjects to recall on the posttest (average item difficulty of 83.5%). This may be due to the fact that these keywords were mentioned several times in the passage. Easiness of these items on the posttest is in line with Finn's (1978) hypothesis that the information content of these rare words is reduced by their high text frequency.

Roid and Haladyna (1978b) found no statistically significant main effect for writers or foil type, nor was there a significant two-way interaction between writers and foil. This result is somewhat surprising in that different writers would be expected to write easier or harder items when they had the latitude to choose their own foils. Apparently, the method of writing foils, which allowed the choice of only single words to replace the question word, did not provide as much latitude as was expected. If the item writer were allowed to rewrite or replace the entire noun phrase, perhaps the differences between writers would have been magnified. New studies are currently underway to examine this hypothesis.

Variance among Writers

Variability of item difficulties across item writers was examined in the Roid and Haladyna study to answer the question, Do the difficulties of items constructed with the 'writer's choice' foils vary more widely across writers than the difficulties of items constructed with the algorithmic foils? The expectation was that some writers would choose very difficult foils for a given transformed sentence and other writers would choose very easy foils for that same sentence. In contrast, the algorithmic foils chosen at random from matched groups of similar words from the passage would seem to be free of any item-writer bias, and, hence, less variable in their effects on item difficulty.

In examining the variability across writers, the focus was on each sentence that was to be transformed by each writer. There were a total of 20 sentences taken from the passage on insect development. For example, each of the four item writers produced items from the sentence *In most cases each egg produces a single immature insect,* for which the keyword adjective was *immature.* It was, therefore, possible to identify four item difficulties for a given combination of sentence and foil techniques. For instance, for the sentence containing the word *immature,* each writer generated an item using the *writer's choice* foil method, and this resulted in pretest difficulties of 38, 65, 52, and 37%. Posttest item difficulties for these items were 67, 63, 74, and 52%, in that order. The pretest and posttest variances could then be calculated across these item difficulties.

After all variances of item difficulties across writers were calculated, they were subjected to a repeated-measures analysis of variance in which the dependent variable was the natural logarithm of the variances (Scheffé, 1959, p. 83). The design for this analysis was $2 \times 2 \times 2 \times 2$ with the following factors: (*a*) foil type (writer's choice versus algorithmic); (*b*) part of speech (noun versus adjective); (*c*) stem type (keyword versus rare singleton question word); and (*d*) the repeated measure (pretest versus posttest).

The only factor that approached statistical significance in this analysis was the foil type. The writer's-choice foil method had an average variance of 115.31% (*SD* of 10.74%) and the algorithmic foil method had a variance of 73.97% (*SD* of 8.60%); this difference was statistically significant at $p =$ .07. Although this result is not significant beyond the .05 level, I mention it because in a subsequent study employing the same item writers on a new prose passage, a similar result was found, this time at $p = .003$. This new study involved more than 400 grade school students who read a story about animals and took pretests and posttests designed in a manner similar to the Roid and Haladyna (1978b) study. The same analysis of variance on the variances of item difficulties was computed and the main effect for foil type was the strongest effect obtained, with writer's-choice foils having a higher variance (219.2%) than the algorithmic method (98.4%).

Thus, higher variances in item difficulties are obtained when human item writers choose the foils using whatever mental process they employ. This variance between writers is exactly the source of bias in item writing described by Bormuth (1970), Anderson (1972), and Millman (1974).

Conclusions

The Roid and Haladyna (1978b) study seems to indicate that the concept of identifying high information words from prose passages for use in selecting sentences to be transformed into questions is a workable methodology. Words identified as rare singletons, which have a standard frequency index of 60 or less (they are relatively rare in American textbooks) and yet occur only once in a prose passage, are useful candidates for questions that test learning from prose. In contrast, words that are rare in American textbooks yet highly frequent in a prose passage, particularly if these are nouns, are apparently not very good candidates for question words, since they are too simple even on a pretest.

Algorithmic methods of constructing foils for multiple-choice versions of sentence-derived questions are apparently feasible as implemented in the Roid and Haladyna study. Words can be selected from the prose passage itself if they are relatively uncommon words from the same semantic classification as the question word. This suggests, for example, that this type of item writing could be computer-assisted. When prose passages are entered into a computer file or if prose segments are already present in computer-administered instructional programs, question words and foils can be identified for the item writer. The actual transformation of sentences into questions by computer may also be feasible, but, to my knowledge, has not yet been implemented in an instructional system.

The Roid and Haladyna study provides evidence to support the theory of processing in reading proposed by Finn (1977). Items constructed from sentences containing rare singleton nouns, as compared to keyword nouns, were shown to be much more difficult for subjects to answer. In other words, rare singletons are truly high information words. Roid and Haladyna (1978b) further suggested that rare words that occur on two or three occasions in a passage may have the same attributes as a rare singleton.

DIRECTIONS FOR FUTURE RESEARCH AND DEVELOPMENT

Bormuth (1970) discusses

> three logical divisions in achievement test theory: (a) the development of descriptive systems for defining items (item writing theory), (b) the study of the processes underlying the responses to items (item response theory), and (c) the study of the relationships of responses on test items to responses in real world situations referred to by the instruction (item validity theory) [p. 66].

Bormuth describes some of the types of research that could be conducted in each of these areas. The topic of this chapter has been on item writing theory with some overlap into the arena of studying students' responses to different methods of constructing items.

Further research and development is needed to extend the work of Roid and Haladyna (1978a, 1978b) and Finn (1978), as well as the work of Millman and Outlaw (1977) in computerized testing and Tiemann and Markle (1978a) in concept testing. Another area of new research is the application of facet design (Guttman, 1969) to item-writing technology, as is being explored by Engel and Martuza (1976). One emphasis in this ongoing work could be to compare the characteristics of items written by objective-based methods versus algorithmic or semi-algorithmic methods. One of the major questions of my own research in this area, supported by the Defense Advanced Research Projects Agency, will be, Do algorithmic methods of item writing significantly reduce the variability among item writers? Sets of item writers will write items using both learning objectives on the one hand and algorithmic methods on the other. The variability of the item difficulties of each type of item produced will be computed across item writers. The hypothesis first presented by Bormuth (1970) and Anderson (1972) would be that the algorithmic methods would tend to reduce the variability among item writers. In the wording of the

Roid and Haladyna (1978a) study, a reduction in variability across item
difficulties would be a reduction in item-writer bias.

Another area of future research and development would be to explore
the feasibility of algorithmic methods. Several questions of feasibility
seem possible:

1. Can algorithms be developed at higher levels of typologies of educational objectives (Williams, 1977)?
2. Are there certain constraints of particular subject matters that make them less amenable to the development of algorithmic item writing schemes?
3. What is the practical implication of a "trade-off" that seems to be inherent in automated methods—that algorithmic methods may produce items that are somewhat easier than those written by highly skilled item writers and yet they produce a multitude of items very quickly and efficiently?
4. Will algorithmic methods be more of an aid to item writers who will be given computer analyses of instructional materials, or will widespread use be more oriented to completely automated implementations of the techniques?

Clearly, one of the most important areas of research in item response
theory will be to examine the differential performance of subjects on items
constructed at various levels of educational objectives. Anderson (1972)
has claimed that true comprehension cannot be tested unless the items
used in testing have material that is paraphrased or somewhat different
from the verbatim material included in the instruction. However, some
studies, such as Roid and Haladyna (1978a), have been unable to detect
significant differences in performance of students on verbatim versus
paraphrased versions of items that test learning from prose material. In
developing test items that are paraphrased versions of sentences from
stories used in grade school classrooms, I have found that paraphrasing
can introduce a possible bias that must be noted. Bias can be present if the
paraphrased words used to construct a test question are of higher reading
difficulty or are unfamiliar words as compared to the verbatim words from
the instructional materials used by students. If students encounter unfamiliar words in the test, they may answer incorrectly because of that
unfamiliarity, rather than because of a lack of comprehension of the story.
Clearly, more research needs to be conducted on the processes underlying responses to items constructed at various levels of learning objectives
for prose passages and other types of materials.

Another interesting area of research related to that discussed under the
section entitled "An Exploratory Study of a Linguistic-Based Algorithm"

in this chapter is the whole question of the information content of words in prose passages. If rare singleton words are indeed high information words in the passage, it would seem that learning might be promoted if a student were tested systematically on those words in a posttest following reading of the material. Experiments could compare students who are given test questions on the high information words versus questions on keywords in the passage. Because rare singletons occur only once and are relatively unfamiliar words in a text, students could tend to pass over these important words in a quick reading of a passage. Testing specifically on high information words might promote attention to text.

In addition to various research interests, there are many practical reasons why the development of algorithmic methods of item writing should be encouraged. Item writing is still a time-consuming business if done by an individual teacher or item writer. In my own experience with editing a nationally distributed set of programmed texts that required coordinated classroom tests, the use of algorithmic methods was invaluable in creating large item banks to produce parallel test forms to accompany these texts. Clearly, even if algorithmic methods are used only to suggest test items and not to construct entire test forms for a teacher, a contribution to the quality of tests and the implementation of mastery learning systems will be made. The next chapter, by Conoley and O'Neil, provides a "first cut" at this approach.

SUMMARY

A number of investigators have strongly argued for the development of a technology for item writing. Bormuth (1970) has probably made the most thorough statement of this position. An item-writing technology is proposed to reduce some of the problems of item writers' subjectivity and bias. The technology promises to bring a more scientific basis for test development, both for application to the technology of instructional development and for more rigorous educational research. One of the most compelling reasons for an interest in the technology of item writing would appear to be the need for a logical, publicly defined relationship between tests and teaching.

The two major strands of research and development in item-writing technology are represented by the work of Hively (1974) on item forms and Bormuth's (1970) linguistic transformation methodology. These two pioneering developments have encouraged a large number of applications of the technology.

A promising new area of algorithmic test development is being examined by Tiemann and Markle (1978a, 1978b; Tiemann, Kroeker, & Markle, 1977). This work is a development of a domain-referenced testing system for concept learning. Sets of examples and nonexamples that vary on defined attributes are used as a pool from which items can be constructed in systematic ways in order to test comprehension of concepts or principles. This work has the promise of extending algorithmic methods to the higher levels of learning objectives.

The work of Finn (1975, 1978) and Roid and Haladyna (1978b) is an interesting new extension to the work of Bormuth. In Bormuth's 1970 work, the methodology for selecting sentences from prose material to be transformed into test items was not developed in great detail. Finn (1978) has developed a theory of processing in reading that would predict that important questions can be written from sentences in which high information words occur. High information words are defined as nouns or adjectives which are relatively rare in American textbooks and occur only once in a prose passage. In the absence of such a theory one might be tempted simply to draw a random sample of sentences from a text and to pick a verb or other possibly unacceptable keyword from that sentence to transform into a question word.

The technology proposed by Finn creates an interesting contrast to the popular method of writing items on the basis of learning objectives that might be specified for a prose passage. The Bormuth and Finn methods are domain-based rather than objective-based, in that sentences (or types of words such as rare singletons) constitute the domain of elements to be learned. This domain specification takes the place of written objectives. However, it should be noted that there is a "hidden" objective in the Bormuth and Finn work—that the student will comprehend the important elements of the prose material. The sentence-transformation technology has provided an operational definition of what constitutes a test of reading comprehension for a prose passage. For example, this technology provides tests that are precisely matched in reading difficulty to the reading level of the passage, and it can assist in defining and counting all of the elements (e.g., important words) that a student should comprehend from a prose segment. In this sense, the sentence-transformation technology is a tool for implementing a learning objective of reading comprehension.

An interesting area of exploration would be to examine the relationship between learning objectives defined by teachers for a prose passage and the high information words selected by a computer analysis of the passage. Perhaps learning objectives can be mapped to specific segments of prose in instructional materials. If so, the high information words in those segments could be linked to the matching learning objectives. In a recent analysis of a passage describing the characteristics of sharks, in preparation for a testing experiment, I found that there was, indeed, a mapping of learning objectives to specific sentences in the passage. For example, the objective "List the differences between sharks and most bony fish" is discussed in a four-paragraph segment of the materials. In those four paragraphs, words such as *cartilage* and *swimbladders* are rare singletons that appear in key sentences explaining the differences between sharks and bony fish. The questions created from the sentences in which *cartilage* and *swimbladders* occurred were directly related to the learning objective. This mapping of words to objectives could increase the applicability of the Finn technique to instructional programs that are objective-based. Also, it points out that learning objectives can and should be designed to generate a domain of items so that domain-based, criterion-referenced tests can be constructed. As Hambleton *et al.* (1978) have convincingly argued, domain-based tests provide scores that are more generalizable and interpretable than objective-based tests, because "If the proper domain of test items measuring an objective is not clear, it is impossible to select a representative sample of test items from *that* domain [p. 32]." And further, "Since we desire to interpret an examinee's test performance on the sample of test items measuring a particular objective as an estimate of that examinee's level of mastery in the larger domain of items measuring an objective, it is essential to have the domain of test items specified clearly and to choose a representative sample of test items [p. 32]."

Clearly, the Bormuth and Finn technology can be useful in specifying the domain of test items for learning objectives involving reading comprehension.

In conclusion, it seems that a technology of item writing has several promises. The technology has the practical advantage of allowing a large number of items to be produced for use in instructional systems where there is repeatable testing. Algorithmic item writing can be used to produce test forms that are relatively equivalent in difficulty. The effect of item-writing methods on the difficulty of items is important for criterion-referenced testing in instructional systems, because item difficulty will be directly related to the magnitudes of the scores obtained by students. If the item difficulties of different test forms vary in unknown ways, a precise passing score cannot be set accurately. The use of algorithmic methods can help to produce equivalent test forms and field testing can be conducted at the item form level to assess the characteristics of items of a particular type. The greatest benefit of a technology of item writing, however, is the benefit of having educational achievement tests operationally defined. If an educator can describe in precise terms the relationship between test items and instruction and the method of producing test items, this can be communicated to colleagues. This public sharing of the precise nature of tests will help to advance the sciences of evaluation and educational research.

ACKNOWLEDGMENTS

The help of Tom Haladyna, Patrick Finn, Gerald Lippey, John Bormuth, and Jason Millman in the conceptual development of the research reported in this chapter is gratefully acknowledged. Also, the author expresses thanks to Joan Shaughnessy and Penny Lane for their assistance.

REFERENCES

Anderson, R. D. How to construct achievement tests to assess comprehension. *Review of Educational Research*, 1972, *42*, 145–170.

Atkinson, R. D., & Wilson, H. A. *Computer-assisted instruction: A book of readings*. New York: Academic Press, 1969.

Bloom, B. S. Learning for mastery. *Evaluation Comment*, UCLA, May 1968, *1*(2).

Bormuth, J. R. *On the theory of achievement test items*. Chicago: University of Chicago Press, 1970.

Bormuth, J. R., & Cocks, P. *Rules for classifying and scoring responses to wh-questions*. Paper presented at the meetings of the American Educational Research Association, Washington, D.C., March 1975.

Carroll, J. B., Davies, P., & Richman, B. *Word frequency book*. Boston: Houghton-Mifflin, 1971.

Cronbach, L. J. John R. Bormuth: On the theory of achievement test items (Book review). *Psychometrika*, 1970, *35*, 509–511.

Culhane, J. W. CLOZE procedures and comprehension. *The Reading Teacher*, 1970, *23*, 410–413.

Dale, E., & Chall, J. S. A formula for predicting readability. *Educational Research Bulletin*, 1948, *27*, 11–28.

DeWarrd, E. J. *What insect is that?* Columbus, Ohio: American Education Publications, 1964.

Engel, J. D., & Martuza, V. R. *A systematic approach to the construction of domain-referenced multiple-choice test items*. Paper presented at the meetings of the American Psychological Association, Washington, D.C., September 1976.

Faw, H. W., & Waller, T. G. Mathemagenic behaviours and efficiency in learning from prose materials. *Review of Educational Research*, 1976, *46*, 691–720.

Finn, P. J. A question writing algorithm. *Journal of Reading Behavior*, 1975, *4*, 341–367.

Finn, P. J. *Word frequency, information theory and cloze performance: A lexical-marker, transfer-feature theory of processing in reading*. Unpublished manuscript, State University of New York at Buffalo, School of Education, 1977.

Finn, P. J. *Generating domain-referenced, multiple-choice test items from prose passages*. Paper presented at the meetings of the American Educational Research Association, Toronto, March 1978.

Frederiksen, C. H. Representing logical and semantic structure of knowledge acquired from discourse. *Cognitive Psychology*, 1975, *7*, 371–458.

Fremer, J., & Anastasio, E. J. Computer-assisted item writing—I (Spelling items). *Journal of Educational Measurement,* 1969, *6,* 69–74.

Guttman, L. Integration of test design and analysis. In *Proceedings of the 1969 invitational conference on testing problems.* Princeton, N.J.: Educational Testing Service, 1969.

Hambleton, R. K., Swaminathan, H., Algina, J., & Coulson, D. B. Criterion-referenced testing and measurement: A review of technical issues and developments. *Review of Educational Research,* 1978, *48,* 1–47.

Hively, W. Introduction to domain-referenced testing. *Educational Technology,* 1974, *14,* 5–10.

Hively, W., Patterson, H. L., & Page, S. A "universe-defined" system of arithmetic achievement tests. *Journal of Educational Measurement,* 1968, *5,* 275–290.

Hsu, T., & Carlson, M. Test construction aspects of the computer assisted testing model. *Educational Technology,* 1973, *13*(3), 26–27.

Johnson, K. J. Pitt's computer-generated chemistry exam. *Proceedings of the Conference on Computers in Undergraduate Curricula,* 1973, 199–204.

Markle, S. M. They teach concepts don't they? *Educational Researcher,* 1975, *4*(6), 3–9.

Markle, S. M., & Tiemann, P. W. Some principles of instructional design at higher cognitive levels. In R. Ulrich, T. Stachnik, & T. Mabry (Eds.), *Control of human behavior* (Vol. 3). Glenview, Ill.: Scott-Foresman, 1974.

McClain, D. H., Wessels, S. W., & Sando, K. M. IPSIM—Additional system enhancements utilized in a chemistry application. *Proceedings of the Conference on Computers in Undergraduate Curricula,* 1975, 139–145.

Millman, J. Criterion-referenced measurement. In W. J. Popham (Ed.), *Evaluation in education: Current applications.* Berkeley, Calif.: McCutchan Publishing Company, 1974.

Millman, J., & Outlaw, W. S. *Testing by computer.* Ithaca, N.Y.: Cornell University Extension Publications, 1977.

Nunnally, J. *Psychometric theory.* New York: McGraw-Hill, 1967.

Olympia, P. L., Jr. Computer generation of truly repeatable examinations. *Educational Technology,* 1975, *15*(6), 53–55.

Osburn, H. G. Item sampling for achievement testing. *Educational and Psychological Measurement,* 1968, *28,* 95–104.

Popham, W. J. Selecting objectives and generating test items for objectives-based tests. In C. W. Harris, M. C. Alkin, & W. J. Popham (Eds.), *Problems in criterion-referenced measurement* (CSE monograph series in evaluation, No. 3). Los Angeles: Center for the Study of Evaluation, University of California, 1974.

Popham, W. J. *Educational evaluation.* Englewood Cliffs, N.J.: Prentice-Hall, 1975.

Roid, G. H. Selecting CAI author languages to solve instructional problems. *Educational Technology,* 1974, *14*(5), 29–31.

Roid, G. H., & Haladyna, T. M. A comparison of objective-based and modified-Bormuth item writing techniques. *Educational and Psychological Measurement,* 1978, *38,* 19–28.(a)

Roid, G., & Haladyna, T. *A comparison of several linguistic-based, multiple-choice item writing algorithms.* Paper presented at the meetings of the American Educational Research Association, Toronto, March 1978.(b)

Scheffé, H. *The analysis of variance.* New York: Wiley, 1959.

Shannon, C. E., & Weaver, W. *The mathematical theory of communication.* Urbana: University of Illinois Press, 1949.

Sherman, J. G. *Personalized system of instruction: 41 germinal papers.* Menlo Park, Calif.: W. A. Benjamin, Inc., 1974.

Shoemaker, D. M. Toward a framework for achievement testing. *Review of Educational Research*, 1975, *45*, 127–147.

Suppes, P., Jerman, M., & Groen, G. J. Arithmetic drills and review on a computer-based teletype. *Arithmetic Teacher*, 1966, *13*(7), 303–308.

Tiemann, P., Kroeker, L. P., & Markle, S. M. *Teaching verbally-mediated coordinate concepts in an on-going college course.* Paper presented at the meetings of the American Educational Research Association, New York, April 1977.

Tiemann, P. W., & Markle, S. M. *Domain-referenced testing in conceptual learning.* Paper presented at the meetings of the American Educational Research Association, Toronto, March 1978.(a)

Tiemann, P. W., & Markle, Susan M. *Analyzing instructional content: A guide to instruction and evaluation.* Champaign, Ill.: Stipes, 1978.(b)

Vickers, F. D. Creative test generators. *Educational Technology*, 1973, *13*(3), 43–44.

Williams, R. A behavioral typology of educational objectives for the cognitive domain. *Educational Technology*, 1977, *17*(6), 39–46.

4

A Primer for Developing
Test Items[1]

JANE CLOSE CONOLEY and
HAROLD F. O'NEIL, JR.

In the previous chapter Roid has suggested the "radical" argument that
tests are the "most important" components of an instructional system.
Although some may disagree over the relative ordering of instructional
system elements, there is probably little disagreement that a vital part of
any instructional development is a well-designed testing component.

Despite general agreement on this premise, directions for test-item
development have traditionally contained the statement that test writing is
an art much like baking a cake, where a good recipe and a talented cook
produce great successes. General guidelines such as the following have
been suggested (Ebel, 1972; Gronlund, 1971; Nunnally, 1964):

1. Make an outline of the topics dealt with in the instruction. This
   provides a useful basis for generating test items that will representatively sample the desired achievement.
2. Consult the behavioral objectives of the instruction to ensure that
   the evaluation is in line with the stated desired outcomes, and that
   the mental processes that are to be tested are clearly in the construc-
   tor's mind before starting to write.
3. Draft the items some time in advance, making sure there is a surplus
   of items, since this is desirable.
4. Borrow ideas from curriculum makers, textbook writers, and classroom teachers.

---

[1] Early stages of the research associated with this chapter were supported in part by
the McDonnell Douglas Corporation. The opinions expressed, however, are those of the
authors and do not reflect the views of McDonnell Douglas.

Copyright © 1979 by Academic Press, Inc.
All rights of reproduction in any form reserved.
ISBN 0-12-526660-X

5. Construct tests so that items dealing with the same content or skill are grouped together.
6. Have items examined and critiqued by colleagues.

Emphasis is placed on the subjective intuitions of the writer to choose what to test, to choose the form of the item, and to judge the relevance of the item to the instruction. No procedures are given for actually generating the items or for ascertaining that test items are closely related to the instruction.

If the evaluation is based on criterion-referenced tests, care must be taken to construct test items that will discriminate among students who have achieved the objectives of the course and those who have not. The validity and reliability of tests can be affected by poorly designed items that either allow students who have marginally mastered the material to choose correct answers or confuse students who have mastered the material with irrelevant sources of difficulty.

In addition to reliability and validity concerns, a new technology for test-item development is needed just because of the emergence of criterion-referenced testing. This orientation makes the construction of a number of parallel forms for each mastery test a necessity.

The new technology of test-item development must also be responsive to the needs of test constructors to assess at various levels of learning. Anderson (1972) and Piaget (1960) have deplored the encouragement of mere rote learning. Piaget calls this "learning in the narrow sense," mere acquisition of knowledge resulting in no real growth in intellectual capacities.

Our approach to the problem of test-item development went through stages mirroring the three concerns expressed above. Our first strategy to improve the test items was to gather together all the guidelines offered by writers in the field of testing about multiple-choice items. Multiple-choice items were chosen because of their widespread use in criterion-referenced systems. That done, we realized that the guidelines, though helpful especially in editing, did not provide a method for systematically generating items.

Stage 2 of our work, then, involved applying Bormuth's (1970) method of item generation for knowledge-level items. We thought this method was a technology that could be used to generate test items at alternative levels of learning. Thus, Stage 3 was begun.

This chapter is the end product of this three-stage evolution in our thought. It contains preliminary information regarding multiple-choice questions, Bloom's (1956) taxonomy of educational objectives, guidelines for the review of multiple-choice items, and a method for generating items at the knowledge, comprehension, application, and analysis levels. Original examples are generated from the material in the chapter itself.

The major weakness and limitation of our work is that the system taken from Bormuth (1970) for item construction has not been empirically validated by us. We have responded to numerous requests for earlier unpublished segments of this chapter and received good feedback regarding the usefulness of the Bormuth approach. It remains an empirical question, however, whether items constructed in this way are psychometrically superior to items using traditional guidelines. Roid, in the preceding chapter, has presented data that are encouraging.

A set of activities not described in this chapter is that which surrounds matching instruction with objectives. The initial step in instructional development is having and stating clear instructional objectives. Then appropriate instruction is developed or discovered to meet those objectives. No simple task! We are, in this chapter, describing the next phase in instructional systems—that of developing evaluation tools. The objectives give direction to the evaluation both by highlighting important textual material and by describing the level of learning at which the student should be performing upon exiting from the instructional system.

The first section of preliminary information will contain information to consider before test construction begins—the advantages and disadvantages of the multiple-choice question, the forms the item stem can take, and some ways of varying the difficulty of the items. The second part of the preliminary information section will define some of Bloom's (1956) work.

PRELIMINARY INFORMATION

To increase the validity of criterion-referenced tests, the objectives of the course of study must be identified and defined in terms of concrete desired changes in pupil behavior. The subject matter content should be outlined so that transitional goals are identified and representative sampling from course content is facilitated.

The type of item chosen for the evaluation procedure is preeminently determined by the subject matter of the course and the overall objectives. The multiple-choice item is currently the most widely used type. Multiple-choice questions have two parts—the problem and the response. The problem presented is called the *stem* of the item. The responses are called the *alternatives*. The alternatives that are incorrect are called *distractors*.

The multiple-choice item has the advantages of:

1. Efficient measurement of knowledge, understanding, thinking skills, and other complex outcomes
2. Extensive sampling of course content because of the large number of questions that can be included in the test
3. Preventing bluffing on answers and the influence of writing skills
4. Objective scoring, which is quick, easy, and consistent
5. Encouraging pupils to develop a comprehensive knowledge of specific facts and the ability to make fine discriminations among them

Certain disadvantages of multiple-choice items must also be considered:

1. They are inefficient for measuring ability to select and organize ideas, writing abilities, and some types of problem-solving skills.
2. A large number of items are needed—preparation is difficult and time-consuming.
3. Items are subject to guessing.

ITEM FORMS

If the multiple-choice item is chosen as the appropriate type of question for evaluation, it can assume a number of forms. Throughout this chapter an asterisk will be used to indicate the correct answer.

The item can be the *correct-answer type,* which contains just one correct answer, the alternatives being thoroughly wrong. This type is useful for the who, what, where, and when questions.

EXAMPLE: Correct-answer type

Correct-answer-type items
*A. contain just one correct response
 B. are easy to prepare
 C. have structures for measuring writing ability
 D. measure problem-solving ability

However, not all knowledge can be stated in such precise terms that there is only one absolutely correct response. Moreover, when questions concern the how and why, answers of varying degrees of acceptability are the rule rather than the exception. Thus, another form of item is the *best-answer type.* The best-answer type is more difficult than the correct-answer type partly because of the finer discrimination called for, and partly because of the fact that such items are used to measure learning outcomes that require comprehension, or application, of factual information.

EXAMPLE: Best-answer type
What is the particular strength of the best-answer-type item?
A. It prevents bluffing.
B. It allows for a thorough covering of the domain of knowledge.
*C. It allows the finer discriminations of knowledge to be made.
D. It reduces the influence of writing skills on the grade.

The form the stem takes many also vary. As illustrated by the previous examples, an incomplete statement (correct-answer type) or a direct question (best-answer type) can be used to state the problem. The incomplete statement has the advantage of conciseness but is often confusing to the student. To increase clarity, the omitted part of the statement should usually be at the end. A common procedure is to start each problem as a direct question, shifting to an incomplete statement form only when clarity of the problem can be retained and greater conciseness achieved.

ITEM DIFFICULTY

The difficulty of the item (percentage correct) can be varied by varying either the difficulty of the problem or the difficulty of the responses. Generally, the difficulty is most effectively controlled by problem modification. Once a problem has been stated, the domain from which plausible alternatives can be selected is limited. If an attempt is made to provide easier responses, it is probable that the correct answer will stand out very obviously from the others. The difficulty of a test should be established by selecting those problems which the pupils should be able to solve if they have achieved the objectives of the course.

Amount of Information

The amount of information contained within each alternative may be varied and thus have influence on item difficulty. Compound alternatives have at least two bits of information that are examples of separate desired learning outcomes or that are redundant. If the compound elements measure different learning outcomes, the difficulty level of the item is increased, whereas if the compound elements are redundant—that is, knowing either one will provide the correct answer—the item difficulty is decreased. In the examples below, difficulty is increased by asking the student what and why, and decreased by giving redundant answers to a "what" question.

EXAMPLE: Increased difficulty due to compound responses

Item difficulty can be varied in two ways. What are the ways, and which is the more appropriate method?

*A. Varying the difficulty of the responses or, more appropriately, the difficulty of the problem
 B. Varying the length of the alternatives or more appropriately, the difficulty of the responses
 C. Most appropriately, varying the form of the stem, and also using the correct-answer-type item
 D. Reducing irrelevant sources of confusion or, more appropriately, varying the difficulty of the problem

EXAMPLE: Decreased difficulty due to compound responses

Item difficulty is decreased when

 A. alternatives have two bits of information
*B. parts of alternatives are redundant or measure the same learning outcome
 C. parts of the problem formulation contain at least two bits of information
 D. the domain of information is limited and has few plausible distractors

At times it is better to break an item that has compound alternatives into two items, thereby testing the student's knowledge of the two facts independently. This prevents a student from getting points for an item he would have failed if it had been presented singly, and pinpoints the area in need of remediation.

Levels of Learning

Another factor that bears on item difficulty is, of course, the level of learning that the item tests.

In 1956, Bloom and his collaborators made six distinctions among various levels of learning. They listed knowledge, comprehension, application, analysis, synthesis, and evaluation as making up a taxonomy of educational outcomes.

The synthesis and evaluation levels are not dealt with in this chapter, since we believe that these levels cannot be tested using an item-generation procedure that relies on the instructional text. The Bormuth (1970) system to be presented in subsequent sections is based on the text. Brief distinctions among Bloom's (1956) levels follow:

Knowledge is defined as remembering what was seen in the instructional material.

Comprehension of instruction results in ability to deal with the material in a form somewhat different from that in which it was originally presented. (Evaluation of a student's comprehension of instructional material can, according to Bloom, take at least three forms: *translation, interpretation,* and *extrapolation.*

Translation of instructional material means that students are able to put the instruction into another form or in other terms. They can state the problem in their own words.

Interpretation means that students can reorder the instruction in some way. They are able to make inferences, generalizations, or summaries.

Extrapolation indicates the ability to make estimates or predictions based on an understanding of the instruction.

Application is distinct from comprehension in that it results in a student's applying a learned principle to a new problem without being prompted as to which principle is relevent. Comprehension implies that the principle is specified and it is the student's task to use it.

Analysis results in the student's ability to break down material into its constituent parts, to detect relationships among the parts and the way the parts are organized. It necessitates that the student recognize unstated assumptions, distinguish facts from hypotheses, and determine which are the pivotal points in an argument. Analysis is distinct from comprehension and application in its emphasis on understanding and generalizing from the underlying structure of instruction.

Synthesis is defined as the putting together of elements and parts so as to form a whole. The students must work with elements or parts to form a structure or yield a product that is clearly more than the materials they began to work with.

Evaluation is the making of judgments about the value, for some purpose, of ideas, works, solutions, methods, or materials. This level relies on all the previous levels and has the added element, or component, of values.

It is clear from the preceding that the form of the item, the appropriateness of the multiple-choice format for instructional goals, the level of learning tested, and the difficulty of the item are all important considerations in item construction.

Based on these general considerations we now provide a set of eight guidelines for construction with illustrative examples, some more general guidelines without examples, twelve undesirable constructions to be avoided, and some desirable constructions to be included.

TRADITIONAL GUIDELINES

Guidelines for Item Construction with Examples

In constructing items, the following guidelines should be considered. For each suggested guideline a poor example is given, followed by a better one.

1. **The stem should be meaningful by itself, and should present a definite problem.**

The stem should present a problem before all the alternatives have been read. It is useful to construct the stem in such a way that it could serve as a short-answer item.

POOR EXAMPLE:

Multiple-choice items
A. are effective question for measuring problem-solving skills
B. cannot be the sole criterion for measuring learning outcomes
*C. are the most widely used item type
D. are suitable for measuring knowledge and complex learning outcomes

BETTER EXAMPLE:

Multiple-choice items are widely used by test constructors because they
A. are effective in measuring problem-solving skills
B. are easy to generate and edit
*C. are suitable for measuring a wide array of thinking skills
D. take into account the writing and organizational skills of the student

2. **The item stem should include as much of the problem as possible and should be free from irrelevant material.**

Words or phrases that would need to be repeated in all the alternatives should be included in the stem. The most conciseness is achieved with the incomplete-statement stem. Of course, in testing some types of problem-solving ability, irrelevant material might be included in the stem of an item to determine whether the student is capable of identifying and selecting the material that is relevant to the solution of the problem. Also, sometimes repetition of common words is necessary for grammatical consistency and greater clarity.

POOR EXAMPLE: Redundancy in stem and in alternatives

Repetition of common words in stem and alternatives is sometimes necessary. Why is repetition necessary?
A. Repetition sometimes reduces irrelevant sources of difficulty.
B. Repetition determines whether the student is capable of identifying relevant material.
*C. Repetition occasionally facilitates grammatical consistency.
D. Repetition and redundancy are ways of varying item difficulty.

BETTER EXAMPLE: Incomplete-statement stem and brief alternatives add clarity.

The incomplete-statement stem is
A. a popular item type
B. a phrase repeated in alternatives
C. free from irrelevant material
*D. the most concise

3. Avoid negatively stated item stems.

A negative stem is not desirable for the following reasons: A student may overlook the negative, and the negative makes for less problem clarity, not greater item difficulty.

POOR EXAMPLE:

Which item characteristic does not result in greater item difficulty?
A. Irrelevant information in stem or alternatives
B. Compound alternatives measuring separate learning outcomes
C. Measurement of levels of learning above knowledge
*D. Alternatives with redundant components

BETTER EXAMPLE:

Which item characteristic tends to reduce item difficulty?
A. Irrelevant information in stem or alternatives
B. Compound alternatives measuring separate learning outcomes
C. Measurement of levels of learning above knowledge
*D. Alternatives with redundant components

In addition, the negative stem often measures relatively insignificant learning outcomes—for example, the least important method, the principle that does not apply, or the poorest reason. In contrast, a negatively stated item stem is desirable when having the wrong information has important consequences. It is helpful to capitalize the negative form.

POOR EXAMPLE:

Which of the following is not an appropriate way to generate parallel forms?
A. Sample from other parts of a domain of knowledge
*B. Permutations of original test items
C. Develop novel problems
D. Different questions based on the learning objectives

BETTER EXAMPLE:

All of the following are appropriate ways to generate parallel forms except
A. sampling from other parts of a domain of knowledge
*B. permutations of original test items
C. developing novel problems
D. different questions based on the learning objectives

4. All of the alternatives should be grammatically consistent with the stem of the item.

Careful attention to grammatical usage in the stem and alternatives prevents irrelevant clues from creeping into the item. Tense of verbs, proper use of the articles *a* and *an,* and the use of plurals in the stem or alternative should be checked.

POOR EXAMPLE:

Careful attention to grammatical usage in the stem and alternatives
*A. prevents irrelevant clues from creeping in
B. checking the proper use of articles *a* and *an*
C. to use plural in both stem and alternatives
D. to prevent disagreement between tense of verbs

BETTER EXAMPLE:

Careful attention to grammatical usage in the stem and alternatives
*A. prevents irrelevant clues from creeping in
B. is important only with incomplete-statement stems
C. is rarely a problem in multiple-choice item construction
D. prevents item difficulty from varying

5. An item should contain only one correct or clearly best answer.

Including more than one correct answer, and asking the student to select all correct responses, has two major shortcomings:

1. such items are usually no more than a collection of true–false items presented in multiple-choice form. They do not present a definite problem in the stem and do not require a comparison of all alternatives.

2. since the number of alternatives selected as the correct answer varies from pupil to pupil, there is no satisfactory method of scoring.

POOR EXAMPLE:

Which of the following are advantages of the multiple-choice item?
A. Easy and quick to prepare
*B. Allows extensive sampling from knowledge domain
*C. Prevents bluffing
D. Measures writing skills

BETTER EXAMPLE:

Advantages of the multiple-choice item include

	True	False
A. easy and quick preparation		*
B. extensive sampling from a knowledge domain	*	
C. prevention of bluffing	*	
D. measurement of writing skills		*

The better example above is known as a *cluster-type true–false item*. In this way accurate scoring is simplified.

It is important that the "best" answer to a problem be agreed upon by most experts. A careful check of wording in the stem can prevent confusion. It is often helpful to make the criterion for "best" explicit in the stem.

POOR EXAMPLE: Criteria for best answer is ambiguous.

The best item type to use in evaluation strategies is the
A. essay question
*B. multiple-choice item
C. short-answer item
D. true–false question

BETTER EXAMPLE: Criteria are clearly stated.

The item type that best allows for extensive sampling of a domain and prevents the influence of writing skills is the
A. essay question
*B. multiple-choice item
C. short-answer item
D. true–false question

6. All alternatives should be plausible.

In a test each alternative should be selected by some pupils. The alternatives should be homogeneous; that is, they should be drawn from the same domain of information. The stem should clearly point to the theme of the correct alternative. The alternatives should not be uncorrelated facts, one of which is true and the others false. In constructing the distractors, the learning experience of the student must be considered. All the alternatives should be familiar to the student in some way. Common misconceptions, errors of judgment, and faulty reasoning that appear during the learning process should be recorded during formative evaluation. These provide sound alternatives. Also, the inclusion of irrelevant or unfamiliar technical terms as alternatives is undesirable since such terms can often be immediately eliminated by the student.

POOR EXAMPLE: Distractors are from different domain than correct answer.

The two highest of Bloom's levels of learning are
A. multiple and cluster forms of learning
B. subjective intuition and evaluation
C. writing and problem-solving skills
*D. synthesis and evaluation

BETTER EXAMPLE: Alternatives are all examples of Bloom's taxonomy.

The two highest of Bloom's levels of learning are
A. application and evaluation
B. synthesis and comprehension
C. comprehension and analysis
*D. synthesis and evaluation

7. Verbal association between stem and correct answer should be avoided.

A word in the correct answer will provide an irrelevant clue if it looks or sounds like a word in the stem of the item. Often a reading aloud of the items and alternatives will uncover such cases. Words similar to those in the stem might be included in distractors to increase their plausibility. It is important not to overdo irrelevant clues in alternatives, however, since pupils catch on quickly and will learn to avoid alternatives with pat verbal associations.

POOR EXAMPLE: Verbal association between word in stem (*application*) and word in correct answer (*apply*).

Application of learning describes a student's ability to
A. deal with the material in a different form
*B. apply what has been learned
C. remember the material as presented
D. break down the material into component parts

BETTER EXAMPLE: Verbal associations are used to distract from the correct answer.

Application of learning describes a student's ability to
A. deal with the material in a different form
*B. use what has been learned on new problems
C. remember applications of material that have been presented
D. apply skills to break down the material into component parts

8. The relative length of the alternatives should not provide a clue to the answer.

The correct answer tends to be longer than the distractors, since it usually needs to be qualified. Lengthening distractors increases their plausibility and disguises long correct answers. The relative length of the correct answers should vary with no discernible pattern, sometimes longest, sometimes shortest. In general, suggested answers should be as brief as possible.

POOR EXAMPLE:

The relative length of the correct answers should
A. usually be short
B. be long enough to allow for qualifiers
C. usually be long
*D. vary with no discernible pattern, sometimes longest, sometimes shortest

BETTER EXAMPLE:

The relative length of the correct answer should
A. usually be short, since longer alternatives draw choices
B. be long enough to allow for necessary qualifications
C. usually be long, since students are drawn to short, simple statements
*D. be variable, long and short, with no discernible pattern

Guidelines for Construction without Examples

The following guidelines are self-explanatory and need no examples to make them useful to the item writer or editor.

1. **Use special alternatives such as "none of the above" or "all of the above" sparingly.**

There is some disagreement among test constructors as to the feasibility of the alternatives "none of the above" and "all of the above." The "all of the above" response may cause students to give an incorrect answer for not reading through all of the alternatives. They also can give a correct answer on the basis of partial knowledge. If students know that two or more of the alternatives are correct, they can safely choose "all of the above."

The use of "none of the above" is, of course, restricted to correct-answer-type items. It is often successfully used in quantitative problems.

2. **The correct answer should appear in each of the alternative positions approximately an equal number of times, but in random order.**

Test constructors should avoid the tendency to overload the middle positions with the correct answer, and should develop some convenient system for randomizing.

3. **The test items should be independently reviewed by a competent colleague for clarity and correctness of response.**

Even with careful editing by the writer, the test-item bank is likely to be improved with a review by another reader.

Undesirable Constructions with Examples

In addition to these general guidelines, there are a number of undesirable constructions that should be **avoided**.

1. **Items using citation of authority. It is generally better to test the student's knowledge of what experts tend to say about a subject than one person's opinion of a subject.**

POOR EXAMPLE:

What does Roid say about the relative importance of testing in an instructional system?
A. It is equal in importance to the textual material.
B. Testing, though vital, must be seen as less important than instructor preparation.

*C. It is the most important component of the system.
 D. Testing's importance is overlooked by many instructional system developers.

BETTER EXAMPLE:

Most instructional system developers see evaluation as
A. the most difficult component to develop
B. equal in importance to the instructional material
*C. a vital part of an instructional system
D. a frequently weak link in an instructional system

2. Items dealing with incidental details. Trivial details are rarely important learning outcomes.

POOR EXAMPLE:

How many "Guidelines without Examples" were presented in this chapter?
A. 1
B. 2
*C. 3
D. 4

BETTER EXAMPLE:

Special alternatives such as "all of the above" should
A. be placed in random order as alternatives
B. appear as often as "none of the above"
*C. be used sparingly
D. be checked by a reviewer for clarity

3. Items using label alternatives. It is usually more difficult to get good distractors for one- or two-word correct answers than for a phrase or a sentence.

POOR EXAMPLE:

Criterion-referenced orientations demand the construction of many alternative tests known as
A. permutations
B. mastery tests
C. cluster tests
*D. parallel forms

BETTER EXAMPLE:

A parallel or alternate form of a test
A. samples from alternate domains of knowledge
B. can appropriately be generated using permutations of the original questions
C. is rarely needed if a criterion-referenced system is being used
*D. can increase the standard error of measurement

4. Items asking examinee his opinion. If the item asks for the student's opinion, no alternative can be marked wrong. A more feasible approach is to ask the opinion of experts on a particular subject.

POOR EXAMPLE:

How often do you think small details should be included as test items?
A. Occasionally, to ensure that students read carefully
*B. Rarely, since they hardly ever are important learning outcomes
C. Frequently, since they are often examples of higher learning outcomes
D. Depends on the type of instructional material

BETTER EXAMPLE:

What is generally felt about test items dealing with incidental detail?
A. They are useful to ensure careful reading by students.
*B. They rarely test for important learning outcomes.
C. They are useful to test for higher learning outcomes.
D. No general statement can be made.

5. Items involving an "instructional aside."

POOR EXAMPLE:

Test writers should avoid the tendency to overload the middle positions with the correct answer. How often should correct answers appear in each of the alternative positions?
A. More frequently at the first position
B. More frequently at the last position
C. A random number of times
*D. An equal number of times

BETTER EXAMPLE:

How often and in what order should test items appear in each of the alternative positions?
A. More frequently at the first position, but only every fifth or sixth time
B. More frequently at the last position, but only every fifth or sixth time
C. A random number of times in random order
*D. An equal number of times in random order

6. Items using stereotyped phrases in the correct answer. Stereotyped phrases may provide irrelevant clues, since the student may choose an alternative simply because it looks familiar.

POOR EXAMPLE:

Traditional guidelines for test-item construction have typically contained a statement like the following:
*A. A good recipe and a talented cook produce great successes.
B. Tests are the most important components of an instructional system.
C. Subjective intuitions of the writer are most relevant.
D. Generate items closely related to instruction.

BETTER EXAMPLE:

Traditional guidelines for test item development suggest that test writing is a(n)
*A. rather intuitive skill
B. highly developed technology
C. area in need of empirical validation
D. area where "too many cooks spoil the broth"

7. Items having nonparallel responses, especially time and place.

POOR EXAMPLE:

The organization of this chapter is such that some textbooks dealing with test-item construction are
*A. listed in the reference section
B. cited and quoted from extensively
C. mentioned only when a quotation is used
D. all pre-1956 publication dates

BETTER EXAMPLE:

The organization of this chapter is such that some textbooks dealing with test-item construction are
*A. listed in the reference section
B. cited and quoted from extensively
C. mentioned only when a quotation is used
D. cited in footnotes

8. Items that interlock—that is, provide answers to other questions in the same test.

POOR EXAMPLE:

Question 1. Interlocking items are those which
A. are placed in tandem
B. use a stereotyped phrase
*C. provide answers to other questions
D. have some logical relevance to each other

Question 2. Undesirable constructions, to be **avoided,** in test-item development include
A. nonparallel alternatives and different levels of learning
B. incomplete statements and tandem construction
*C. interlocking items that provide answers, and stereotypic phrases
D. instructional asides, and items with just one clearly best answer

9. Items with responses placed in tandem instead of listed.

POOR EXAMPLES:

Interlocking items are those which (A) are placed in tandem, (B) use a stereotyped phrase, (C) provide answers to other questions, (D) have some logical relevance to each other.

BETTER EXAMPLE:

Interlocking items are those which
A. are placed in tandem
B. use a stereotyped phrase
*C. provide answers to other questions
D. have some logical relevance to each other

10. Items that contain irrelevant sources of difficulty because of complex sentence structure in the stem or the alternatives, or difficult vocabulary.

POOR EXAMPLE: Complex sentence structure in stem

Compound alternatives, which have at least two (perhaps many more) bits of information or statements that are examples of either separate desired learning outcomes or that are examples of redundant information or statements, can be used to
A. teach as well as test
*B. vary item difficulty
C. vary levels of learning
D. distract from the correct alternative

BETTER EXAMPLE:

Compound alternatives—that is, alternatives having redundant or separate bits of information—can be used to
A. teach as well as test
*B. vary item difficulty
C. modify levels of learning
D. distract from the correct alternative

POOR EXAMPLE: Complex sentence structure in alternatives

Multiple-choice questions differ from essay questions mainly in that
A. Although many complex thinking skills can be measured quite effectively through multiple-choice questions, only knowledge levels of learning are tapped, unlike essay questions, where evaluation of higher levels of learning is possible.
B. Though guessing is a problem in evaluting the responses on any test, the problem of guessing is especially acute with multiple-choice questions though not with essay questions, where bluffing is virtually impossible.
*C. The number needed of multiple-choice questions is much greater than the number of essay questions in addition to the fact that although there is the chance to evaluate complex learning outcomes with multiple-choice questions, essay questions are the more appropriate choice for measuring writing, organizing, and some problem-solving skills.
D. Though writing skills are of virtually no importance in multiple-choice problems, neither are problem-solving skills, which are mainly important in responses to essay questions.

BETTER EXAMPLE:

Which is the characteristic of essay questions that distinguishes them from multiple-choice questions?
A. extensive sampling of course content
B. large number of questions included on test
*C. potential for evaluating writing skills
D. quick scoring

POOR EXAMPLE: Difficult vocabulary

An evaluation methodology with the primary requisite of surplus examples of items might best be based on
A. essay questions
B. true–false items
C. short-answer items
*D. multiple-choice questions

BETTER EXAMPLE:

A testing strategy requiring large numbers of items is best met with
A. essay questions
B. true–false items
C. short-answer items
*D. multiple-choice questions

11. **Items that contain inclusive terms such as** *never, always, sole,* **and** *all*
    in the wrong alternatives. (Statements involving such broad
    generalizations are likely to be wrong, and the test-wise student
    knows this and can use such clues to get credit for knowledge he or
    she does not possess. *Sometimes, generally,* and *usually* should be
    used in both correct and incorrect responses.)

POOR EXAMPLE: Inclusive terms in distractors

A good rule to follow when writing alternatives is to
A. never make the vocabulary or sentence structure difficult
B. always use the "all of the above" or "none of the above" alternatives
*C. generally avoid use of inclusive terms
D. use alternatives that are opposites

BETTER EXAMPLE:

A good rule to follow when writing alternatives is to
A. make the vocabulary or sentence structure difficult
B. usually use the "all of the above" or "none of the above" alternatives
*C. generally avoid use of inclusive terms
D. usually use alternatives that are opposites

12. **Items with alternatives that are opposite. This leads students to**
    suppose that one of the opposites is the correct answer.

POOR EXAMPLE:

To increase clarity, the omitted part of the item stem should
*A. be at the end
B. not be very long
C. be at the beginning
D. contain the most important element of the statement

BETTER EXAMPLE:

To increase clarity, the omitted part of the item stem should
*A. be at the end
B. not be very long
C. be carefully placed to increase difficulty
D. contain the most important element of the statement

Desirable Construction with Examples

Some aspects of construction which are useful to **include** are the following:

1. **All distractors should be true statements.** (The following item contains all true statements concerning advantages of multiple-choice questions. The student must decide which advantage is particularly important for a particular evaluation methodology.)

GOOD EXAMPLE:

Which is the advantage of multiple-choice items that makes them very appropriate for criterion-referenced evaluation?
A. They measure thinking skills efficiently.
B. They prevent bluffing.
*C. They allow large numbers of items from course content.
D. They encourage students to develop comprehensive knowledge of content.

2. **Stereotyped phrases in the distractors.** (The use of phrases that have often been heard but possibly not understood will sometimes distract students who have only marginal mastery of the subject matter from the correct answer.)

GOOD EXAMPLE:

Synthesis and evaluation levels of learning are
*A. dependent on original production from the student
B. the *raison d'etre* of learning
C. impervious to the correction for guessing formula
D. the most common levels learning to come under evaluation scrutiny

3. **Items whose responses are kept in some natural sequence, either quantitative or qualitative.**

GOOD EXAMPLE: A qualitative sequence

All of the following are examples of traditional guidelines for test item construction **except**
A. make an outline of the topics
B. consult behavioral objectives and determine the mental processes that are to be tested
C. draft items sometime in advance, making sure there is a surplus
*D. construct test so that item groupings are heterogeneous for skills and content to be evaluated.

4. **Items whose numerical responses are different from each other by approximately equal amounts. Numbers that are very different from the other numerical alternatives are usually immediately eliminated by students.**

POOR EXAMPLE:

How many levels of educational objectives are described in Bloom's (1956) taxonomy?
A. 3
B. 4
*C. 6
D. 15

BETTER EXAMPLE:

How many levels of educational objectives are described in Bloom's (1956) taxonomy?
A. 3
B. 4
C. 5
*D. 6

A SYSTEM FOR DEVISING ITEMS USING
OPERATIONAL DEFINITIONS

Despite the obvious usefulness of the preceding suggestions, criticism has been directed at these traditional guidelines, and suggestions made for deriving test items using operational definitions (Anderson, 1972; Bormuth, 1970). An *operational definition* describes the manner in which items are derived from the instruction. It has two major components:

1. A set of operations by which a syntactic structure is assigned to the instruction
2. A set of operations performed on that syntax that transforms the relevant segments of the instruction into test items

This method can be contrasted with the traditional methods. First, when operational definitions are used to generate items, the results are closely replicable. The writer using a particular operational definition has little freedom in phrasing the item. In contrast, conventional methods place so few constraints on the item writer that it is improbable that two writers could replicate each other's results even using the same text as a source.

A second contrast between the two methods is in the item's logical relevance to the instruction. Logical relevance is the relationship of the item to a specific segment of instruction. Using operational definitions, it is possible to state the exact manner in which the structure of the test item is related to the relevant segment of the instruction. Traditional writers must rely on subjective, judgmental procedures. Even if a panel of judges is used to review the items, their judgment is based primarily on introspection about the relevance of the items.

The subsequent sections of this chapter will present suggestions for test-item development that are based on operational definitions. The suggestions are meant to facilitate analysis of relationships between questions and preceding instruction and to provide a rationale for selecting questions. If the suggestions for test writing that will be given are rigorously followed, numerous questions can be generated, far more than are ordinarily needed for actual testing purposes. As mentioned previously, a surplus of items is desirable. Surplus items can be used to construct parallel or equivalent forms of tests. Parallel forms should not be simple permutations of the original questions with the multiple-choice responses given different letters. Using permutations of original questions will actually increase the standard error of measurement in the second form. This occurs since any errors in sampling present in the first form will also be present in the second form plus error from specific sources. Parallel forms should cover the same material—that is, sample from the same domain, asking different questions and presenting novel problems to the student.

Those interested in a more rigorous treatment of the rules and operations used to transform instruction into questions than is presented here are referred to *On the Theory of Achievement Test Items* by John Bormuth (1970), to Anderson (1972, 1973), and to Chapter 3 of this volume.

Suggestions for deriving two types of items at the knowledge level will be given. Also, the limitations of the transformational system will be discussed before providing suggestions for generating items at the comprehension, analysis, and application levels. The final section of the chapter will suggest a method for choosing items. *Base sentence* will refer to sentences taken directly from the instruction; *transformed sentence* will indicate that an operation has been performed in order to transform the base sentence into a question. Special cases will be appropriately labeled.

Suggestions for Item Development with Examples

The operations by which questions and their responses are derived from instruction are called *item transformations*. All that is needed to construct items using this method is a rudimentary understanding of nouns, verbs, adjectives, adverbs, and prepositions. Mature users of the language are cognizant of sentence structure even if they are unable to verbalize it formally. Therefore, assigning a syntactic structure to a sentence can be done with no extra study of grammar.

Assigning a syntactic structure means that a sentence is broken down into its constituent parts—for example, subject phrase, verb phrase, object phrase, and prepositional phrase.

EXAMPLE:
Base sentence: The operations by which questions and their responses are derived from instruction are called item transformations.
Subject phrase: The operations
Verb phrase: are called
Object phrase: item transformations
Prepositional phrase: by which questions and their responses are derived

The prepositional phrase in the above example refers back to the subject phrase *The operations.*

Once this kind of simple structure has been seen in the instructional sentences the second step in item transformation can be accomplished. An operation can be performed on the sentence to transform it into a question. Examples of the various operations are given below. Most operations will be illustrated with multiple-choice questions.

Questions at the Knowledge Level

Verbatim Items

It is occasionally desirable to test the student's rote memory of the instruction. A first example of a verbatim item is a *yes–no item.* Sentences can be taken directly from the instructional material, and (*a*) the period deleted and (*b*) a question mark added. These items require only a yes–no answer.

EXAMPLE:
Base sentence: It is occasionally desirable to test the student's rote memory of the instruction.
Transformed sentence: It is occasionally desirable to test the student's rote memory of the instruction.

Instructions at the beginning of verbatim items can make them *true–false items.* In this case the period would not be deleted and no question mark would be necessary.

EXAMPLE:
Base sentence: It is occasionally desirable to test the student's rote memory of the instruction.
Transformed sentence: Mark the following sentence true or false: It is occasionally desirable to test the student's rote memory of the instruction. T F
                                                                    —* —

When this transformation is used for true–false items there will be a disproportionally large number of true statements, since ostensibly most instructional sentences are true. Three ways to derive false items are to

1. Insert negative into the sentence. This must be done sparingly or the student will realize that most negative items are false.

EXAMPLE:
Base sentence: Instructions at the beginning of verbatim items can make them *true–false items.*
Transformed sentence: Instructions at the beginning of verbatim items cannot make them *true–false items.* T F
                                    — *—

2. Draw negative sentences from the instruction and transform a random half of them into positive statements. This can usually be done by deleting the form of *not* that is present.

EXAMPLE:

Base sentence: Parallel forms should not be simple permutations of the original questions with the multiple-choice responses given different letters.
Transformed sentence: Parallel forms should be simple permutations of the original questions with the multiple-choice responses given different letters.   T F
— —*

3. Select the base sentences to be tested, and for a random half of these, select paired sentences with both identical syntactical constituents and logical consistency—that is, the elements are matched according to some category. The identical syntactical constituents are then switched from one sentence to the other. The derived sentences are then false statements.

EXAMPLE:

Base sentence: An operational definition *describes the manner in which items are derived from the instruction.* Logical relevance *is the relationship of the item to a specific segment of instruction.*
Transformed sentence: An operational definition is the relationship of the item to a specific segment of instruction.   T   F
— —*

Logical relevance describes the manner in which items are derived from the instruction.   T F
— *—

Verbatim items can also be used for *short-answer questions*. The test writer can decide to generate items through, for example, subject-phrase deletion. This decision would entail (*a*) identifying the subject phrase in each relevant instructional sentence and (*b*) deleting the subject phrase.

EXAMPLE:

Base sentence: *An operational definition* describes the manner in which items are derived from the instruction.
Transformed sentence: A(n) ＿＿ describes the manner in which items are derived from the instruction.

This same sentence could be transformed by verb-phrase deletion, or object-phrase deletion.

EXAMPLE: Adverbial-phrase deletion

Base sentence: An operational definition describes the manner in which items are derived from the instruction.

Transformed sentence: An operational definition describes the manner in which items are
derived from the ___.

Notice that in the adverbial-phrase-deletion example the whole phrase
from the instruction was not deleted. In generating questions with this
method, care should be taken that results concur with recommendations
made earlier in the chapter. Short-answer questions should usually test
for one important fact—that is, leave only one blank. The important part
of the phrase is *instruction*.

Verbatim transformations can also be used for *multiple-choice items*.
Base sentences can be transformed into stems: (*a*) identify the
segment to be deleted, and (*b*) delete the segment. Alternatives can be
generated: (*a*) identify the structure of the correct response, and (*b*) take
words, phrases, or sentences with similar structure from the instructions
and use them as distractors. Distractors should be plausible.

A strategy we used to generate the examples that accompanied the 30
guidelines presented in the preceding sections of this chapter was to use
the transformational method to develop the test items and then revise the
items, if necessary, according to traditional suggestions.

EXAMPLE:

Base sentence: Logical relevance is the relationship of the item to a specific segment of the
instruction.
Transformed sentence: Logical relevance ___.
*A. is the relationship of the item to a specific segment of the instruction
B. describes the manner in which items are derived from the instruction
C. can be taken directly from instructional material
D. provides a useful basis for generating test items that will representatively save the
desired achievement

Transformed Verbatim Items

For clarity and variety, sentences can be rearranged using the same
words but in a somewhat different form.

EXAMPLE:

Base sentence: Logical relevance is the relationship of the item to a specific segment of the
instruction.
Rearranged sentence: The relationship of the item to a specific segment of the instruction
is called logical relevance.

The rearranged sentence can be made into a question: (*a*) identify the
segment to be deleted, and (*b*) delete the segment.

EXAMPLE:

Rearranged sentence: The relationship of the item to a specific segment of the instruction
is logical relevance.

Transformed sentence: The relationship of an item to a specific segment of the instruction is called ____.
A. operational definition
*B. logical relevance
C. a behavioral objective
D. a parallel form

Transformed verbatim operations are good to apply when the rearrangement will add clarity to the stem. Deleted segments should usually be near the end of the stem, especially if the stem is lengthy.

Transformations that involve inserting a wh-question can be made through verbatim transformation. There are four groups of wh-words.

1. *Who* and *what* are used to replace human and nonhuman nouns, respectively.
2. *Which* is used to replace noun modifiers.
3. *How, when, where,* and *why* are used to replace the various adverbial categories.
4. A form of *what do* is used when the verb is deleted.

In order to accomplish the wh-transformation the writer must (*a*) study the structure of the sentence; (*b*) select the segment to be tested; (*c*) delete that segment; (*d*) replace the deleted phrase with a wh-word; and (*e*) shift the wh-word to the front of the sentence.

Distractors are constructed: (*a*) study the structure of the correct response; (*b*) choose sentences from the instruction with similar structures. The sentences chosen from the instruction should be plausible, be matched grammatically (i.e., same tense, same number, etc.).

EXAMPLE:

Base sentence: Surplus items can be used to construct parallel or equivalent forms of tests.
Transformed Sentence:
Noun deletion: What can be used to construct parallel or equivalent forms of tests?
A. Outline of topics
B. Behavioral objectives
*C. Surplus items
D. Judgmental procedures

EXAMPLE:

Base sentence: Traditional writers must rely on subjective, judgmental procedures.
Transformed sentence:
Object-phrase deletion: Which procedures must traditional writers rely upon?
A. Operational definition procedures
B. Logical relevance systems
C. Behavioral objective analyses
*D. Subjective judgmental analyses

EXAMPLE:

Base sentence: Transformed verbatim operations are good to apply when the rearrang-
ment will add clarity to the stem.
Transformed sentence:
Adverbial deletion: When are transformed verbatim operations good to apply?
A. When deleted segments are near the end of the stem
B. When the deleted phrase is a wh-word
*C. When the rearrangement will add clarity to the stem
D. When sentences chosen from the instruction are plausible

EXAMPLE:

Base sentence: Surplus items can be used to construct parallel or equivalent forms of the
test.
Transformed sentence:
Verb deletion: What can surplus items be used for?
A. To prevent sampling errors
*B. To construct equivalent forms of the test
C. To prevent a decrease in the standard error of measurement
D. To test at comprehension levels of learning

Limitations of the Transformational System

Before proceeding with step-by-step guidelines for item generation at
the comprehension, analysis, and application levels, certain limitations of
this adaptation of Bormuth's (1970) work should be made explicit. The
main purpose of this system is to ensure that test items bear logical
relevance to the instruction that they concern. Logical relevance is the
relationship of the item to a specific segment of instruction. Using operational definitions, it is possible to state the exact manner in which the
structure of the test item is related to the segment of the instruction.

When generating items above the knowledge level, however, much
depends on the skill of the test writer in paraphrasing, mediating, and
selecting particular and superordinate terms. Although the operational
definitions can be exactly specified, the results are not perfectly replicable—a goal of Bormuth's.

Furthermore, by remaining closely tied to the text, certain nuances of
Bloom's taxonomy are sacrificed. Operational definitions are always
based on the text. Bloom suggests, however, that performance at the
application and analysis levels may require generation of new material. It
is the assumption of this chapter that the strategies to be described
generate enough novel material to fulfill Bloom's definitions.

The preceding sections have illustrated verbatim and verbatim-
transformation question types that lend themselves to testing only rote
memory or knowledge. Comprehension of the instruction cannot be in-

ferred from successful performance on verbatim and verbatim-transformation items, since students could be responding to phonological or orthographic overlap—that is, sound or sight memory. In the next sections strategies will be suggested that can be used to generate questions at the comprehension, application, and analysis levels. Four strategies are of particular importance. They are paraphrasing, substituting superordinate terms for particular terms, substituting particular terms for superordinate terms, and identifying the mediating or underlying structure of sentences.

Questions at the Comprehensive Level:
Paraphrase Questions

Comprehension can be inferred from the capacity to answer a question based on a paraphrase of a test statement. As noted in earlier chapters of this book, statements are defined as paraphrases of one another if

1. They have no substantive word in common—that is, nouns, verbs, and modifiers
2. They are equivalent in meaning

The judgment of equivalence in meaning will require some introspection on the part of the writer. Phrases may be paraphrased by single words or single words by phrases. A number of sentences may be paraphrased by one sentence or one sentence may be paraphrased by more than one. To form a paraphrased test item, (*a*) paraphrase the base sentence; (*b*) delete a segment from the paraphrase; or (*c*) transform the paraphrase into a wh-question. Alternatives may be formed by paraphrasing other sentences from the instruction.

EXAMPLE: Comprehension question

Base sentences: The preceding sections have illustrated verbatim and verbatim-transformation question types that lend themselves to testing only rote memory or knowledge. Comprehension of the instruction cannot be inferred from successful performance on verbatim and verbatim-transformation items, since students could be responding to phonological or orthographic overlap—that is, sound or sight memory.

Paraphrase: Because items built with words taken directly from the text test only for memorization, higher levels of understanding of text material cannot be guaranteed by a passing grade on these items.

Transformed sentence: Items built from words taken directly from the text

A. are necessary to infer comprehension of the text
B. are appropriate paraphrases of the basic meaning of the material
C. are not verbatim or verbatim transformations unless equivalence of meaning is established
*D. cannot guarantee higher levels of understanding of text material

Not all sentences can be paraphrased. Proper nouns and words of a highly specific or technical nature are difficult or impossible to communicate precisely in a paraphrase. In such cases, these words can be kept verbatim in the paraphrase to avoid introducing irrelevant sources of difficulty to the student.

EXAMPLE: Proper name cannot be paraphrased

Base sentence: Those interested in a more rigorous treatment of the rules and operations used to transform instruction into questions than is presented here are referred to *On the Theory of Achievement Test Items* by John Bormuth (1970), to Anderson (1972, 1973), and to Chapter 3 by Roid.

Paraphrase: Readers desiring an in-depth discussion of procedures useful in generating test items from text material are urged to read *On the Theory of Achievement Test Items* by Bormuth (1970), Anderson (1972,1973), and Chapter 3 by Roid.

Transformed sentence: What book provides readers with an in-depth discussion of procedures useful in generating questions from text material?
  A. *Measurement and Evaluation in Teaching*
  B. *Generating Test Items*
 *C. *On the Theory of Achievement Test Items*
  D. *Rigorous Test Production and Review: Achievement Testing*

Note that the distractors were constructed from (A) another bibliographic citation, (B) verbal association with stem, and (D) paraphrases of stem.

Questions at the Application Level

Questions Formed by Substituting Particular Terms for Superordinate Terms

A term is superordinate if at least some of the members of the class can be named without repeating the superordinate term. For example, *tool* is a superordinate term because each new instance of the class has a particular name (e.g., pliers, hammer, wrench). The word *wings* is not superordinate because although there are numerous examples of wings, the examples cannot be stated without repeating the word *wings*.

Superordinate terms are often found in instruction illustrated by a few examples. Instruction sets out to teach students cognitive behaviors on a few examples in order to enable them to deduct the answers to all the remaining problems. Test items can be generated by using examples of the superordinate terms that have not appeared in the instruction.

To derive a question formed by substituting particular terms for superordinate terms, (*a*) replace every superordinate term in the base sentence with a particular term; (*b*) substitute synonyms for every remaining substantive word; (c) delete a segment; or (d) form a wh-question. Distractors should be similar, in structure and grammatical features, to the correct response in addition to being plausible alternatives. Questions aimed at evaluating the student's ability to apply what he has learned can be formed by this method.

EXAMPLE: Application question that replaces superordinate terms with particular terms

Base sentence: The operations by which questions and their responses are derived from instruction are called item transformations. Most operations will be illustrated with multiple-choice questions.

Particular instance: The Bormuth method can be used to generate essay items.

Transformed sentence: What might characterize essay items generated by the Bormuth method?

*A. Essay questions would most likely be formed through paraphrase, substitutions of superordinate and particular terms, and the identification of structure.

B. There might be a series of complex operations based on the logical relevance of the item to the instruction.

C. Essay questions meant to measure organizational abilities might well be formed through careful use of verbatim transformations.

D. The evaluation and synthesis levels appropriate for essay questions cannot be derived from the Bormuth method.

If answered correctly, the transformed sentence using particular terms for superordinate terms gives evidence that the student can apply what he has learned. Knowing the antecedent conditions (operations of item transformation) he can supply or select the consequent condition (possible way to generate essay questions). Questions that have explicit or implicit "if–then" statements are good examples of items that require application of knowledge. That is, *if* one understands the chapter, *then* one is able to generate essay-test items. This type of question permits evaluation at a higher level of skill than the paraphrased questions described previously.

Questions Formed by Substituting Superordinate Terms for Specific Terms

Questions can be formed by replacing specific terms with superordinate terms. When this substitution is made, the meaning of the sentence is enlarged but not changed completely.

If the instruction has provided the student with many particular instances, it is desirable to construct questions that evaluate whether the student has seen the general principles, or "main idea," behind the instruction. This is accomplished by (a) replacing particular terms with superordinate terms; (b) replacing all substantive words with synonyms, or paraphrasing where appropriate; (c) deleting a segment; or (d) forming a wh-question. Questions of this type are meant to test a student's grasp of the material and so should not be confined to information that he can read directly from the instruction. The answers may require some synthesis or original thought.

EXAMPLE:

Base sentence: This is accomplished by (*a*) replacing particular terms with superordinate terms; (*b*) replacing all substantive words with synonyms, or paraphrasing where appropriate; (*c*) deleting a segment; or (*d*) forming a wh-question.

Superordinate terms: Item generation is done by performing structural and semantic operations on text material.

Transformed sentence: What is done by performing structural and semantic operations on text material?

  A. Text improvement
*B. Item generation
  C. Structural and semantic clarifying
  D. Test-item revision

In this example the particular steps in item generation were subsumed under the superordinate terms *structural and semantic operations*. The questions formed from these substitutions may be very flexible, since the purpose of the question, in this case, is to test not for specific activities but for the underlying principle.

Questions at the Analysis Level: Formed by Identifying Mediating Structure

Mediating (or underlying) *structures* of instruction are general statements that put the instruction in symbolic language. The purpose of discovering and making explicit the underlying structure of instruction is to give the test-item writer a clean look at the relationships contained within the instruction. Once these relationships are made explicit, questions concerning constituent parts of the instruction can be generated.

Questions designed to evaluate a student's ability to analyze the instruction are difficult to construct. They require, even more than the previous levels, a thorough understanding of the instructional material on the part of the test writer. This kind of in-depth understanding is facilitated by the explicit statement of the lesson's underlying structures.

A way of explaining mediation might be to consider it as an outline of this chapter, as is shown in Figure 4.1. Another graphic illustration of mediation is shown in Figure 4.2 (just a portion of the chapter is shown). All of these methods of elucidating underlying structure can result in a clear picture of the hierarchical relationships within instruction and may facilitate item generation.

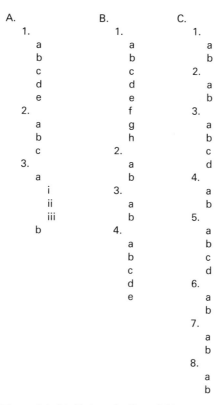

Figure 4.1. Mediation: Outline of Chapter 4.

Strategies discussed previously regarding paraphrasing and substitution of particular and superordinate terms can be combined with the use of mediating structure to devise items that present the students with novel problems while maintaining logical relevance to the textual material.

EXAMPLE: Analysis question formed by identifying underlying structure of instruction

Base sentence: See pages 100 and 101 of this chapter for a discussion of Bloom's (1956) taxonomy.

Mediated sentence: Learning occurs at Levels 1, 2, 3, 4, 5, and 6. Level 2 depends upon Level 1, Level 3 depends on Levels 1 and 2; Level 4 depends upon Levels 1, 2, 3; Levels 5 and 6 depend upon the previous levels plus other undefined factors. Each level past 1 is a prerequisite for other levels. Higher levels are more valued.

Transformed sentence: An analysis of Bloom's (1956) taxonomy of educational objectives might lead to which of the following generalizations?

A. The process of learning is both a sequential phenomenon and a process that relies upon insight to reach its highest expression.

A.
1.   2.   3.
abcde abc   a
         i ii iii   b

B.
1.   2.   3.   4.
abcdefgh ab ab   abcde

C.
1.   2.   3.   4.   5.   6.   7.   8.
ab   ab   abcd   ab   abcd   ab   ab   ab

Figure 4.2. Mediation: Outline of part of Chapter 4.

B. The content of the instruction is, by far, the best predictor of which levels of learning take place; test writers operate with a "ceiling effect."
*C. There is a similarity between this taxonomy and the constructs of *stages, fixation,* and *self-actualization* suggested by writers such as Piaget, Freud, and Maslow.
D. Taxonomies of learning, like taxonomies of species or plants in biology and botany, are descriptive but not evaluative.

A METHOD FOR SELECTING ITEMS

Once a number of items have been generated using operational definitions, they can be chosen for testing in a partly random fashion. There are two constraints on the randomness of selection:

1. Each objective is tested by at least one item and more if it is necessary.
2. A certain percentage of the items test comprehension, application, and analysis skills, in contrast to merely rote memory or knowledge.

The operations used to generate the items, and actual items chosen, would be random choices.

As an alternative strategy a writer may decide that each step in a programmed instruction should have one test item. In this case the writer could randomly choose which operational definition to apply to each step. The writer would choose the test item randomly from the number of items generated within the step. The same constraints previously mentioned also apply to this method.

CONCLUDING REMARKS

This chapter has presented a very detailed and pragmatic set of guidelines for multiple-choice-item generation and review. We hope that readers will attempt to use our adaptation of the Bormuth method to generate items based on the instructional texts they currently use.

Though lacking in a review of relevant literature (refer to the preceding chapter by Roid) the goal of this chapter was to provide a set of strategies for accomplishing the difficult task of test-item writing. This accounts for its rather handbook-like organization. In summary, traditional guidelines for item review were given, many with examples from this chapter's text and the Bormuth method for item generation was illustrated at the knowledge, comprehension, application, and analysis levels of learning. Bloom's levels of learning and important preliminary information about multiple-choice items were also provided.

Though some of the methods presented are relatively complex and may appear rather burdensome we are confident as to their usefulness. Applying our own methods in order to generate the necessary examples for this chapter was a strong indication to us of the feasibility of our approach.

REFERENCES

Anderson, R. C. How to construct achievement tests to assess comprehension. *Review of Educational Research,* 1972, *42*(2), 145–170.

Anderson, R. C. Learning principles from text. *Journal of Educational Psychology,* 1973, *64*(1), 26–30.

Bloom, B. S. (Ed.). *Taxonomy of educational objectives: Handbook I, cognitive domain.* New York: Longmans, Green, 1956.

Bormuth, J. *On the theory of achievement test items.* Chicago: University of Chicago Press, 1970.

Ebel, R. L. *Essentials of educational measurement* (2nd ed.). Englewood Cliffs, N.J.: Prentice-Hall, 1972.

Gronlund, N. E. *Measurement and evaluation in teaching.* New York: Macmillan, 1971.

Nunnally, J. C. *Educational measurement and evaluation.* New York: McGraw-Hill, 1964.

Piaget, J. P. *Psychology of intelligence.* Patterson, N.Y.: Littlefield, Adams & Co., 1960.

5

Computerized Adaptive Achievement Testing[1]

DAVID J. WEISS

INTRODUCTION

For the instructional process to be effective, its effects on each student must be evaluated. That is, the instructor must determine whether or not the students are learning from their exposure to instruction. In traditional instructional environments, tests or examinations are scheduled at regular intervals to assess the acquisition of knowledge or skills by students. This approach has also been utilized in individualized instruction, except that testing occurs when the student has completed one or more units of instruction.

Although considerable research has been done during the 1960s on the improvement of instruction by the application of computer technology, comparatively little effort has been expended in the improvement of the measurement of achievement. Regardless of the sophistication of instructional design, with regard to both conceptualization and use of computer hardware, the testing procedures used are almost invariably those designed and implemented in the 1920s. Almost without exception, paper-

[1] The research reported in this chapter was supported by funds from the Defense Advanced Research Projects Agency, Army Research Institute, Air Force Human Resources Laboratory, Navy Personnel Research and Development Center, and Office of Naval Research, and monitored by the Office of Naval Research under contract N00014-76-C-0627, NR150-389. Views and conclusions contained in this chapter are those of the author and should not be interpreted as necessarily representing the official policies, either expressed or implied, of the funding agencies or of the United States government. More detailed information on the studies reported is available in Bejar, Weiss, and Gialluca (1977) and Brown and Weiss (1977).

129
Copyright © 1979 by Academic Press, Inc.
All rights of reproduction in any form reserved.
ISBN 0-12-526660-X

and-pencil tests based on classical test theory (e.g., Gulliksen, 1950) are used to measure student achievement. Where the tests are computer-administered because computer terminals are available, such as in a computer-assisted instructional environment, the tests are simply computer-administered versions of the same kinds of tests usually administered by paper and pencil.

As a consequence of this lack of research and development in achievement testing during the last decade, sophisticated instructional systems are being burdened with excessive amounts of testing time. As a consequence, many instructors or designers of instructional systems simply ignore testing, or use as little testing as possible. The result, of course, is a lack of information on the impact of the instruction on the individual student, with a likely decrease in the effectiveness of instruction. Where testing is eliminated altogether because it consumes too much instructional time, individually designed instruction becomes impossible, and inefficient group-oriented instruction models must be used.

Even if sufficient amounts of testing time are available during the instructional process, the use of classical approaches to the construction of tests can result in very poor measurement for some students and, consequently, poor instructional decisions. The results can be movement to another instructional unit when the students have not really learned prerequisite units, although because of poorly constructed tests it appears that they have. Or, similarly, a test may erroneously indicate that a student has not learned the content of an instructional unit; the result is that students waste time while repeating units already learned.

Tests built on classical test theory are bound to make these kinds of errors in the individual evaluation of instructional outcomes because the current classical wisdom of test construction is based on a **group**-oriented approach to measurement rather than an **individual**-oriented approach. That is, tests are usually constructed to measure well for the "typical" member of a group or at a certain level of difficulty or achievement. If a given student is not "typical" of the group for which the test was designed, is not a member of that group, or has a score higher or lower than the level for which the test was designed, the test will measure that student very poorly. The result of such poor measurement will be erroneous instructional decisions.

Since the 1960s, a new approach to test construction has emerged. This approach, based on latent trait theory (Hambleton & Cook, 1977; Lord & Novick, 1968) is designed for **individual** measurement. Consequently, it can be integrated into computer-administered testing systems in which tests are administered to each student on an item-by-item basis. Such testing has been termed *tailored* (Lord, 1970) or *adaptive* (Weiss & Betz,

1973) *testing*, the latter term emphasizing its relationships with adaptive instructional procedures. In adaptive testing, the test items to be administered to a student are selected dynamically based on the student's responses to previous items administered. The test is thus adapted to each student's measured level of ability or achievement during the process of testing, much as adaptive instruction adapts the sequence of instruction to the student's previous performance.

By contrast with adaptive instruction, which was well researched and refined during the 1960s, very little research has been done in adaptive testing, particularly as it applies to the measurement of achievement and performance. Consequently, through the impetus of the Defense Advanced Research Projects Agency and the Office of Naval Research a research program was begun at the University of Minnesota in 1976 to study approaches to improving the measurement of achievement by applying latent trait test theory in combination with computerized adaptive test administration. This chapter provides an overview of that 3-year research program, and describes the results of two studies showing how these approaches can be used to improve the measurement of achievement in an instructional context.

OVERVIEW OF THE RESEARCH PROGRAM

Figure 5.1 provides an overview of the research in progress on the computerized adaptive measurement of achievement and performance at the University of Minnesota. The objective of this research program is to develop and evaluate some psychometric approaches for improving achievement and performance testing by combining aspects of modern test theory and computerized adaptive test administration. The first step was to determine how achievement testing differs from ability testing. In general, both ability testing and achievement testing are concerned with measuring an individual's performance on a certain type of task, such as defining words, doing arithmetic problems, comparing geometric figures, or finding the x's in a line of letters. Generally, when a test is used to measure how well a person can do one of these tasks during or at the end of a specific period of instruction or training, the test is an *achievement* test. The same test items can be used to measure a person's *ability* when the capability to perform the task has developed over a long period of interaction with a variety of environments. Thus, ability is the capability of performing a task that results from an unspecified learning history over a long period of time; achievement may be the capability to perform the same task as the result of specific instruction or training.

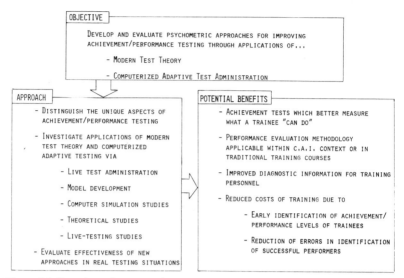

Figure 5.1 Overview of computerized adaptive achievement and performance measurement research program.

The vast majority of the work that has been done in computerized adaptive testing during the last 7 or 8 years (e.g., Urry, 1977; Weiss, 1976) has been in the context of ability measurement. But there are unique problems in achievement testing, such as the complex content structure of many achievement domains, that demand special attention.

Several integrated approaches are being used in combination. These include the development of psychometric models, computer simulation studies, and theoretical studies. These then lead to live-testing and/or real-data studies simulations, which in turn may generate the need for additional model development, followed by new theoretical studies and/or simulation studies. Live-testing studies, of course, involve the computerized administration of adaptive tests directly to students. In real-data simulation studies (Weiss & Betz, 1973, pp. 4–12), responses of students to conventional paper-and-pencil tests already administered are used for after-the-fact administration of hypothetical adaptive tests. That is, the students' responses are used to answer the question, What if we had selected these items in a different order for each student? Computer simulation studies, on the other hand, use a mathematical model to administer hypothetical test items to hypothetical students.

Benefits of the Research

Figure 5.1 also summarizes some of the potential benefits of this research. The adaptive measurement of achievement should result in achievement tests that better measure what a student can do during, or at the end of, some period of instruction. Thus, the methodologies to be developed in this research will be oriented toward performance-evaluation methodologies that are applicable both within a computer-assisted instruction context and within traditional training approaches. Improved testing procedures should also provide improved diagnostic information for training personnel.

In addition, improved measurement of performance should help to reduce the cost of training. This should be particularly true in a military environment where training is very expensive. Reduced costs should accrue by the early identification of students who cannot benefit by instruction, or by the early identification of students who have mastered a content area early in training.

Approaches to Measurement of Achievement

Figure 5.2 summarizes four major approaches to the measurement of achievement and performance that are under investigation in this research program; each of these has been identified in the psychometric literature and studied to varying degrees. Population- or norm-referenced testing has been the primary focus of achievement testing since it began early in this century. In this type of achievement testing a student's performance level is compared to that of other individuals in order to evaluate the student's relative level of achievement or performance. Content- or criterion-referenced testing is an attempt to obtain a more absolute statement about a student's level of performance. It approaches this problem by referencing an individual's performance level to (a) an item pool, which must adequately represent the content of the instructional domain, and (b) an arbitrarily chosen level of "mastery." Criterion-referenced testing rejects most of the rationale of population-referenced testing. As a consequence, it has little psychometric rationale of its own. One goal of our research program is to improve the quantitative underpinnings of this approach to achievement testing.

In time-referenced testing an individual's performance level is expressed as a function of time in training. Thus, each student's performance is considered relative to the time base of the training procedure. A special case of time-referenced testing can be called stage-referenced testing. In this type of achievement testing, a structure or theory is imposed upon the time continuum that indicates where a student should be in the instructional process at a given point in time. Both time-referenced and stage-referenced testing have been little studied in the measurement of achievement, primarily because existing test theory resulted in a

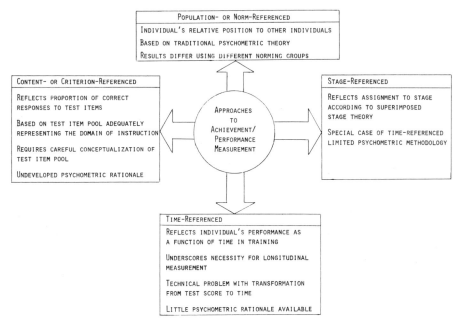

Figure 5.2 Approaches to achievement/performance measurement.

number of intractable psychometric problems, such as the problems involved in the measurement of change (e.g., Cronbach & Furby, 1970).

In summary, our research program is concerned with effecting a marriage of computerized adaptive administration of tests and modern test theory in an attempt to develop more adequate approaches for measuring achievement than the predominant population- or norm-referenced approaches based on traditional test theory. In the process, the research effort is concerned first with the improvement of achievement testing by applying modern test theory and adaptive test administration within a population-referenced viewpoint. Then, the special problems raised by criterion-referenced, time-referenced, and stage-referenced testing will be considered. Finally, the expected result will be a point of view and a set of computer-based adaptive testing methodologies that will integrate these various approaches into a comprehensive system for the measurement of achievement and performance.

A Reconceptualization of the Criterion-Referenced Testing Problem

Typical content- or criterion-referenced measurement has been concerned with measuring a student's achievement status with regard to one content area. That is, the student has mastered a particular content area within a course of instruction. In doing so, criterion-referenced measurement also measures the student with regard to one population at one particular point in time. On the left of Figure 5.3 is shown a content–population–time cube that summarizes the three kinds of referents for achievement measurement. That is, any student's progress can be evaluated with respect to (a) different content areas, within one course of instruction; (b) different populations, such as age levels or grade levels; or (c) time, such as the beginning or the end of training. In the lower left-hand corner of Figure 5.3 is shown the single cube, out of the more comprehensive content–population–time cube, which is considered in typical applications of criterion-referenced measurement—an individual is measured with regard to one content area and population (i.e., one "mastery" score) at one point in time. For example, a student's knowledge of "general biology" might be tested to an 85% criterion level at the end of 3 weeks of instruction.

A more realistic conceptualization of the problem is shown on the right-hand side of Figure 5.3. This improved multivariate conceptualization considers achievement as occurring differentially within content areas for a given student. Thus, the criterion-referenced or content-

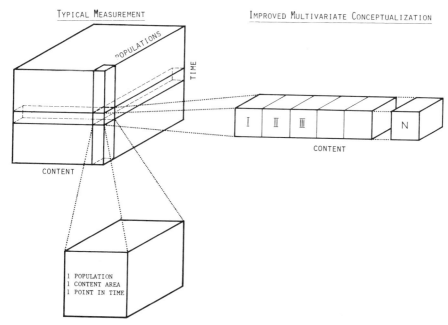

Figure 5.3 Content- or criterion-referenced measurement.

referenced problem should be to determine whether or not an individual has mastered not only one content area at one point in time, but a number of content areas, still holding time constant. For example, the student's biology knowledge at the end of 3 weeks of instruction might be separately measured in three content areas, each at a different mastery level (e.g., reproduction at 90% mastery, cells at 80% mastery, and ecology at 85% mastery).

Figure 5.4 illustrates the effect of measuring achievement as a heterogeneous content domain as opposed to breaking down the content domain into its components and separately measuring an individual's achievement status within each content area. The ranking of individuals shown on the left of Figure 5.4 shows that Individuals A, E, and F have all achieved mastery in the heterogeneous content domain at the same level of performance at a given point in time. Student B has passed the mastery level but has performed at a lower level, whereas Students C, G, and H not only have not reached the mastery level but have all performed at the same low level.

The right-hand side of Figure 5.4 shows the effects of considering the heterogeneous content domain as four homogeneous content domains (population is held constant by use of a constant mastery cutoff). For example, Student C, who did not exhibit mastery in the heterogeneous content test, has not mastered Content Areas I or II, but has mastered Areas III and IV. Similarly, Student B, who did pass the mastery criterion on the heterogeneous test, has mastered Content Areas I, II, and III, but not IV. Student B's performance exhibits the same patterns of mastery as Student A, but at different levels of performance. That is, both Students A and B mastered the same areas, but Student A did better than B on Content Area I, whereas B performed better than A in Area III.

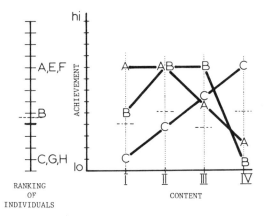

Figure 5.4 A multivariate conceptualization of criterion-referenced measurement. (- - - indicates mastery level.)

Thus, it is important in the criterion-referenced measurement of achievement to consider mastery as occurring separately for each identifiable subdomain within the course. At the same time, an individual's achievement levels should be monitored with respect to both time and populations (i.e., different mastery criteria). The problem of achievement measurement, therefore, becomes one of simultaneously and continuously measuring an individual's achievement levels on the multivariate multicontent, multitime, multipopulation cube. To do this within the framework of traditional achievement testing would require the student to spend so much time in testing that instructional time would be severely reduced in order to meet the testing demands.

Thus, one goal of our research program is to use adaptive testing techniques to reduce testing time by reducing the number of items administered to each student while measuring the student's achievement level accurately. This can be approached by reducing test length without sacrificing any of the measurement characteristics of the test scores. Conversely, the problem can be defined as one of holding test length constant while increasing the "goodness" of the test scores.

UNIDIMENSIONAL ADAPTIVE TESTING:
THE STRADAPTIVE TEST

Adaptive testing involves selecting for administration to a given individual the set of test items, from all the items available, that is likely to measure that individual best. This is in contrast to a conventional test in which everyone is administered the same items, as has been done in paper-and-pencil tests almost since psychological testing began. In an adaptive test different people are administered different test items.

Figure 5.5 shows an item pool structure for one kind of adaptive test, the *stratified adaptive*, or *stradaptive test* (Vale & Weiss, 1975a, 1975b; Weiss, 1973, 1974). In its current stage of development, the stradaptive test assumes that all the items in its pool measure a single dimension. All the very easy items are combined into a subgroup called a *stratum* (e.g., Stratum 1). As Figure 5.5 shows, these very easy items vary somewhat in difficulty, but only within a very restricted range. Stratum 2 contains a group of items with difficulty levels slightly greater than those in Stratum 1, but still within a restricted difficulty range. Continuing up the difficulty scale, Stratum 5 contains items of average difficulty, whereas Stratum 9 contains a subset of very difficult items. Thus the stradaptive test operates from a pool of test items that are stratified by difficulty levels; easy items are those which can be answered correctly by both high- and low-

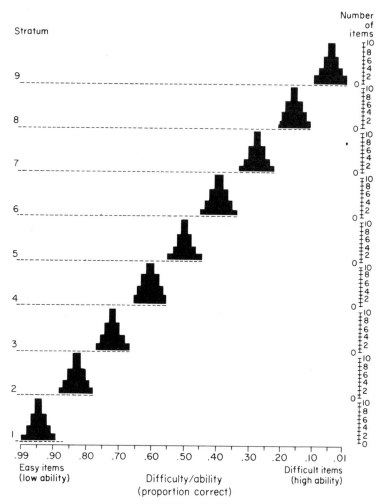

Figure 5.5 Distribution of items, by difficulty level, in a stradaptive test.

ability people, whereas difficult items are answered correctly only by high-ability people. Given a pool of achievement test items structured in this way, the next problem is to determine rules for adaptively administering the items in the test in order to minimize the number of items to be administered to each student, thereby reducing testing time. Since computers are becoming increasingly used in the instructional process, it is logical to have the computer control the adaptive administration of the test items.

Report on stradaptive test

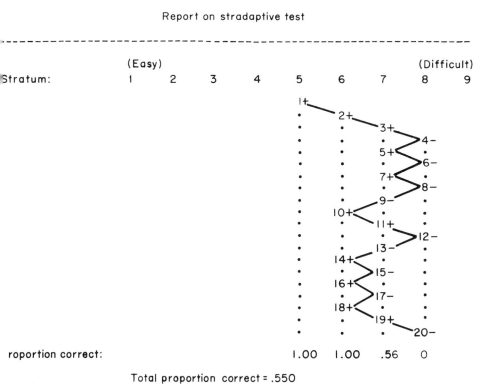

Figure 5.6 Report on a stradaptive test for a student.

Figure 5.6 shows an example of the response record of a person who took a stradaptive test, and serves to illustrate a number of characteristics of this testing procedure. The stradaptive test is designed to make use of prior information on a student to determine at what level of difficulty testing is to begin. For example, for the person whose response record is illustrated in Figure 5.6, it was assumed from observation that he or she was an average student in the domain being measured; thus, testing was begun with an item of average difficulty in Stratum 5. In the stradaptive test, as soon as a test item is administered, it is scored by the computer. If the item is answered correctly, a more difficult item is administered from the next higher stratum; if it is answered incorrectly, an easier item is administered from the next lower stratum. In either case the next item administered is the next unadministered item in the stratum. Thus, in Figure 5.6 movement to the left indicates an incorrect answer to the previous question, and movement to the right follows a correct answer. In the response record shown in Figure 5.6 the first 3 items were answered correctly, the next one (Item 4) incorrectly, the fifth correctly, and so on. For this person, testing continued until 20 items were administered.

The number of items administered to each person in a stradaptive test depends on the person's response pattern. At the bottom of Figure 5.6 is shown the proportion of correct answers given by this person at each level of difficulty. For example, for Stratum 5 it was 1.00, whereas for Stratum 8 it was .00. In general, this proportion will decrease as a function of difficulty level; that is, students will tend to answer easy items correctly and difficult items incorrectly. Since these proportions can be recalculated after each test item is administered, they can be used to terminate the administration of a stradaptive test. Specifically, testing can be terminated when the level of difficulty is identified at which the individual answers items correctly at the chance level or less. Assuming five-alternative multiple-choice items, testing would terminate when the student answered correctly fewer than 20% of the items in a given stratum; a minimum of five items per stratum is required as the data base for making this decision. This is an individualized termination rule, which resulted in the administration of 41 items to the person shown in Figure 5.6. In this example, since the proportion of correct responses for Stratum 8 (.00) was less than chance responding (.20), the test was terminated.

Figure 5.7 shows the response record of another person completing a stradaptive test. In this case the student was assumed to be of higher ability; thus testing was begun at Stratum 8. Using the up-one-stratum branching rule for correct answers and the down-one-stratum rule for incorrect answers, in conjunction with the same termination rule, assessment of this student's achievement level required 41 items. Thus the stradaptive test is individualized in three ways:

1. The test begins at the student's estimated achievement level, rapidly adjusting if that estimate is erroneous.
2. Different items are administered to each student, depending on the student's responses to each item.
3. The test terminates when the testee answers at or below a chance level.

Because each student is administered different test items, the traditional number-correct score cannot be used in adaptive testing. In the stradaptive test, almost everyone will answer about half the items correctly. The person whose response record is shown in Figure 5.7 answered about 49% of the items correctly. The response record in Figure 5.6 shows that 55% of the items were answered correctly. Shown in Figure 5.7 are some of the scores that can be derived from a stradaptive

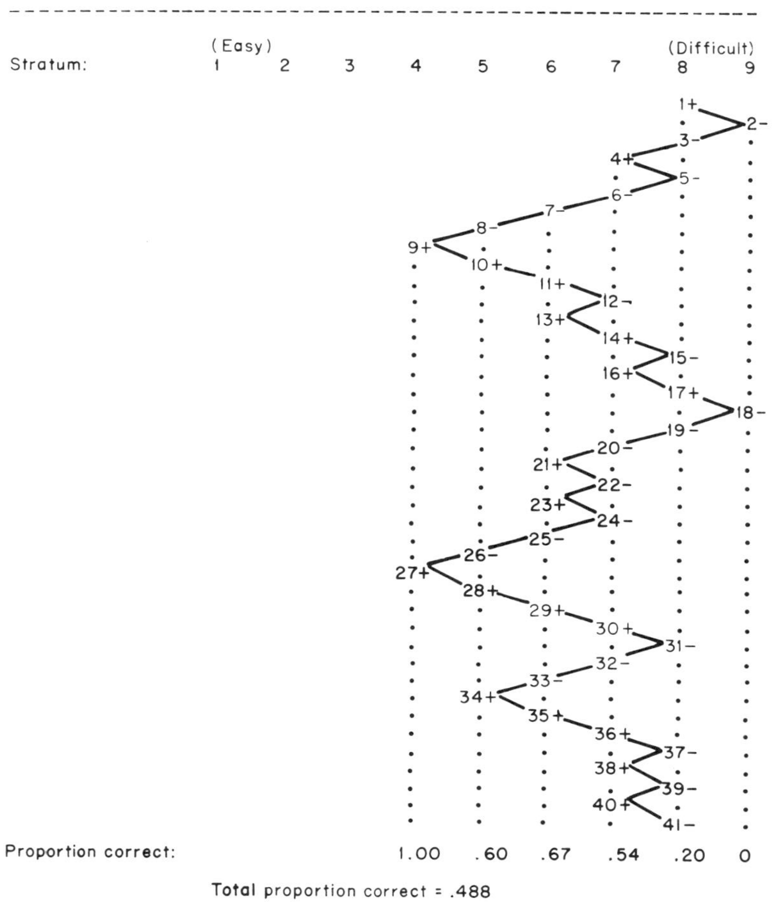

Scores on stradaptive test

Ability level scores

1. Difficulty of most difficult item correct = 1.89
2. Difficulty of the N+1th item = 1.01
3. Difficulty of highest nonchance item correct = 1.53
4. Difficulty of highest stratum with a correct answer = 2.01
5. Difficulty of the N+1th stratum = 1.33
6. Difficulty of highest nonchance stratum = 1.33
7. Interpolated stratum difficulty = 1.36
8. Mean difficulty of all correct items = .72
9. Mean difficulty of correct items between ceiling and basal strata = .76
10. Mean difficulty of items correct at highest nonchance stratum = 1.24

Consistency scores

11. SD of item difficulties encountered = .86
12. SD of difficulties of items answered correctly = .74
13. SD of difficulties of items answered correctly between ceiling and basal strata = .50
14. Difference in difficulties between ceiling and basal strata = 2.64
15. Number of strata between ceiling and basal strata = 3

Figure 5.7 Report on a stradaptive test for another student.

141

test. The "level" scores are achievement estimates, whereas the consistency scores are experimental scores used to determine a person's "reliability." There are 10 level scores shown, varying from the "difficulty of the most difficult item correct" to the "mean difficulty of items correct at the highest non-chance stratum." In all these scores, difficulty and achievement level are expressed on a standard-score scale with mean of 0 and standard deviation of 1; this scale is derived from latent-trait test theory (Lord & Novick, 1968). High achievement levels are indicated by high positive scores, low achievement levels by high negative scores. The choice among scoring methods still awaits further data, although some data suggest that the mean difficulty scores (specifically Score 8) may be most useful (Vale & Weiss, 1975b).

Comparison with Conventional Achievement Tests

The following study uses the stradaptive test in live testing to determine how it would perform in the measurement of achievement. Research by Hansen (1969) utilized a different adaptive testing approach to measure achievement levels, but the present study evaluated the adaptive testing strategy on different criteria than Hansen used. The stradaptive test was compared with conventionally administered paper-and-pencil classroom achievement tests. For this purpose approximately 350 volunteer students were recruited from a general biology course at the University of Minnesota. This course has a traditional lecture and laboratory structure, although the lectures were delivered on videotape.

Method

An adaptive testing item pool was constructed using multiple-choice test items from three content areas: chemistry, the cell, and energy. For purposes of this study, items from the three content areas were combined to measure the single common factor underlying the three content areas (Bejar, Weiss, & Kingsbury, 1977). Table 5.1 shows the number of items available for the stradaptive test structure. Using data on the items from previous academic quarters, latent-trait item parameters of difficulty,

TABLE 5.1
Number of Items Available and Number of Usable Items by Content Area

	Chemistry	Cell	Energy	Total
Items available	53	60	33	146
Items rejected	16	13	3	32
Usable items	37	47	30	114

discrimination, and guessing (Lord & Novick, 1968) were calculated for each item. The original group of 146 test items was reduced to 114 after eliminating some items, primarily those with low discriminations (Bejar, Weiss, & Kingsbury, 1977). These items were structured for a stradaptive test, similar to the structure illustrated in Figure 5.5. The items were assigned to one of nine strata in such a way that there were approximately the same number of items in each stratum. Within strata the items were placed so that, although the content areas were alternated, the items in the strata were ordered by discriminations, with the most discriminating items placed first in the strata.

The first item to be administered to a student in the stradaptive test was determined by the student's reported grade point average. For example, if the student reported an average of 3.75 or higher, testing was begun at the ninth stratum. At the other extreme, if the student's grade point average was less than 2.00, the first item administered was from the first stratum (i.e., the easiest stratum).

The standard stradaptive item selection rule was used in the computerized administration of the stradaptive biology test. That is, after responding to the first item in the entry stratum, the student was given the first item from the next lower stratum if the answer was incorrect or the first item from the next higher stratum if the answer was correct. Thereafter, the student was branched to the next unadministered item in the next higher or lower stratum, depending on whether the answer was correct or incorrect. The exception to this rule occurred if the testee was at the most difficult stratum. In that case, after a correct answer the next item in that same stratum was given. Similarly, for the student in the least difficult stratum, an incorrect response led to the next item in that same stratum.

The stradaptive test was compared with the conventionally administered paper-and-pencil classroom exam (the "conventional classroom test"). The comparison was based on scores derived from the 39 out of the 55 items in the classroom test for which latent-trait item parameter estimates were available. In addition, an "improved conventional test" was constructed from the stradaptive test item pool. Since the classroom test was constructed by the biology course staff using a combination of pedagogical, content, and psychometric considerations, it was not designed to function optimally in comparison with the adaptive test. Consequently, the improved conventional test was designed to be similar to the stradaptive test in terms of both item discrimination and length, thereby providing a more equitable comparison between the testing methods.

All tests were scored by a common method, the method of maximum likelihood (Birnbaum, 1968, p. 459). Use of this scoring procedure also permitted the computation of test information characteristics (Bejar, Weiss, & Gialluca, 1977; Birnbaum, 1968) in order to compare the different tests directly. Test information is related to the precision of measurement as a function of achievement level. The higher the information value, the more precise the measurement at that level; conversely, the lower the information value, the less precise the measurement. Information can also be interpreted as the inverse of the standard error of measurement at a given achievement level. High levels of information imply low standard errors of measurement, whereas low information levels imply high standard errors of measurement (and, therefore, imprecise measurement). Thus, information curves were computed for the conventional classroom test, the improved conventional test, and the adaptive test. Both the conventional classroom test and the adaptive test data were derived from live test administration; information data for the improved conventional test was derived from a theoretical analysis based on the latent-trait item parameters.

Results

Figure 5.8 shows information curves for the conventional classroom test and the adaptive test. Although 39 items were scored in the conventional test, some items were omitted by students, so the average test length was 35 items. The adaptive test had a maximum test length of 50 items, but because of its variable-termination rule, an average of only 27 items was administered. In addition, the adaptive test was rescored at a

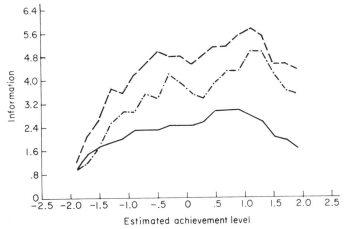

Figure 5.8 Information curves for classroom conventional test (———) and adaptive test for a maximum test length of 50 (– – –) and 20 (–·–). Mean number of items were 35, 27, and 17, respectively.

maximum length of 20 items, yielding an average length of 17 items. In Figure 5.8, information levels are plotted as a function of students' achievement levels on a standard score scale with mean of 0 and standard deviation of 1.0.

As Figure 5.8 shows, the adaptive test with an average of 27 items provided higher levels of information (more precise measurement) at all achievement levels than did the conventional test. Measurements provided by the full-length adaptive test were of considerably higher precision (information) at all achievement levels than those of the conventional test, even though the adaptive test was, on the average, 8 items shorter than the conventional test. However, even when the adaptive test was half the length of the conventional test (17 items average versus 35 items average), it still provided measurements of considerably higher precision than the conventional test, with the exception of a range of achievement below 1.5 standard deviations below the mean, where the two testing strategies measured with little difference in precision. Thus, these data show that adaptive tests can administer as few as 50% of the number of items in conventional tests and still provide measurements of higher quality.

Figure 5.9 provides information curves comparing the *improved 25-item conventional test* with the adaptive test at mean lengths of 25 items and 17 items. The relevant comparison is for achievement levels greater than about −.5, since in the construction of the improved conventional test, item difficulties were concentrated to measure well for the upper half of

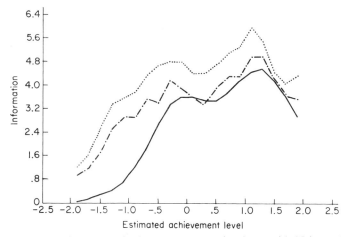

Figure 5.9 Information curves for improved conventional test with 25 items (——) and adaptive test with a maximum test length of 20 (–·–) and 30 (· · ·). Mean number of items on each adaptive test were 17 and 25, respectively.

the achievement distribution (i.e., between achievement levels of 0 and 2.0). In that range it is clear from Figure 5.8 that the adaptive test with an average of 25 items provided more precise measurement than the improved 25-item conventional test. When the length of the adaptive test was reduced to an average of 17 items, there was little difference in information levels between the adaptive and conventional tests, although there was a tendency for the adaptive test to measure somewhat more precisely.

Thus, with number of items equal, adaptive testing provided measurements of better quality than even a well-constructed conventional test drawn from the same pool. With one-third fewer items, on the average, the precision of the adaptive test still equaled or exceeded that of the improved conventional test.

Implications

The implications of these results for instructional testing should be obvious. With number of items in a test held constant, adaptive testing—in which test items are dynamically selected for each student during the process of testing—provides measurements of much higher quality than does conventional testing. Even with substantially fewer items—as much as 50% fewer—adaptive tests measure with less error than conventional tests. Consequently, it is possible to reduce testing time and to improve the quality of measurement simultaneously by using adaptive tests rather than conventional tests. The result should be more time available for instruction combined with better instructional decision making due to the increased precision of test scores.

ADAPTIVE ADMINISTRATION OF AN ACHIEVEMENT TEST BATTERY

All the previous research in adaptive testing, including the study just described, has been concerned with tests that covered only a single content area. Thus, all of the branching procedures implemented for the adaptive selection of items to be administered to a testee have been designed exclusively for intra-test branching within a single, presumably unidimensional, content area.

Frequently, however, achievement tests span several content areas, measuring specific subdomains of achievement. Consequently, in many cases the assumption of a single dimension may not be appropriate. For these kinds of achievement tests, or for achievement test batteries covering a number of separable content areas for which separate scores are required, none of the existing adaptive strategies (Weiss, 1974) are directly applicable.

There are two reasons why many of the adaptive testing strategies developed for single-content-area ability tests may not be appropriate for achievement tests that cover several content areas. The first reason is that although the unidimensional branching models can be applied to separate content areas, they are not designed to take into account the information available between content areas. The second, and more practical, reason is that it might not be possible to generate relatively large numbers of items, such as those required for many adaptive testing strategies, within one content area in an achievement test. Consequently, in the application of adaptive testing to the unique problems in the measurement of achievement, an important research issue is the identification of adaptive testing strategies that make efficient use of existing item pools, rather than requiring the redesign of test-item pools to meet the requirements of specific adaptive testing strategies.

Thus, an adaptive testing strategy was designed for use with achievement test batteries comprised of a number of subtests. The adaptive testing strategy operates within a fixed item pool containing a relatively small number of items for each subtest. Real-data simulation techniques were used to evaluate the testing strategy. That is, the adaptive testing strategy was applied to item-response data obtained from the administration of an achievement test battery that had been previously administered conventionally by paper and pencil. Results for the conventional testing strategy were compared with those for the adaptive testing strategy in terms of both test information and test length.

Method

Test Items and Subjects

Achievement test data were provided by the Personnel and Training Evaluation Program of the Naval Guided Missile School at Dam Neck, Virginia. These data were from a systems achievement test (SAT F17603) battery administered to 365 fire control technicians; these technicians are concerned with monitoring potential fire sources on submarines and controlling fires that do occur. The test battery included 12 subtests, each covering knowledge areas for different equipment or subject matter. Table 5.2 shows the content and number of items in each subtest. The test battery was administered in one booklet containing 232 items. The number of items per subtest ranged from 10 to 32; all of the items were multiple-choice with four response choices.

TABLE 5.2
Number of Items in Each Subtest

Subtest	Content	Number of items
A	Fire control system casualty procedures	10
B	Optical alignment group	10
C	Control console and power subsystem	18
D	Platform positioning equipment	22
E	Multiplexed equipment	18
F	Digital control computer and software	18
G	Digital control computer—operator interface	14
H	Magnetic disk file	12
I	Digital control computer—missile interface	24
J	Guidance and guidance testing	29
K	MTRE MKG MOD3	32
L	Spare guidance temperature monitor	25
Total		232

As in the previous study, items were parameterized by a computer program (Urry, 1977, p. 99) for latent-trait item parameterization employing the three-parameter normal ogive model. This program provided estimates of the item discrimination, item difficulty, and guessing parameters of latent-trait test theory (Lord & Novick, 1968). In contrast to the previous study, however, the items in each subtest were parameterized independently of items in other subtests.

Adaptive Testing Strategy

The adaptive testing procedure was developed in order to reduce to a minimum the number of items administered to each individual, with as little impact as possible upon the measurement characteristics of the test battery. Both intra-subtest (within subtest) adaptive branching and inter-subtest (between subtest) adaptive branching were used in the development of the procedure.

Intra-subtest Branching. The basic concept for intra-subtest adaptive branching was that the order in which the items were to be administered was to be dependent upon values of the item information curve (Birnbaum, 1968, p. 462). Item information curves are similar to the test information curves reported above in Figures 5.8 and 5.9. However, while the test information curve indexes precision of measurement for test scores as a function of achievement level, the item information curve reflects precision of measurement for a single item, also as a function of achievement level. Thus, values of item information indicate how well a given item measures for testees at a given level of the variable being measured.

This study used a different adaptive testing strategy than the first study, since there were not enough items in each content area to construct a stradaptive item pool. Items were selected within a subtest for each testee by computing the value of all item information curves at the current estimated achievement level ($\hat{\theta}$) for that testee. The item selected for administration was the item that had the highest information value at the testee's current level of $\hat{\theta}$. Once an item was administered to a testee, it was eliminated from the subtest pool of available items for that testee.

Achievement levels were estimated using Owen's (1975, p. 353) Bayesian scoring procedure. This scoring procedure provides an achievement level estimate ($\hat{\theta}$) after each test item is administered. The procedure begins with a prior estimate of θ and its variance. An item is administered and scored as correct or incorrect. The revised estimate of $\hat{\theta}$ is determined and is used for the selection of the next test item, based on the maximum information rule just described. That item is administered, and a new value of $\hat{\theta}$ is determined, which is then used to select the next item. This procedure is repeated until a termination criterion is reached.

Two criteria were used in determining when administration of items within a subtest should be stopped: (a) when all of the remaining items provided less than a predetermined small amount of information, or (b) when the within-subtest item pool was exhausted. Testing was terminated for a given testee at the first occurrence of one of these criteria within a given subtest. In applying the first criterion, testing was terminated when there was no item available that provided an information value greater than .01 at a given testee's current level of $\hat{\theta}$.

Illustration of Intra-subtest Adaptive Branching. Figure 5.10 shows estimated item information curves for six items from one of the subtests.

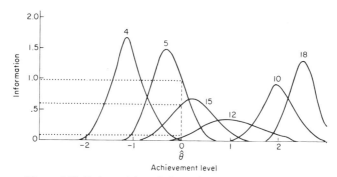

Figure 5.10 Estimated item information curves for six items.

(There were a total of 15 items in the subtest from which only six were chosen to simplify the illustration.) The height of the information curve at a given achievement level indicates the amount of information provided by the item. Most of the items are fairly "peaked"—that is, they provide information over a relatively narrow range of the achievement continuum. Though the information curves overlap to some degree, different items provide different amounts of information at a given point on the achievement continuum. The guiding principle for the adaptive procedure was to administer the item that provides the most information at the current achievement estimate.

For a testee beginning the subtest the initial achievement level estimate was $\hat{\theta} = 0$ (this varied by individual for subsequent subtests); this is shown by the vertical dashed line in Figure 5.10. Of the six items in the example, only three items had essentially nonzero information values at $\hat{\theta} = 0$; these values, shown by the horizontal dotted lines in Figure 5.10, were .95 for Item 5, .60 for Item 15, and .10 for Item 12. Applying the rule that the item selected is the one that provides the most information at the current $\hat{\theta}$, Item 5 would be selected for administration.

Figure 5.11 shows the revised value of $\hat{\theta} = .46$ derived from the Bayesian scoring routine, assuming that a correct answer was given to Item 5. The information curve for Item 5, which was already administered, is not shown in Figure 5.11. At the new value of $\hat{\theta}$, only Items 15 and 12 provide nonzero values of information. Since Item 15 has an information value of .60 and Item 12 has a value of .20, Item 15 is selected as the second item to be administered to this testee.

Assuming that the testee had correctly answered Item 15, the value of $\hat{\theta}$ increased to .88; this is shown by the dashed vertical line in Figure 5.12. At that value of $\hat{\theta}$ Item 12 provides .35 information and Item 10 provides

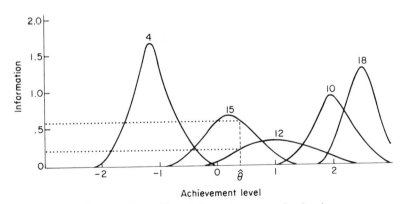

Figure 5.11 Estimated item information curves for five items.

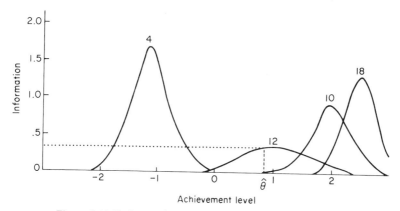

Figure 5.12 Estimated item information curves for four items.

.02 information. Item 12 is thus administered next. Assuming that Item 12 was answered incorrectly, the $\hat{\theta}$ decreased to .62, which is plotted in Figure 5.13. The figure shows that of the three items remaining, none provides any information at the current level of $\hat{\theta}$. Thus, there is no need for administering additional items from that subtest, and testing in that subtest is terminated. The achievement level estimate of $\hat{\theta} = .55$ is taken as the testee's score on the subtest, since it is based on all items providing more than nontrivial amounts of information about that testee's achievement level.

Inter-subtest Branching. In addition to reducing the number of items administered in each subtest by selecting items based on the maximum information procedure just described, the adaptive testing strategy was designed to begin each testee at his or her estimated achievement levels

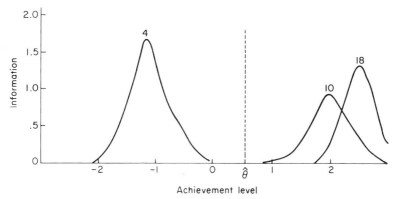

Figure 5.13 Estimated item information curves for three items.

on each subtest after the first. That is, the starting items for administration of tests 2 through 12 were based on each testee's estimated achievement levels from tests administered earlier in the battery.

The order of administration for the various subtests was chosen to take maximum advantage of the intercorrelations among them, thereby utilizing the redundant information in previously administered subtests. This was accomplished through linear multiple regression. First, the number-correct subtest scores for the 12 subtests were intercorrelated, and the highest bivariate correlation was chosen from the intercorrelation matrix. One of these two subtests was arbitrarily designated to be administered first; the other was designated to be administered second.

Multiple correlations were then computed using the subtests previously designated first and second as predictor variables. Each of the 10 remaining subtests, in turn, was designated as the criterion variable. Of these 10 subtests, the one that had the highest multiple correlation with the first and second subtests was designated as the third subtest. This procedure was repeated to select each subsequent subtest for the adaptive administration, computing multiple correlations with the previously ordered subtests as predictor variables and each of the remaining subtests, in turn, as the criterion variable. That subtest having the highest multiple correlation with the previous subtests was selected as the next subtest to be administered. By adding one subtest to the predictor set at each subsequent stage, this procedure was continued until all 12 subtests were ordered.

As a result of this procedure, the order in which the subtests were administered was the same for all testees. However, the selection of items within each subtest and the order in which those items were administered varied with testees as a function of the amount of item information provided at the testee's current achievement estimate.

The entry point into the item pool for the second and succeeding subtests was determined from both the examinee's $\hat{\theta}$s at the end of the previously administered subtests and the linear multiple regression of scores from the previously administered subtests on the next subtest. This regression equation was based not only on scores for the items administered adaptively, but also on the correlations derived from number-correct scores for all items in each of the subtests. The $\hat{\theta}$ from the regression equation was used as the initial prior achievement level estimate for intra-subtest branching in a subsequent subtest and the squared standard error of estimate from the regression equation was used as the initial prior variance of the Bayesian achievement level estimate for each subtest. Item selection and scoring within a subtest were then based on the intra-subtest item selection procedure described earlier.

Data Analysis

In order to facilitate comparison of results with the adaptive strategy, Bayesian scoring was used for the 12 conventional tests originally comprising the achievement test battery. Pearson product-moment correlations were computed between subtest achievement level estimates ($\hat{\theta}$) from the conventional and adaptive testing procedures in order to examine the extent of the relationship between the scores. These were computed separately for each of the 12 subtests. High correlations between the scores would suggest that the tests ranked the examinees in a similar order along the achievement continuum.

Information curves were also used to compare the adaptive and conventional testing strategies as a function of achievement levels. Estimated test information curves were generated separately for each subtest for both conventional and adaptive testing strategies. In the conventional testing strategy, an examinee's subtest information value was computed by summing the item information values at the examinee's final estimated achievement level ($\hat{\theta}$) for that subtest. An estimated information curve was then plotted for the total group of examinees from their individual achievement level estimates and corresponding information values.

Subtest information curves were generated similarly for the adaptive testing strategy. The estimated value of test information was computed at each testee's final achievement estimate for the subtest by summing the information values at that $\hat{\theta}$ for the particular subset of items administered to that testee. Thus, for both adaptive and conventional testing, each test information value was computed at the final value of $\hat{\theta}$ for the subtest, based on the information provided by the items actually administered.

Results

Test Length

The number of items administered under both the adaptive and conventional testing strategies is summarized in Table 5.3. These data show substantial reductions in test length as a result of the adaptive testing strategy. For Subtest 1, 15 items were administered by the conventional procedure and from 4 to 13 items were administered by the adaptive procedure. Fifty percent of the group answered between 7 and 10 items in the adaptive test. The mean number of items administered by the adaptive strategy in Subtest 1 was 8.73, which represents a 41.8% reduction from the number of items required by the conventional test.

Similar results were observed for the other subtests. Reduction of

TABLE 5.3
Number of Items Administered in 12 Adaptive and Conventional Subtests

Ordered subtest	Number of conventional test items	Adaptive test		Range		Percentage reduction[a]
		Mean	SD	Minimum	Maximum	
1	15	8.73	1.86	4	13	41.8
2	24	14.12	2.90	4	20	41.2
3	17	9.87	3.38	2	17	41.9
4	22	12.57	4.60	2	22	42.9
5	19	11.55	3.58	1	18	39.2
6	13	4.70	2.10	1	12	63.8
7	18	7.44	3.21	1	15	58.7
8	10	7.07	1.71	1	10	29.3
9	10	6.44	1.72	1	9	35.6
10	23	8.42	5.54	1	22	63.4
11	12	5.52	2.97	1	12	54.0
12	18	5.41	3.20	1	15	69.9
Mean	16.75	8.49	3.06	1.67	15.42	49.3
Test battery	201	101.84	24.08	27	153	49.3

[a] Computed by the formula 100 − [(Mean number of items in adaptive test − mean number of items in conventional test) × 100].

154

number of items required by the adaptive test varied from a low of 29.3% for Subtest 8 to a high of 69.9% for Subtest 12, in which a mean of 5.41 items was administered by the adaptive strategy. In Subtest 12, between 3 and 7 items were administered to 50% of the testees in the adaptive strategy as compared to 18 items for each testee in the conventional test. Subtest 12 had the highest percentage of reduction. In all probability, this was attributable to the increased accuracy of the test entry point from the multiple regression of the scores on the 11 prior subtests.

It is interesting to note that for Subtests 5 through 12, the minimum number of items administered by the adaptive procedure was one. For several of these subtests, a relatively substantial number of testees was administered only one item—that is, almost 10% of the total group for Subtests 6, 11, and 12. The minimum number of items administered by the adaptive strategy was less for tests later in the adaptive testing sequence. This also probably resulted from the increased use of prior test information for determining the initial item to be administered.

Although minimum numbers of items were administered at relatively high frequencies by the adaptive strategy, the maximum numbers of items were administered to very few testees. For Subtests 3, 4, 8, and 11 the maximum number of items administered by the adaptive strategy was the same as that administered by the conventional test; the numbers of testees associated with these maximums were two, one, five, and one, respectively. For the remaining eight subtests, none of the testees received the same number of items in the adaptive tests that they did in the conventional test.

The conventional test battery consisted of 201 items administered to all testees. The average number of items administered by the adaptive strategy (see Table 5.3) was 101.84, representing a 49.3% reduction in number of items administered. Fifty percent of the testees received between 86 and 119 items in the adaptive battery, representing reductions of 57.2% to 40.8% for half of the testees. None of the testees required all of the items in the adaptive administration. The longest adaptive battery administered required 153 items for one testee, representing a 23.9% reduction in test length; the shortest adaptive battery for one testee required only 27 items, representing a total test length reduction of 86.6%.

Correlation of Achievement Estimates

Table 5.4 shows the Pearson product-moment correlations of the Bayesian achievement level estimates ($\hat{\theta}$) for the conventional and adaptive testing strategies. Eleven of the 12 correlations were greater than .90. The highest correlations were .98 for Subtests 2 and 8; the lowest was .74 for Subtest 6.

TABLE 5.4

Correlation (r) of Bayesian Achievement Level Estimates ($\hat{\theta}$) for the Adaptive and Conventional Testing Strategies by Subtest, and Cronbach's Alpha Coefficient for the Conventional Subtests

Subtest	Number of items	r	Cronbach's alpha
1	15	.91	.57
2	24	.98	.69
3	17	.96	.54
4	22	.97	.65
5	19	.93	.59
6	13	.74	.44
7	18	.90	.50
8	10	.98	.56
9	10	.95	.39
10	23	.92	.61
11	12	.91	.51
12	18	.94	.40

The items contributing to the Bayesian subtest achievement level estimates in the adaptive test were a subset of those used in the conventional test. Thus, to some extent, the magnitudes of the correlations in Table 5.4 were a function of this part–whole relationship. This is supported by a comparison with the alpha internal consistency estimates for the conventional subtests also shown in Table 5.4. If there were no part–whole relationship, the correlations between the achievement level estimates would be restricted by the internal consistencies. However, all the correlations were substantially higher than the alpha values.

If the magnitude of the correlations of the two achievement estimates were primarily determined by the part–whole relationship attributable to common items, the longer subtests should have higher correlations and the shorter subtests should have lower correlations. This was not generally the case: One of the two highest correlations ($r = .98$) was observed for Subtest 8, which had only 10 items in the conventional test, whereas Subtest 9, which also had 10 items, had an $r = .95$. Although Subtest 9 had the smallest percentage reduction attributable to the adaptive administration, 20.3% (see Table 5.3), Subtest 9 had a 45.6% reduction; and Subtest 2 ($r = .98$), which had 24 items, had a 41.7% reduction. Subtest 6 (13 items), which had the lowest r (.74), had a 63.8% reduction attributable to adaptive testing; but the highest percentage reduction (69.9%) was observed for Subtest 12 (18 items), for which an $r = .94$ was observed between the adaptive and conventional achievement estimates. Thus, these data suggest that the magnitudes of the correlations shown in Table

5.4 were not a direct function of either the number of items in the conventional tests or the internal consistency of those tests; rather they reflect the similarity of the achievement estimates derived by the conventional and adaptive testing procedures.

Information

The information obtained from the adaptive administration of each subtest was, for all practical purposes, identical to the information from the conventional administration (see Brown & Weiss, 1977). This result was obtained in each of the 12 subtests of the achievement test battery, even though the adaptive test administered considerably fewer items than the conventional test. Thus the data showed that both testing strategies measured with essentially equal precision, even though the adaptive strategy required an average of 50% fewer items than the conventionally administered test.

Implications

This study has demonstrated that an adaptive testing strategy designed specifically for achievement test batteries can substantially reduce the number of items administered in all subtests of the battery without reducing the precision of subtest scores. The data indicate that on this achievement test battery the length of the battery could be reduced by 50% for the typical testee. In no case was it necessary to administer in the adaptive battery all of the items included in the conventional tests. Therefore, adaptive testing can reduce the time spent in testing; the time saved can then be used by the testees for other activities, such as additional instruction. The strategy appears to be generalizable; it should be applicable to a variety of test batteries in which there is a fixed and relatively small subset of items for each subtest. Further research is needed to evaluate the performance of this adaptive testing strategy in other test batteries and in live-testing situations. In addition, research is needed to modify the adaptive testing strategy to identify optimal procedures for the complete individualized administration of an achievement test battery.

SUMMARY AND CONCLUSIONS

The research program on computerized adaptive administration of achievement tests underway at the University of Minnesota is designed to develop and investigate methods for the improvement of the practice of achievement testing. This is being approached by integrating developments in modern test theory with the availability of interactive computing capabilities frequently in use in computer-assisted instructional settings. In addition, the research program is reconceptualizing the problems of both norm-referenced and criterion-referenced achievement testing, as well as developing psychometric models necessary for measuring achievement in a time-referenced framework.

The two studies described above illustrate how adaptive testing techniques can be used to improve the quality of achievement test scores and/or to reduce the length of achievement tests. The first study was a live-testing study in which an adaptive achievement test was administered by computer to students in a biology course. In this study, an adaptive testing strategy designed for use in ability testing was applied to a pool of achievement test items. The achievement test item pool was composed of multiple-choice test items written by the biology course staff, from which the conventional classroom tests were constructed. Whereas the classroom tests used a fixed set of items for all students, in the adaptive test the items were dynamically and individually selected from the entire available pool for each student, based on their answers to previous test questions.

The results of the adaptive test administration were compared with those from the regular classroom test and with an improved conventional test. The improved conventional test was designed to provide a comparison with the adaptive test, equated for both level of item discrimination and test length. The testing strategies were compared in terms of test information curves. These curves reflect the precision of measurement for each of the testing strategies at differing levels of achievement. High precision (information) is equivalent to a low standard error of measurement at a given achievement level, whereas low precision (information) reflects a high standard error of measurement associated with a given achievement level.

Results showed that the adaptive test provided measurements of higher precision throughout the ability range in comparison to both the classroom and the improved conventional tests. Furthermore, rescoring of the adaptive test at a shorter average test length showed that the adaptive tests measured more precisely than the classroom tests, even when the adaptive tests consisted of 50% fewer items. When the adaptive test was compared to the improved conventional test, the adaptive test provided more precise measurement with an average of over 30% fewer items.

This study has demonstrated how adaptive testing can be used to improve achievement testing by using all the available test items in adaptive test administration. Frequently in the construction of classroom achievement tests the instructor has many test items available that were developed and used in previous years. To construct a test for a given class, the instructor usually selects a set of items from this pool and administers all the selected items to all the students. In this process, items not selected for the conventional test are ignored.

But the unused items have potential for measuring some individuals. Modern test theory (e.g., Lord, 1970) indicates that a test measures best when all its items are of about average difficulty **for each student.** If there is any range of individual differences in a class, no conventional test can be of the appropriate difficulty level for all students. Thus, conventional testing in these circumstances guarantees measurement of poor quality for some students. As the data show, adaptive testing in which items are selected from the entire pool of available items to approximately match the achievement levels of each student provides, with fewer test items, measurements of higher precision. Adaptive testing thus permits the instructor to use all the items available to measure each student as well as possible within the constraints of the total pool of items available. At the same time, the number of items each student is required to complete is substantially reduced, and, because each student's test consists of different items, test security is improved.

The second study addressed another problem of importance in achievement testing. This study was concerned with reducing the length of an achievement test battery by adaptive administration. Achievement test batteries are frequently used in the assessment of performance in multicontent achievement domains. The objective of these batteries is to assess an individual's performance levels on each of a number of content areas that are relevant to the domain of instruction. The number and content of each of the subtests are determined by the content of the instructional domain. Though it might be possible to consider these content areas together as measuring a single content domain, for pedagogical reasons it is important to generate separate scores on each of the subtests. The results of such an achievement test battery are frequently reported to the instructional staff as a profile of achievement levels for each student, describing his or her levels of performance on each subarea of the instructional domain.

Because the achievement subdomains measured with achievement test batteries are frequently very specific in nature, there is usually a small and limited number of test items available to measure each content area. Thus, the situation is quite different than in the first study, in which large item pools were available; consequently, the same kinds of testing strategies are not usable. Instead the question becomes one of developing testing strategies that are concerned with administering only the minimum number of test items necessary to measure each individual's achievement levels in each content area. In this situation, because no additional items are available, it is not possible to improve the quality of measurement by adaptive testing. All that can be accomplished is to reduce test length while keeping measurement precision approximately the same as that provided by the full-length conventional test.

In the second study an adaptive testing strategy was developed and evaluated that used both intra-subtest adaptive branching procedures and between-subtest branching to reduce the length of an achievement test battery. Within subtests items were selected on the basis of the amount of information each provided at the testee's current level of achievement. Achievement estimates were computed after each test item was adminis- tered; the next item to be administered was the one providing most information at the given achievement level. After the first subtest, the first item to be administered in subsequent subtests was based on the esti- mated achievement level resulting from the multiple regression of prior subtest scores on later subtests. Performance of the adaptive testing strategy was studied by real-data simulation using a 12-subtest Navy achievement test battery.

Results of this study showed that the adaptive test battery strategy resulted in the administration of an average of 50% fewer items than the conventional test battery with essentially no decreases in test precision (information). For some individuals adaptive administration resulted in reductions of more than 85% of the items in the conventional test battery; that is, 201 items were required to administer the 12 subtests convention- ally, whereas measurements of equal quality were possible through adap- tive testing using only 27 items. None of the testees required in the adaptive administration all the items administered in the conventional test battery. The effect of the inter-subtest branching procedure was illustrated in the general decrease in average number of items required for tests administered later in the adaptive procedure.

Thus, the second study demonstrated that even with a fixed item pool and relatively small numbers of items in each subtest of a multisubtest battery, adaptive testing can result in significantly shorter test batteries than can conventional tests. A further advantage of such adaptive testing is that it administers only those items that provide some information about the testee's achievement levels within each content domain. Thus, the student's time is not wasted responding to items that are not necessary to provide good measurement.

In addition to providing these psychometric benefits of shorter tests with equal or greater precision, it is also possible that adaptive achieve- ment testing might have positive psychological advantages, providing further beneficial effects on the psychometric characteristics of test scores. At the least, reduced testing time might result in more favorable attitudes of the testees toward the testing process. In addition, however, the elimination of very easy and very difficult test items might result in higher testee motivation levels (Betz & Weiss, 1976b) and higher test scores (Betz & Weiss, 1976a) that are more indicative of students' true levels of achievement. In any event, it should be clear that the reductions in test length due to adaptive testing applied within an instructional context can result in increased time available for instruction, or reductions in total time in training or instruction. In addition, the measurements of higher precision that result from adaptive testing under certain circumstances can provide data from which better instructional decisions can be made.

Together these two studies show considerable promise for the improvement of achievement testing by the use of adaptive testing procedures. Where a large item pool is available from which test items can be selected, adaptive testing can provide measurements of higher precision with from 30 to 50% fewer items. If a fixed item pool is used, adaptive testing can reduce average subtest lengths by 30 to 70%, with typical battery-length reductions of 50%. In both cases, adaptive testing accomplishes this reduction by administering to each student only those test items that are near the testee's estimated achievement levels. The result is the elimination of items that are either too difficult or too easy for each student.

The studies reported above describe only two problems in the adaptive measurement of achievement being studied at the University of Minnesota. The research program is concerned with fully investigating the potential of adaptive administration of achievement tests for the improvement of instructional decisions. Other studies in progress include the effects of point-in-training on achievement estimates, effects of immediate knowledge of results, development and investigation of an adaptive approach to mastery testing, studies of the dimensionality of achievement tests at different points in the instructional process, and the development of the concept of adaptive self-referenced testing that is designed to transform the process of achievement testing into a coherent multidimensional framework. As results become available from these studies, it is expected that the application of interactive computers to the measurement of achievement will result in substantial improvements in the assessment of the effects of instruction on individuals.

ACKNOWLEDGMENTS

The author acknowledges with thanks the important contributions of Isaac I. Bejar, Joel M. Brown, Kathleen A. Gialluca, and G. Gage Kingsbury to this research program. Data for

162   David J. Weiss

the second study were generously provided by Lee J. Walker of the Personnel Training and
Evaluation Program.

REFERENCES

Bejar, I. I., Weiss, D. J., & Gialluca, K. A. *An information comparison of conventional and adaptive tests in the measurement of classroom achievement* (Research Report 77-7). Minneapolis: University of Minnesota, Department of Psychology, Psychometric Methods Program, 1977. (NTIS No. AD-A047495)

Bejar, I. I., Weiss, D. J., & Kingsbury, G. G. *Calibration of an item pool for the adaptive measurement of achievement* (Research Report 77-5). Minneapolis: University of Minnesota, Department of Psychology, Psychometric Methods Program, 1977. (NTIS No. AD-A044828)

Betz, N. E., & Weiss, D. J. *Effects of immediate knowledge of results and adaptive testing on ability test performance.* Minneapolis: University of Minnesota, Department of Psychology, Psychometric Methods Program, 1976. (a) (NTIS No. AD-A027147)

Betz, N. E., & Weiss, D. J. *Psychological effects of immediate knowledge of results and adaptive ability testing.* Minneapolis: University of Minnesota, Department of Psychology, Psychometric Methods Program, 1976. (b) (NTIS No. AD-A027170)

Birnbaum, A. Some latent trait models and their use in inferring an examinee's ability. In F. M. Lord & M. R. Novick, *Statistical theories of mental test scores.* Reading, Mass.: Addison-Wesley, 1968.

Brown, J. M., & Weiss, D. J. *An adaptive testing strategy for achievement test batteries* (Research Report 77-6). Minneapolis: University of Minnesota, Department of Psychology, Psychometric Methods Program, 1977. (NTIS No. AD-A04062)

Cronbach, L. J., & Furby, L. How should we measure "change"—Or should we? *Psychological Bulletin,* 1970, *74,* 68–80.

Gulliksen, H. *Theory of mental tests.* New York: Wiley, 1950.

Hambleton, R. K., & Cook, L. L. Latent trait models and their use in the analysis of educational test data. *Journal of Educational Measurement,* 1977, *14,* 75–96.

Hansen, D. N. An investigation of computer-based science testing. In R. C. Atkinson & H. A. Wilson (Eds.), *Computer-assisted instruction: A book of readings.* New York: Academic Press, 1969.

Lord, F. M. Some test theory for tailored testing. In W. H. Holtzman (Ed.), *Computer-assisted instruction, testing, and guidance.* New York: Harper & Row, 1970.

Lord, F. M., & Novick, M. R. *Statistical theories of mental test scores.* Reading, Mass.: Addison-Wesley, 1968.

Owen, R. J. A Bayesian sequential procedure for quantal response in the context of adaptive mental testing. *Journal of the American Statistical Association,* 1975, *70,* 351–356.

Urry, V. W. Tailored testing: A successful application of latent trait theory. *Journal of Educational Measurement,* 1977, *14,* 181–196.

Vale, C. D., & Weiss, D. J. *A simulation study of stradaptive ability testing* (Research Report 75-6). Minneapolis: University of Minnesota, Department of Psychology, Psychometric Methods Program, 1975. (a) (NTIS No. AD-A020961)

Vale, C. D., & Weiss, D. J. *A study of computer-administered stradaptive ability testing* (Research Report 75-4). Minneapolis: University of Minnesota, Department of Psychology, Psychometric Methods Program, 1975. (b) (NTIS No. AD-A018758)

Weiss, D. J. *The stratified adaptive computerized ability test* (Research Report 73-3). Minneapolis: University of Minnesota, Department of Psychology, Psychometric Methods Program, 1973. (NTIS No. AD-768376)

Weiss, D. J. *Strategies of adaptive ability measurement* (Research Report 74-5). Minneapolis: University of Minnesota, Department of Psychology, Psychometric Methods Program, 1974. (NTIS No. AD-A004270)

Weiss, D. J. *Computerized ability testing: 1972–1975* (Final Report). Minneapolis: University of Minnesota, Department of Psychology, Psychometric Methods Program, 1976. (NTIS No. AD-A024516)

Weiss, D. J., & Betz, N. E. *Ability measurement: Conventional or adaptive?* (Research Report 73-1). Minneapolis: University of Minnesota, Department of Psychology, Psychometric Methods Program, 1973. (NTIS No. AD-757788)

6

The Instructional Quality Profile:
A Curriculum Evaluation
and Design Tool[1]

M. DAVID MERRILL, CHARLES M. REIGELUTH,
and GERALD W. FAUST

The Instructional Quality Profile provides a set of detailed procedures for analyzing the quality of instruction in relation to different kinds of objectives and test items. *Instructional quality* refers to the degree to which instruction is effective, efficient, and appealing—that is, the degree to which it works in cost-effectively promoting student performance on a posttest and student affect toward learning. Educators have developed detailed procedures for making reliable tests and for writing well-stated objectives. However, very little attention has been devoted to detailed procedures for analyzing instruction. The Instructional Quality Profile is an analytic tool for diagnosing specific weaknesses and correcting those weaknesses in existing instruction and for providing prescriptions for avoiding such weaknesses in the design of new instruction.

[1] Previous publications on the Instructional Quality Profile referred to it as the Instructional Strategy Diagnostic Profile (Merrill, Richards, Schmidt, & Wood, 1977) and the Instructional Quality Inventory (Ellis & Wulfeck, 1978). The authors gratefully acknowledge support from the following institutions (in alphabetical order) for the development of the ideas presented herein: Brigham Young University, The Church of Jesus Christ of the Latter Day Saints (Education System), Courseware Incorporated, and the Navy Personnel Research and Development Center (San Diego) and Advanced Research Project Agency. The ideas expressed herein are those of the authors and should not be interpreted as necessarily representing the official policies, either expressed or implied, of any of the funding institutions.

PROCEDURES FOR INSTRUCTIONAL
SYSTEMS DEVELOPMENT

165

Copyright © 1979 by Academic Press, Inc.
All rights of reproduction in any form reserved.
ISBN 0-12-526660-X

WHERE DOES IT FIT?

Clearly, there are many different aspects of instruction that influence its quality. We believe it is helpful to classify those aspects as to three kinds: (*a*) ways for *organizing* the instruction, such as the choice of words, diagrams, format, and student responses; (*b*) ways for *delivering* the instruction to the student and for receiving responses from the student, such as textbooks, class lectures, homework assignments, television, and discussion groups; and (*c*) ways for *managing* the interaction between the student and the instruction, such as scheduling, motivation, record keeping, and strategy selection. (See Reigeluth and Merrill [1978a] for a more detailed description of these three aspects of the quality of instruction.)

Within this scheme, the Instructional Quality Profile analyzes only Class 1: ways for organizing the instruction. But it is also helpful to divide this class into two categories: (*a*) ways for organizing the instruction on a **single** concept, principle, or procedure, such as the use of examples, and mnemonics; and (*b*) ways for organizing aspects of instruction that relate to **more than one** concept, principle, or procedure, such as the use of overviews, advance organizers, and various kinds of sequencing (Reigeluth & Merrill, 1978b). The profile analyzes only Category 1: ways for organizing the instruction on a **single** concept, principle, or procedure (see Figure 6.2). However, work is currently in progress to expand the scope of the profile to the second category (Reigeluth, Merrill, & Bunderson, 1978; Reigeluth, Merrill, Wilson, & Spiller, in press) and the profile will eventually be expanded to include the other two classes: the aspects of the quality of instruction that relate to delivery and management.

WHAT DOES IT DO?

The Instructional Quality Profile is a tool for analyzing the quality of instruction in the six areas shown in Figure 6.1: (*a*) purpose-objective

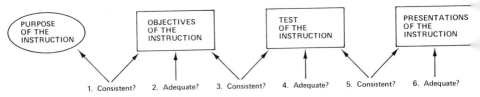

Figure 6.1 The context of the Instructional Quality Profile with respect to the major aspects of instructional quality.

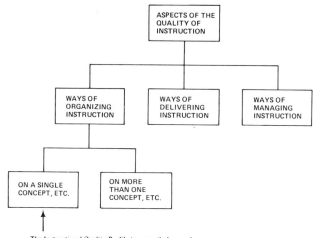

Figure 6.2 The six areas of instructional quality analyzed by the Instructional Quality Profile.

consistency; (*b*) objective adequacy; (*c*) objective–test consistency; (*d*) test adequacy; (*e*) test–presentation consistency; and (*f*) presentation adequacy. The following is a general introduction to what the profile does in each of these six areas.

Purpose–Objective Consistency

The educational literature contains a considerable amount of material about the importance of instructional objectives and about how to write them (Logan, 1978). Though knowing how to write correctly stated objectives is important, there has been relatively little guidance in how to decide whether the objectives that have been written are the objectives that should be taught. There have been no adequate guidelines for justifying the substance of one's objectives. As a consequence, many of the objectives that have been written are either unnecessary or trivial. They often stress memory-level behavior when rule using or problem solving is more appropriate. Though some memory-level objectives are certainly justified, many more are not. Merely stating objectives correctly cannot compensate for inappropriate substance.

The first set of profile prescriptions addresses the question, Is the objective justified? In other words, is the substance of the objective consistent with the purpose of the course?

Objective Adequacy

Knowing that the substance of an objective is consistent with the purpose of the course is very important, but it is not enough. In order to be an effective guide for writing both test items and instructional presentations, an objective must be stated adequately. The educational literature contains many prescriptions for writing objectives in a useful form. Perhaps the classic is Robert Mager's book (1962). Although the profile does not make any new contributions to objective adequacy, it emphasizes the importance of this area of instructional quality.

The second set of profile prescriptions addresses the question, Is the objective adequate? In other words, does the objective contain the characteristics that make it useful for guiding the design of test items and instructional presentations? (See Figure 6.1.)

Objective–Test Consistency

Much of educational psychology over the past 30 years has been directed toward testing. But most of this effort has been devoted to prescriptions for the construction of reliable tests and for the construction and use of good items of various kinds (e.g., multiple-choice and true–false). Although reliability and other aspects of test adequacy are important, validity is critical. If the test items measure the wrong thing, then the careful construction of the test items is of little value.

In spite of the extensive work on tests, relatively little effort has been devoted to correlating tests with objectives. Often the two activities are viewed separately and are not related. Consequently, most tests end up measuring memory, even though it might be more appropriate to measure the ability to use knowledge to solve problems. Some testing of memory is necessary and desirable, but too often we test memory and make inferences about ability to use the information remembered.

The third set of profile prescriptions addresses the question, Are the test items consistent with the justified objectives? In other words, are we measuring the real goals of our instruction?

Test Adequacy

Knowing that the substance of a test item is consistent with a justified objective is critical, but it is not enough. A test item must also be reliable, well-formatted, and in other ways adequately constructed. In the educational literature there are excellent prescriptions available for constructing reliable tests. There are also many guidelines for constructing a wide variety of test formats, such as multiple-choice, matching, true–false, short-answer, and essay (Courseware, Inc., 1977). The profile emphasizes the importance of these aspects of test adequacy and includes them, but it does not contribute anything new to them. What the profile does contribute is the identification of other aspects of test adequacy that have been largely overlooked.

The fourth set of profile prescriptions addresses the question, Are the test items adequate? In other words, do the test items have the characteristics necessary to ensure that they will adequately test the objectives with which they are consistent?

Test–Presentation Consistency

Of the three components of instruction shown in Figure 6.1 (objectives, tests, and presentations), objectives and tests have received considerable attention, as previously described; but the prescription of appropriate instructional presentations has received much less attention in the educational literature. Most instructional presentations are based on tradition, intuition, or the modeling of others. Most of the texts in a given field are modeled after a given best seller. Most professors teach as they have seen others teach. There is almost no information available for judging the appropriateness of an instructional presentation for teaching what is required by an objective and its test item(s). As a consequence, many instructional presentations are inappropriate. Often the information needed to pass the test is not available anywhere in the presentation—either in the text or in the teacher's elaboration of the text.

The fifth set of profile prescriptions addresses the question, Are the instructional presentations consistent with their corresponding test items? In other words, do the instructional presentations provide the kind of information necessary for the student to learn how to perform as required by the test?

Presentation Adequacy

Even when the necessary information is present, it is often hidden in the elaboration or nice-to-know material; it is often inadequately illustrated with examples; and it is frequently unclear to the student. The necessary information may be present, but the student is unable to find it or to understand it if he does find it.

The sixth set of profile prescriptions addresses the question, Is the presentation adequate for effective and efficient learning to occur? In other words, has the student been provided with a complete, concise, easily studied, adequately illustrated, and sufficiently elaborated presentation to enable him or her to acquire the desired performance efficiently?

HOW DOES IT WORK?

A distinction between descriptive and prescriptive principles (Reigeluth, Bunderson, & Merrill, 1978; Simon, 1969) is germane to an understanding of the profile. An experimental psychologist might attempt to describe *predictive relationships,* which are somewhat value-free. That is, under a given set of conditions a given event can be predicted to occur within some range of probability. It does not matter whether someone wants such an event to occur, or whether it is good for such an event to occur; it occurs.

An instructional psychologist, on the other hand, might attempt to state *prescriptive relationships,* which are based on values. Such prescriptions often take this form: "If you want such an event to occur, then do thus and so." In stating prescriptive principles it is important that the desired outcomes be clearly identified. Such specified outcomes enable one to consider the desirability or relative importance of the prescriptions with respect to one's own values and to decide if a given set of prescriptive principles is appropriate in a given situation.

The common goals of an instructional strategy are maximum effectiveness (i.e., the fewest errors and least time to perform), maximum efficiency (i.e., the least time to learn), maximum retention (i.e., continued low error rate and low performance time over time), maximum transfer (i.e., maximum effectiveness in new contexts), and maximum appeal (i.e., students perceive they are learning and seek additional opportunity to interact with the task or similar tasks).

Profile prescriptions are usually stated using the term *should.* This *should* implies that if the prescription is followed, one or more of the desired goals will be promoted. Instructional situations exist in which one or more of these common goals may be inappropriate, destructive of another goal, or impractical. The profile also provides prescriptions for these situations in which only some subset of the common goals is desired.

The following six sections describe how the profile works in each of the six areas of instructional quality shown in Figure 6.1. With the exception of the section on objective adequacy, all sections have three parts: (*a*) a description of concepts essential to the analysis of quality in that area; (*b*) a description of instructional principles that provide the basis for the analysis of quality; and (c) an outline of the procedures for performing each analysis.

Purpose–Objective Consistency

The first set of profile diagnoses is concerned with determining whether or not each objective is one which we really want to teach. This justification of the objectives requires four steps (see Figure 6.3). First, analyze the purpose of the lesson to be taught and classify it on the basis of important characteristics. Second, analyze the objectives and classify them on the basis of the same characteristics. Third, compare the classification of each objective with the classification of the purpose. If they are not the same, the objective should be revised to be consistent with the purpose. Finally, make sure that no important objectives have been left out.

Concepts

The most crucial requirement for estimating the quality of instruction in this area is the nature of the characteristic(s) for classifying the purpose and objectives. After much consideration and experimentation, it was concluded that just one characteristic was of great importance: the level of behavior expected of the student, which is referred to as *task level*. To be justified, an objective must be at an appropriate task level for the purpose of the lesson.

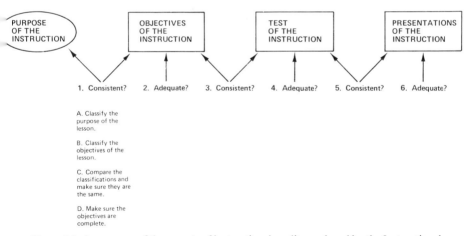

Figure 6.3 A summary of the aspects of instructional quality analyzed by the Instructional Quality Profile.

The profile identifies three major task levels: Remember an instance, remember a generality, and use a generality. A *generality* is an abstract or general statement that can be applied in a variety of specific situations, such as the definition of a concept or the statement of a procedure. An *instance* is a specific object, event, or symbol, such as an example of a concept or an application of a procedure. For every generality there are two or more instances associated with that generality. (See Merrill and Tennyson [1977] for a more detailed definition of generality and instance.)

Principles

The task level of the purpose of a lesson is based on two things: (*a*) the orientation of the lesson and (*b*) the degree of transfer required when the content–behaviors learned are used in a real-world setting. Transfer is the ability to use information in a new situation.

With respect to the orientation of the lesson, some lessons are application-oriented, which means that a major intention of the instruction is for the students to learn to **use** the content of the lesson in some way after completion of the lesson. Other lessons are non-application-oriented, which means that the intention of the lesson is just for the students to **know** the content (such as that the Declaration of Independence was signed in 1776), without any specific use for the content in mind.

With respect to the degree of transfer required after the lesson, some application purposes require no transfer, such as learning to use a procedure with specific, invariant inputs and conditions. Other purposes do require transfer, such as learning to use that procedure with a wide variety of different inputs and conditions. This is a greatly oversimplified notion of transfer, because there are qualitative differences (i.e., different types of transfer) as well as quantitative differences (i.e., different degrees of transfer). The profile itself deals more adequately with the true nature of transfer (see Merrill, Richards, Schmidt, & Wood, 1977), but this simplification allows a basic understanding without being overly technical.

To be consistent, the objectives of a lesson should reflect both the lesson's orientation and its transfer requirements.

Procedures

The profile uses the following procedure to analyze the consistency between the purpose of a course and its objectives.

Step 1. Determine the orientation and transfer requirements of the course on the basis of its purpose. Use this information and the flow diagram in Figure 6.4 to determine the appropriate task level for the major objectives of the course.

Step 2. Determine the task level of each objective by inspection.

Step 3. Compare the actual task level of each objective with its appropriate task level.

Step 4. Make sure that the objectives are complete—that is, that no important objectives have been left out.

Objective Adequacy

Once we have determined that the objectives for a lesson are consistent with the purpose of the lesson, the second set of profile diagoses is intended to determine whether or not each objective is adequate (see Figure 6.5). Because of the extensive treatment of this area of the quality of instruction in the educational literature, the profile has not attempted to contribute anything new. Nor will we discuss this area in terms of concepts, principles, and procedures.

Mager (1962) identified three important criteria of objective adequacy that must be clearly specified: (a) the desired student behavior; (b) the conditions under which the behavior is to be performed; and (c) the standards for the acceptable performance of the behavior. Gagné and Briggs (1974) extend these criteria to include (d) the object of the behavior; (e) the tools and constraints, and (f) the capability to be learned (which overlaps with standards). However, these last three criteria are usually parts of the first three. For an excellent summary of criteria for objective adequacy, see Davies (1976).

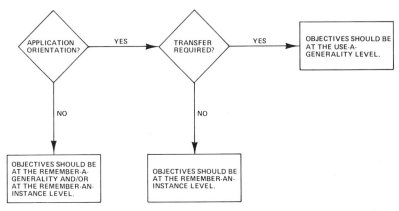

Figure 6.4 The procedure for determining the appropriate task level for the objectives of a course.

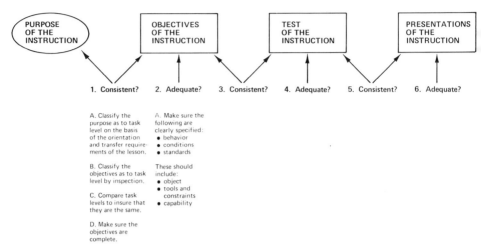

Figure 6.5 A summary of the aspects of instructional quality analyzed by the Instructional Quality Profile.

Objective–Test Consistency

Having determined that the objectives for a lesson are justified and adequate, the third set of profile diagnoses is intended to determine whether or not the test items are consistent with those objectives (see Figure 6.6). This analysis requires four steps. First, classify the objectives on the basis of important characteristics. Second, classify each test item on the basis of those same characteristics. Third, match each test item with the objective it tests (if any), compare their classifications, and (if necessary) revise the test item to be consistent with the objective. Finally, make sure all the objectives are tested.

Concepts

As with the justification of objectives (above), the most important requirement for estimating the quality of instruction in this area is the nature of the characteristics used for classifying the objectives and the test items. After much careful deliberation and experimentation, it was concluded that two characteristics were of great importance for assessing objective–test consistency: the level of behavior expected of the student (which is referred to as task level) and the type of content with which the student is expected to exhibit that behavior.

As indicated above, the profile identifies three major task levels: remember an instance, remember a generality, and use a generality. ("Find a generality" may also be included, but such problem-solving-type objec-

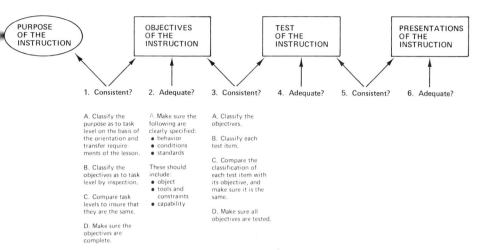

Figure 6.6 A summary of the aspects of instructional quality analyzed by the Instructional Quality Profile.

tives are not yet adequately considered by the profile.) The profile also identifies four major content types: facts, concepts, procedures, and principles. A *fact* is a one-to-one association between objects, events, and/or symbols. A *concept* is a class of objects, events, or symbols that share critical attributes and have discriminably different individual members. A *procedure* is a series of steps required to produce an instance of an outcome class. Each step may involve (*a*) the temporal or spatial ordering of specific objects, events, or symbols, or (*b*) a branching decision based either on a fact or on the classification of an instance of a concept. A *principle* is a change relationship (between concepts) that explains why an instance of a particular concept is changed as a result of a particular change in an instance of another concept.

A fact cannot be represented by a generality, since there is not a class of objects, events, or symbols involved, but only a single specific object, event, or symbol. Hence, the task level for a fact is always the remember-an-instance level (see Figure 6.7).

A concept can be represented by (*a*) a generality (i.e., a statement identifying those critical attributes which determine class membership and the way in which those attributes are combined), or (*b*) an instance (i.e., the individual objects, events, or symbols comprising the class or their mediated representations). Therefore, a student can be asked to respond to a concept at any of the three basic task levels previously defined (see Figure 6.7).

A procedure is often characterized as **how** to do something (as con-

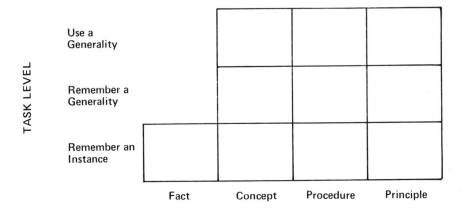

CONTENT TYPE

Figure 6.7 The profile's task–content classification table for analyzing objective–test consistency.

trasted with **why** it works, which characterizes a principle). A procedure can be represented by a generality (i.e., by a listing of the steps involved), or it can be represented by an instance (i.e., by an actual demonstration of the steps using particular objects, symbols, or events). Therefore, a student can be asked to respond to a procedure at any of the three task levels previously defined (see Figure 6.7).

A principle is often characterized as why something happens (as contrasted with how to do something, which is a procedure). Why a given procedure works can usually be explained by a single principle or set of related principles (a theory or model). However, a given principle or theory (model) can often give rise to a number of different procedures, each of which will produce the same outcome. A principle can be represented by a generality (i.e., by a statement of the relationships involved), or it can be represented by an instance (i.e., by its application to specific instances from each of the sets of concepts involved). Therefore, a student can also be asked to respond to a principle at any of the three task levels (see Figure 6.7).

The application of the task levels to the content types as described above results in the 10 classifications for comparing objective–test consistency shown in Figure 6.7. Every test item and every objective can be classified as one of these 10 classifications.

Principles

Adequate student evaluation depends on testing what we intend to teach. Hence determining and rating objective–test consistency is a critical part of good instructional evaluation. An objective and a test item are consistent if they both have the same type of content (fact, concept, procedure, principle) and the same task level (remember an instance, remember a generality, use a generality). Obviously, not only must the content be of the same type, but the subject matter topic stated in the objective and required by the test item must also be the same.

Procedures

The profile uses the following procedure to analyze the consistency between objectives and their respective test items.

Step 1. Classify the objectives with respect to the task–content table (shown in Figure 6.7).

Step 2. Find the test item(s) that correspond to the objective, and classify those test item(s) with respect to the task–content table.

Step 3. Compare the classifications for the objective and its corresponding test item(s). Are they the same? If not, revise the test item(s) to be consistent with the objective.

Step 4. Make sure that all the objectives of the lesson are tested. This may require the generation of additional test items.

Test Adequacy

Once we have determined that the test items for a lesson are consistent with the justified objectives, the fourth set of profile diagnoses is intended to detemine whether or not the test items are adequate. There are two important aspects of test adequacy that have received considerable attention: (a) the reliability of test items and (b) the technical correctness of the format of each test item. The profile calls for the analysis of these aspects of test adequacy (see Figure 6.8). But, because of their extensive treatment in literature, the profile does not attempt to contribute anything new to them.

There are some other aspects of test adequacy that have been largely overlooked or have received considerably less attention. These aspects are of two types: (a) those that apply to the adequacy of single test items, such as some characteristics of the information provided and of the behavior required, and (b) those that relate to sets of test items, such as item sampling, item sequencing, and criterion-level determination. These aspects of test adequacy will now be outlined.

Concepts

Response-level Option. A test item at the remember-an-instance task level or the remember-a-generality task level can require the student

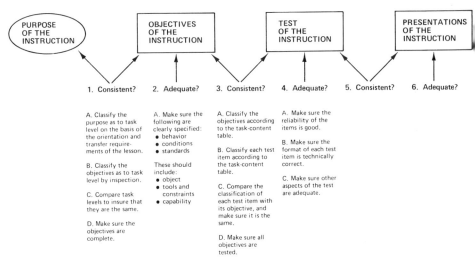

Figure 6.8 A summary of the aspects of instructional quality analyzed by the Instructional Quality Profile.

either to recognize or to recall the instance or the generality. And a test item at the use-a-generality task level can require the student either to identify or to produce the correct answer.

Input–Output Form. Every test item provides the student with some information: a generality name, a generality, or an instance. This is called the student's *input* because it is the information that the student uses. Every test item also asks the student for some information: a generality name, a generality, an instance (or part of an instance, such as a solution), or an explanation of an instance (e.g., telling why or why not it is an example of a concept). This is called the *output* because it is the information the student produces.

Response-time Criterion. On every test, students are allowed a certain amount of time to respond to the items. Response time may or may not be a criterion of acceptable performance specified by the objectives.

Feedback and Prompts. Sometimes feedback as to the correctness of a test response is provided before the test is over. And sometimes prompts are provided within the test itself. There are two basic kinds of prompts: *internal prompts,* such as attribute isolation[2] in the instance given as the input, and *extraneous prompts,* such as the answer to one question being

---

[2] *Attribute isolation* is the use of attention-focusing devices such as color, exploded drawings, arrows, or bold-faced type that enable the student to distinguish more easily the important characteristics of an instance.

facilitated by the wording of an earlier question or (assuming the student can go back and change an answer) by the wording of a later question.

Sampling. Many objectives have a variety of different representations or instances that can be used for testing them, whereas other objectives do not. One important question is the number of test items that should be used to test a given type of objective. And whenever more than one test item should be used, in what ways should the different representations of an instance, or the different instances of a generality, vary from each other with respect to divergence on variable attributes and with respect to item difficulty? *Divergence on variable attributes* refers to the differences between instances of the same generality (Merrill & Tennyson, 1977).

Sequencing. Test items can be sequenced randomly throughout the test, or they can be arranged in such nonrandom sequences as grouping by objective or arrangement in the same order as in the instructional presentation.

Criterion-level Determination. Every test should have a criterion level that indicates the minimum acceptable student performance with respect to an acceptable percentage of student errors.

Principles

Response-level Option. Unless justified, all test items should use the recall option for the remember levels and the produce option for the use levels, rather than the recognize and identify options, respectively.

Input–Output Form. The profile proposes that there is an optimal input form and an optimal output form for each task–content classification. Unless justified, all test items should have the input and output forms indicated in Figure 6.9.

Response-time Criterion. If response time is a criterion of acceptable performance specified by the objectives, then unless justified each test item should test for that criterion. If response time is not specified by the objective, then unless justified the following guidelines should be followed. The response-time criterion should be no delay if the student is to remember an instance or a generality verbatim; it should be short delay if the student is to remember an instance or a generality in a paraphrased form; and it should be untimed if the student is to use the generality.

Feedback and Prompts. Unless justified by the real-world task for which the student is being trained, feedback should be avoided before the student has finished the whole test, because it could influence performance either positively or negatively by such means as teaching something the student did not know or increasing anxiety. Both internal and extraneous prompts should also be avoided, unless justified by the real-

		FACT	CONCEPT	PROCEDURE	PRINCIPLE
Use a Generality	INPUT		Instance and Superordinate Name	Instance and Type of Solution	Instance
	OUTPUT		Name and Attribute Isolation	Solution and Algorithm	Name and Explanation or Name, Prediction and Explanation
Remember a Generality	INPUT		Name	Name	Name
	OUTPUT		Generality	Generality	Generality
Remember an Instance	INPUT	A	Instance	Instance	Instance
	OUTPUT	B	Name	Solution	Explanation

Figure 6.9 The profile's input–output table showing what kind of information should be used as the input and required as the output for each of the 10 task–content classifications. Two boxes are shaded because there are no task–content classifications for those two boxes (i.e., there is no generality for a fact).

world task, because they can allow an insufficiently knowledgeable student to given an "acceptable" performance on the test.

Sampling. The number of test items for an objective should be just one if the objective requires the student to remember an instance or a generality verbatim. For remembering an instance or a generality in a paraphrased form, a variety of representations is necessary, just as for using a generality a variety of instances is necessary. The minimum acceptable sample size for testing these kinds of objectives is estimated on the basis of such factors as the size of the entire population of items, the homogeneity of the population, and the frequency with which the student is likely to encounter different types of items from the population in postinstructional situations. Whenever there is more than one test item for a given objective, those items should be divergent with respect to the variable attributes on which the student is likely to encounter variations in postinstructional situations. Those items should also represent a range of difficulty appropriate for the types of "items" the student is likely to encounter after the instruction.

Sequencing. All test items should be randomly sequenced throughout the test. In addition to testing each objective at different places within a test, it is also preferable to test it at different points in time.

Criterion-level Determination. Unless justified, all tests should entail separate grading and scoring on each objective. The minimum acceptable percentage of student errors is usually specified by the objective. However, if it is not specified (which may particularly be the case for "enabling'' objectives), then the following criteria are recommended: no errors for remembering an instance or a generality, and a *split criterion* for using a generality. A split criterion is something like the following: 100% of all ''easy'' problems correct, 80% of all ''medium'' problems correct, and 40% of all ''hard'' problems correct.

Procedures

The profile requires three separate procedures for analyzing the adequacy of a test. The order of their performance is not important.

1. Empirically determine the reliability of each test item, and improve it as necessary.

2. By inspection, analyze the technical correctness of the format of each test item, and improve it as necessary.

3. By inspection, ensure that each test item has the optimal response-level option (recall or produce), has the optimal input–output form (see Figure 6.9), has the appropriate response-time criterion, and has no prompts or premature feedback; and also ensure that the test as a whole samples the appropriate number, divergence, and difficulty of items for each objective, sequences the items randomly, and has the appropriate criterion for each objective.

Test–Presentation Consistency

Having determined that the test for a lesson is consistent with the justified objectives and is adequate with respect to reliability, item format, and other aspects of quality, the fifth set of profile diagnoses is intended to determine whether or not an instructional presentation is consistent with its test item(s)—that is, to determine whether or not the presentation contains the information necessary for the student to learn how to perform as required by the test (see Figure 6.10).

This analysis requires three steps. First, determine the task level of the test item(s) on an objective. Second, determine what the presentation needs to contain in order to be able to teach at that task level. And finally, analyze the presentation to see whether or not it contains those components and only those components. If it does, the presentation is consistent with its corresponding test item(s). If not, the presentation should be revised.

Concepts

One of the factors that has prevented much progress in the analysis of instruction has been the lack of an adequate description of a presentation.

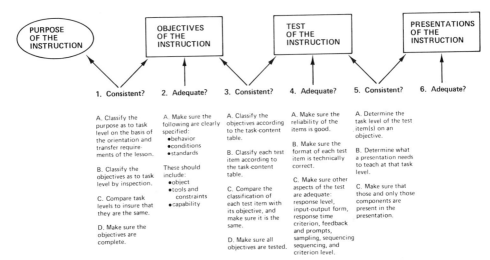

Figure 6.10 A summary of the aspects of instructional quality analyzed by the Instructional Quality Profile.

Concepts like *discussion, lecture,* etc., are far too ambiguous and have little correlation with student performance. A major contribution of the profile to the analysis of instructional quality is the notion that a presentation can be described as a series of *displays* (Merrill & Wood, 1974). A display is different from a frame in that a frame includes only that which is presented simultaneously via the delivery system in use (e.g., for printed materials a frame is synonymous with a page). A single frame may consist of one or more displays, or a single display may require more than one frame. For continuous-type delivery systems—such as lectures, audio tapes, video tapes, or motion pictures—the definition of a frame is somewhat more problematical, but the presentation can still be segmented into a sequence of instructional displays.

The kinds of displays of most importance to the profile's analysis of test–presentation consistency are those called *primary presentation forms* (Merrill & Boutwell, 1973; Merrill & Wood, 1974). Cognitive subject matter—such as concepts, procedures, and principles—can be presented as generalities or as instances (see above under objective–test consistency). Generalities and instances can be presented to the student in two ways: (*a*) The student can be told or shown, and (*b*) the student can be questioned or asked to demonstrate. The combination of these factors creates the four primary presentation forms: *generality, instance, generality practice,* and *instance practice* (see Figure 6.11). In order to analyze

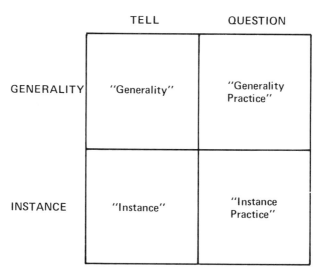

Figure 6.11 The four primary presentation forms.

the consistency between test items and instructional presentations, the profile indicates which primary presentation forms a presentation ought to contain in order to be able to teach the content at the desired task level.

A given presentation, regardless of delivery system, can be segmented into a series of displays, which consist of *primary presentation forms* (i.e., generality, instance, generality practice, and/or instance practice), *secondary presentation forms* (i.e., elaborated or "helped" primary presentation forms), *process displays* (which indicate to the student how he should process the information, such as "Repeat this in your mind"), and *procedure displays* (which indicate to the student how to manipulate the delivery system, such as, "Turn to page 47"). Other types of displays can also be defined but are not pertinent to the profile.

The differences among presentation strategies result largely from the different combinations of primary presentation forms used, the different secondary presentation forms used, and the variations in the characteristics (i.e., strategy components) of each primary and secondary presentation form. The first (i.e., the different combinations of primary presentation forms) is important for analyzing test–presentation consistency, and the latter two (i.e., the different secondary presentation forms and the variations in the characteristics of each presentation form) are important for analyzing presentation adequacy—the sixth set of profile diagnoses (see the discussion to follow).

Principles

Quality instruction depends on teaching what we intend to test. The profile hypothesizes that task level is very important for deciding which primary presentation forms should be presented to the student. For each task level there is an appropriate combination of primary presentation forms that should be used in the presentation. These combinations are as follows (see Figure 6.12).

1. For objectives and test items classified at the remember-an-instance task level, instance and instance practice are the primary presentation forms needed.
2. For objectives and test items classified at the remember-a-generality level, the generality and generality practice are often the primary presentation forms needed. However, it is usually helpful to provide a reference example if the generality is to be remembered in a paraphrased form, as opposed to being remembered verbatim.
3. For objectives and test items classified at the use-a-generality level, the generality, some instances, and some instance practice are the primary presentation forms needed.

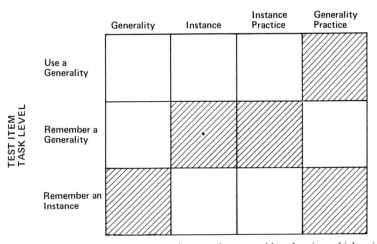

PRIMARY PRESENTATION FORM

Figure 6.12 The profile's test–presentation consistency table, showing which primary presentation forms should comprise an instructional presentation in order for it to be consistent with its test item(s). The shaded boxes show which primary presentation forms should not be included in the instructional presentation for each task level. (*) It is usually helpful to provide a reference example if the generality is to be remembered in a paraphrased form, as opposed to being remembered verbatim.

It should be noted that instance and instance practice at the remember level are of a different nature from instance and instance practice at the use level. At the use level previously unencountered instances should always be used, whereas at the remember level the same instance is always used (sometimes with different representations). The nature of the cognitive processing required is also different at the remember and use levels.

Procedures

The profile uses the following procedure to analyze the consistency between a test item and the presentation intended to prepare the students for it.

Step 1. The test item(s) on an objective are classified as to task level (i.e., remember-an-instance, remember-a-generality, or use-a-generality). This has already been done in the procedure for analyzing objective–test consistency.

Step 2. The test–presentation consistency table (Figure 6.12) is used to determine which primary presentation forms should comprise the instructional presentation intended to prepare the students for the test item(s).

Step 3. The relevant presentation is analyzed to determine whether or not the appropriate primary presentation forms, and only those primary presentation forms, are present. If they are not, then the presentation should be revised to supply missing primary presentation forms. And if inappropriate primary presentation forms are present, they should be deleted. Then the presentation will be consistent with its corresponding test item(s). This step may be split into two parts:

a. Identify all the primary presentation forms in the presentation. Most presentations are composed of some material that cannot be classified as a relevant primary presentation form. Such extra material may be useful, but it is not relevant for rating test–presentation consistency. Therefore, rather than classifying all parts of a presentation, you should just identify the relevant primary presentation forms.

b. Analyze each relevant primary presentation form as to completeness. Often a presentation will have what appears to be a generality or an instance, but upon closer examination it will be found that the generality is incomplete or merely provides context for the concept, procedure, or principle being presented; or it will be found that the example does not contain the attributes necessary for the student to see why it is an illustration of the generality. Such primary presentation forms are not adequate and should not be counted when determining test–presentation consistency.

Presentation Adequacy

Having made sure that each instructional presentation contains the appropriate primary presentation forms for teaching at the desired task level (test–presentation consistency), one can go to the sixth and last set of profile diagnoses, which is intended to determine whether or not each primary presentation form is accompanied by the necessary secondary presentation forms and has the necessary strategy components and characteristics to teach well at the desired task level (presentation adequacy). (See Figure 6.13.) There are two major aspects of presentation adequacy: (*a*) what strategy components should be included in and with each primary presentation form and (*b*) what characteristics each of those strategy components should have.

Concepts

With respect to the inclusion of strategy components, some components should be included in or with all primary presentation forms regardless of the task level of the presentation in which those primary presentation forms appear, whereas the inclusion of other strategy components depends upon the task level of the presentation. Type of content does not influence decisions as to what strategy components should be included, but it does influence decisions as to what characteristics each of those strategy components should have. The next few paragraphs provide a

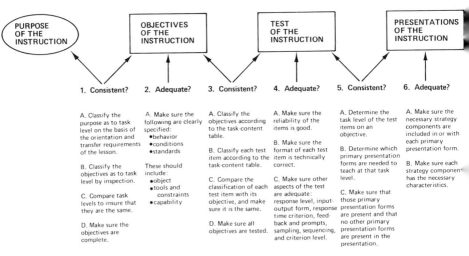

Figure 6.13 A summary of the aspects of instructional quality analyzed by the Instructional Quality Profile.

general description of the important strategy components of which we are aware.

Feedback. Often when practice is provided, the student receives no immediate feedback as to whether or not an answer is correct or (if the answer is not correct) as to what the correct answer is and why.

Isolation. Often a given presentation form (primary or secondary) will be buried in elaboration or in other types of presentation forms so that it is difficult for the students to know what represents the information that they will be required to remember or to use, as opposed to what represents information that is presented only to clarify or to help them see how to apply the ideas. This situation is characterized facetiously as "instructional hide-and-seek": the instructor hides the critical information and the students try to find it. Isolation of a presentation form refers to (a) separating it from other presentation forms and other kinds of displays and (b) clearly labeling it for the student so that there is no ambiguity as to what is the main idea and what is illustration, elaboration, or clarification.

Helps. Helps are various kinds of information that can be added to a presentation form to help the student to reach mastery. Descriptions of some kinds of helps follow.

A mnemonic help, which is a secondary presentation form, is a memory aid to help the student to remember the necessary information. Mnemonic help can include songs, rhymes, schematics, chunking devices, acronyms, and much more.

Attention-focusing help entails the use of various kinds of "flags" to focus the student's attention on critical aspects that are either especially important or are frequently overlooked by the student. Such flags include underlining, color, arrows, and other kinds of verbal or schematic highlighting.

An algorithm help, which is a secondary presentation form, gives the student a step-by-step description of what to do, whether it is for a concept-classification task (identification algorithm) or for a procedure-using or problem-solving task (transformation algorithm)—see Landa, 1974.

An alternative representation help, which is also a secondary presentation form, may be a graphic or schematic representation or even just a rewording of the generality or instance.

Sampling. There are various aspects of sampling instances and practice items that can greatly help a student to reach mastery. Some of them will now be described.

One of the most frequent problems of much instruction, second only to the too heavy use of memory-type test questions, is the lack of a sufficient number of instances. Somehow the notion seems to have been adopted that instances are fine for grade school students, but that adult students should be able to grasp abstract ideas without any illustrative material. This problem is characterized as "generality-rich but example-poor" instruction. However, most advanced concepts and principles cannot be adequately understood without illustrative material. Closely related to example-poor instruction is the lack of a sufficient amount of practice. Most of us learn by doing, not merely by listening or looking. In the hard sciences—mathematics, physics, chemistry, etc.—there seems to be considerable use of practice problems. But in the humanities and social sciences there is usually an almost total absence of relevant practice. Students cannot learn to use ideas unless they have an opportunity to practice using those ideas, with guidance (i.e., feedback) on that practice.

Divergence. Instances and instance practice items can be fairly different, or divergent, with respect to variable attributes (for concepts) or contexts (for procedures and principles). To be different from each other, instances must be divergent in at least one way. The number of ways in which two instances are different is a measure of their divergence.

Difficulty Level. Because they can be divergent, instances and instance practice can usually be at a range of difficulty levels, from very easy to very hard. Even when there is only one instance to be learned (i.e., at the remember-an-instance task level), the various possible representations of that instance usually form a range of difficulty.

Matching. Instances and noninstances can be arranged as matched pairs, which means that an instance and a noninstance are as similar as possible. For example, a ketch and a yawl (types of sailboats) could be the same size, be the same color, and have the same type of hull.

These aspects of the adequacy of each presentation form do not vary with content type. But the optimal characteristics of many of these strategy components do vary with content type. Generalities, instances, practice items, and the various kinds of helps are usually written or arranged differently for each of the different types of content (to be discussed later).

Principles

Presentation adequacy is the sum of the adequacies of all of the required primary presentation forms (generality, instance, generality practice, and/or instance practice) in a presentation. The adequacy of each required primary presentation form is determined by its conformance to principles of presentation adequacy. Some of these principles are valid across all task levels and all content types, others vary with task level only, and still others vary with both task level and content type. The following is a brief description of the major principles that we have discovered or abstracted from the literature (see Figure 6.14 for a summary).

Feedback Principle. A presentation is of higher quality to the degree to which each instance practice or generality practice is followed by immediate feedback as to whether or not the response is correct, what the correct response is, and why it is the correct response. This principle applies to the two practice primary presentation forms at all task levels and for all content types. Practice alone does not make perfect; only

The following principles apply for the indicated primary presentation forms across all task levels and all content types.

PRINCIPLES:	Generality	Instance	Instance Practice Question	Instance Practice Feedback	Generality Practice Question	Generality Practice Feedback
Feedback				✓		✓
Isolation	✓	✓	✓	✓	✓	✓
Mnemonic help	✓	✓		✓		✓
Attention-focusing help	✓	✓		✓		✓

The following principles apply for the indicated primary presentation forms at the indicated task levels, across all content types.

PRINCIPLES:	Generality	Instance	Instance Practice Question	Instance Practice Feedback	Generality Practice Question	Generality Practice Feedback
Algorithm help	UG	UG		UG		UG
Alternative-representation help	UG,(RG)	UG,(RI)				
Number of items		UG	UG			
Divergence		UG	UG			
Difficulty level		UG	UG			
Matching		UG				

The following principles apply for the indicated content types at the indicated task levels.

PRINCIPLES:	Fact	Concept	Procedure	Principle
Make-up of generalities		RG,UG	RG,UG	RG,UG
Make-up of instances	RI	RI,UG	RI,UG	RI,UG
Make-up of instance practice	RI	RI,UG	RI,UG	RI,UG
Make-up of generality practice		RG	RG	RG
Make-up of helps { mnemonics	ALL	ALL	ALL	ALL
attention-focus	ALL	ALL	ALL	ALL
algorithm		UG	UG	UG
alternative-representation		UG,(RI)	UG,(RI)	UG,(RI)

Key: UG — Use-a-generality task level.
      RG — Remember-a-generality task level.
      RI — Remember-an-instance task level.
      ALL — All three task levels.
      ( ) — In a paraphrased form only.

Figure 6.14 A summary of the areas of applicability of each principle of presentation adequacy.

practice with immediate feedback makes perfect. Too often the feedback is delayed long enough to be of questionable value; and too often it does not contain sufficient information—namely what the correct response is (if the student's response was wrong) and why it is the correct response.

Isolation Principle. A presentation is of higher quality to the degree to which the presentation forms are separated and labeled in such a way that the student can easily skip over or skip to each of these separate presentation forms. This principle applies to all primary and secondary presentation forms, including feedback for practice, alternative representations, and algorithms; and it applies across all task levels and content types. If such displays within a presentation are separated and labeled so that the student is told what is the main idea, then processing time can be spent on *encoding* the substance of the message instead of on trying to *find* the substance in a complex game of instructional hide and seek.

Help Principle. A presentation is of higher quality to the degree to which effective information is added to the presentation forms (both primary and secondary) to help the student to learn the information presented. More specific versions of the help principle are described below.

Mnemonic help. A presentation is of higher quality to the degree to which it provides the student with mnemonic aids to facilitate the ability to remember a generality or an instance accurately. This principle applies to all four primary presentation forms, except that mnemonics should only be presented on the feedback display of the practice items; and it applies across all task levels and content types (see Figure 6.14). One should be careful to use mnemonic aids that work well. If the mnemonic may interfere with subsequent performance, then it is better to omit it.

Attention-focusing help. A presentation is of higher quality to the degree to which it provides the student with attention-focusing help. This principle applies to all primary and secondary presentation forms, again with the qualification that attention-focusing aids should only be presented on the feedback display of the practice items; and it applies across all task levels and content types. If attention-focusing help is not provided, the student may miss important attributes or be forced to play another version of instructional hide-and-seek by guessing whether or not a given attribute is important. The student may end up processing a considerable amount of irrelevant information, which may interfere with learning what was important.

Algorithm help. A presentation at the use-a-generality task level is of higher quality to the degree to which it provides the student with algorithm help. This principle applies to all four primary presentation forms, again with the exception of only the feedback on practice items; it applies across all content types; but it applies only to the use-a-generality task level (see Figure 6.14). Most generalities require, at the use level, a series of ordered operations. The algorithm should identify all the important component operations and the order in which those operations should be performed.

Alternative-representation help. A presentation at the use-a-generality task level (and sometimes at the remember-an-instance and remember-a-generality levels) is of higher quality to the degree to which it provides the student with one or more alternative representations. This principle applies to just two primary presentation forms—generality and instance. It applies across all content types. And it applies to the use-a-generality task level, the remember-an-instance task level (in a paraphrased form only), and the remember-a-generality task level (in a paraphrased form only). Some students are more verbally inclined and others are more pictorially inclined. If a given generality or instance can be presented via two or more different representations, then it is likely that more of the students will be able to understand it.

Sampling Principle. A presentation is of higher quality to the degree to which instances are selected to represent adequately the class of possible instances that the student will likely encounter in the real world. The following are some more specific versions of the sampling principle.

Number of items. A presentation is of higher quality to the degree to which the number of instances and instance practice available to students is sufficient for even the slowest students to learn the material well (e.g., learned with the appropriate amount of generalization or transfer). This principle applies to two primary presentation forms—instances and instance practice. It applies across all content types. But it applies principally to the use-a-generality task level.

Divergence. A presentation is of higher quality to the degree to which the instances and instance practice are divergent with respect to variable attributes (for concepts) or with respect to contexts (for procedures and principles), to a degree consistent with postinstructional instances. This principle applies to two primary presentation forms—instances and instance practice. It applies across all content types. But it applies only to the use-a-generality task level. If students are not exposed to a representative set of instances during the presentation, then they will be unlikely to generalize to the types of instances not presented, and there will be a decrement in their performance. Divergence enables students to see the variety of forms that the critical attributes can take or the variety of contexts within which the critical attributes can occur.

Difficulty level. A presentation is of higher quality to the degree to which the instances and instance practice represent the range of difficulty representative of postinstructional instances. A presentation is also of higher quality to the degree to which the early instances and early instance practice are presented in an easy-to-difficult sequence. This may entail the use of a simplified representation for early instances and instance practice. These principles apply to two primary presentation forms—instances and instance practice. They also apply across all content types. But they apply only to the use-a-generality task level. Students confronted immediately with all of the embedded complexity of the real world may be confused and find it difficult to discriminate critical attributes from variable attributes. Once the critical attributes have been identified and internalized, subsequent exposure to difficult, high-fidelity instances is advisable.

Matching. A presentation is of higher quality to the degree to which the instances are matched with noninstances. This principle applies to one primary presentation form only—instances. It applies across all task levels. But it applies only to instances at the use-a-generality task level (see Figure 6.14). Matching enables a student to eliminate quickly potentially confusing, irrelevant attributes or inappropriate operations by being able to compare attributes simultaneously. This promotes discrimination. Matching is especially helpful for the concept type of content but also plays a role for procedures and principles. For procedures, common inappropriate procedures are demonstrated. For principles, common inappropriate explanations are provided for the student.

None of the above-mentioned principles of presentation adequacy varies with content type. But the optimal *characteristics* of many of the strategy components do vary with content type. Generalities, instances, practice items, and many kinds of helps should usually be written or arranged differently for each of the different types of content. Since the optimal characteristics of such strategy components for different task levels are described in some detail elsewhere in this book (see Chapter 1 of this volume), we merely outline the areas of applicability of those principles within our conceptual scheme. This outline is provided in Figure 6.14.

Procedures

The profile uses the following two steps for analyzing the adequacy of each required presentation form in each presentation.

Step 1. Determine whether or not each strategy component that ought to be present in or with each primary presentation form is indeed present. The profile provides a different diagnostic form for each task level for tabulating such information. If each required component is not present, add it.

Step 2. Determine whether or not all the characteristics that ought to comprise each strategy component actually do comprise it. The same diagnostic forms just mentioned are used to tabulate such information. If each required characteristic is not present, add it.

APPLICATIONS

The Instructional Quality Profile was designed primarily for analyzing the quality of existing instruction. However, because of the prescriptive nature of the profile's diagnoses, it is possible to apply the principles of this instrument in a variety of ways. These include (a) diagnosing specific weaknesses in existing instruction; (b) rating the effectiveness of existing instruction; (c) prescribing ways to revise the instruction so as to eliminate those weaknesses; (d) prescribing ways to design more effective new instruction and (e) prescribing effective learning strategies for students.

Detailed descriptions of procedures for each of these areas of application are beyond the scope of this chapter. In the following paragraphs, however, an attempt is made to outline briefly some procedures that may be used for these various applications.

Diagnosing Weaknesses

The starting point for diagnosing specific weaknesses in existing instruction is somewhat variable. It may not be necessary to perform any of the first four sets of diagnoses shown in Figure 6.13. Usually, the diagnosis procedure will start with the fifth set of diagnoses because often only the instruction is to be diagnosed and the test is often assumed to be good. In such cases, the following is a procedure that may be used to diagnose specific weaknesses in existing instruction.

First, classify each of the test items using the task–content table (Figure 6.7).

Second, locate the presentation that corresponds with each test item.

Third, use the test–presentation consistency table (Figure 6.12) to determine which primary presentation forms should be present in each presentation.

Fourth, analyze each presentation to see whether or not it contains all the required primary presentation forms and no unnecessary primary presentation forms. Also, develop a profile that lists all test–presentation inconsistencies.

Fifth, analyze each presentation to determine the adequacy of each of its required primary presentation forms that is present, and develop a

194 M. David Merrill, Charles M. Reigeluth, and Gerald W. Faust

profile that lists all presentation inadequacies. Profile forms have been created to facilitate these last two steps (see Merrill, Richards, Schmidt, & Wood, 1977).

Rating Instruction

There are at least two ways of rating the effectiveness of existing instruction. One is by predicting the level of student achievement that is likely to result from the instruction, and the other is by comparing two or more pieces of instruction on the same subject matter to predict which of the two will result in higher student achievement. The procedure is basically the same for both types of rating, and it is also similar to the procedure just described, except that indexes are needed to rate the presentations on the basis of their weaknesses. Assuming again that only the instruction is to be rated and that the test is of high quality, this procedure would also start with the fifth set of profile analyses.

First, classify each of the test items using the task–content table (Figure 6.7).

Second, locate the presentation that corresponds with each test item.

Third, use the test–presentation consistency table (Figure 6.12) to determine which primary presentation forms should appear in each presentation.

Fourth, analyze each presentation to see whether or not it contains the required primary presentation forms, and develop a different index of consistency for the presentation corresponding to each test item. (There may be some duplication if the same presentation corresponds to more than one test item, but such duplication is necessary for an accurate prediction of student performance on the test.)

Fifth, analyze each presentation to determine the adequacy of each of its required primary presentation forms that is present, and develop an index of adequacy for the presentation corresponding to each test item. (Again there will probably be some duplication.)

Sixth, add up the consistency and adequacy indexes for the presentation corresponding to each test item. This will provide a rating of how well a student should perform on each test item. Those ratings can then be added, to provide a rating of how well a student should perform on the test (the measure of student achievement). To compare two or more instructional programs on the same subject matter, merely compare their ratings.

Procedures for developing the consistency and adequacy indexes are explained in the *Instructional Strategy Diagnostic Profile Training Manual* by Merrill *et al.* (1977). Space constraints prohibit including their specifications here. Also, index forms have been developed to facilitate those procedures (see Merrill *et al.*, 1977).

Revision Procedures

The procedure for revising a given instructional product to increase its probable effectiveness often requires all six sets of profile analyses. Such a procedure is outlined as follows.

First, analyze purpose–objective consistency. With respect to the orientation and transfer requirements of the instruction, are the objectives at the appropriate level? Do they include objectives that are irrelevant to the purpose of the instruction? Do they omit objectives that are important to that purpose? A survey of the test items and instruction may reveal important objectives that are not stated. Objectives should be written, modified, and/or deleted as is necessary to make them consistent with the purpose of the instruction.

Second, analyze objective adequacy. It is important to ensure that the justified objectives contain the characteristics that make them useful for guiding the design of test items and instructional presentations, because the objectives will serve as the basis upon which the remainder of the revisions will be made.

Third, analyze test–objective consistency on the basis of the 10 task–content classifications (Figure 6.7). Each test item that has a different task–content classification than its justified objective should be revised so as to represent the correct classification. Test items that have no objective should be deleted, and test items should be written for those objectives that have none.

Fourth, analyze test adequacy and revise the test items as necessary to ensure that they are reliable, correctly formatted, and adequate with respect to the other aspects of quality previously described.

Fifth, analyze test–presentation consistency. The first four steps outlined under "Diagnosing Weaknesses" can be used to identify whether or not each presentation contains the required, and only the required, primary presentation forms for the task level of its test item(s). If the analysis reveals the absence of required primary presentation forms, these should be written and added to the presentation. Primary presentation forms that are present but not required—and other types of material that do not contribute to the attainment of the objective—should be deleted. Often, instruction contains much that is irrelevant, redundant, or distracting from the presentation. A comparison of all the included material with the objectives can help determine its necessity or desirability.

Sixth and finally, analyze presentation adequacy by determining the adequacy of each required primary presentation form for each presentation. Often this analysis leads to the most extensive revisions. The required primary presentation forms may be buried in text, may need more concise statement, may need the addition of help, may need additional instances, and often—especially in the nonscience areas of the curriculum—may need additional practice. Also, the composition of each of these strategy components may be inadequate. Therefore, this sixth and last step in the revision of existing instruction should entail the revision of each of these aspects of the adequacy of each required primary presentation form in the instruction until they all meet the standards outlined under "Presentation Adequacy" earlier in this chapter.

One of the purposes of the profile was to provide an evaluation tool that could be used to guide the revision of an instructional package without an expensive and time-consuming empirical evaluation. Since the profile has been subjected to extensive validation of the principles involved (see the next section), it is possible to use it for revision without the costs of a prior empirical evaluation. However, it is recommended that you conduct an empirical evaluation of the revised instruction in order to check the validity of this instrument in your unique setting. You may even wish to compare it with the original instruction in the empirical evaluation. Once you have verified its validity in your particular setting, it should not be necessary to subject every revision of similar instruction to a complete empirical analysis.

Designing New Instruction

Although it was developed to evaluate existing instructional materials, the profile can also be used as a very effective design tool for the production of new instructional materials. Because it is prescriptive in nature, it is very easy merely to apply the prescriptions when designing materials. Very briefly, the procedure for designing more effective new instruction could be as follows.

First, perform the necessary task analysis and content analysis in order to determine the subject matter to be taught (all of which is beyond the scope of the profile in its current version).

Second, use the task–content table to help in writing your objectives. The task–content table suggests that there are only 10 kinds of objectives that can be written, with respect to task level and content type. Each category of the task–content table provides a formula for writing a different kind of objective, complete with all the aspects of objective adequacy. To have an adequately stated objective, it is necessary only to determine the task–content combination desired, specify the subject matter topic to be taught, and then complete the formula. The specific formula for each type of objective has been specified by the profile, but their inclusion here would unnecessarily lengthen this chapter.

Third, after the objectives have been justified and adequately written, the test items should follow. Objectives are a form of generality for which test items are instances. Not only does the task–content table provide a set of formulas for writing quality objectives, but it also provides a set of formulas for writing test items that correspond to those objectives. These formulas also include the profile's aspects of test adequacy, as well as its aspects of objective–test consistency.

Fourth, with a consistent set of objectives and test items now developed, the profile provides a formula for preparing consistent presentations. The primary presentation forms that correspond to each task level (see Figure 6.12) represent a guide as to what the presentation should include. Using the prescriptions for these primary presentation forms, one can map out a skeleton lesson.

Fifth, and finally, the adequacy prescriptions indicate what each of the primary presentation forms needs to include, how additional examples should be designed and arranged, how feedback should be specified, etc. Again, the task–content table provides a set of formulas for designing each primary presentation form. There are at most 10 ways in which each primary presentation form should be designed, depending upon its task level and content type. These formulas include the aspects of which strategy components should be present in or with each presentation form (e.g., what kinds of helps), as well as aspects of the optimal makeup of each of those strategy components.

Using the profile as a design tool provides instruction that should already (i.e., without formative evaluation) have a high degree of effectiveness because of the previous validation of most of the principles that constitute the profile (see following section). It is advisable, of course, to subject the newly designed lesson to an empirical test in order to validate a particular application of these principles. It should not be necessary, however, to conduct as extensive an evaluation or as extensive revisions as would be required for a more intuitive approach to the design and development process.

Learning Strategies

The last application of the profile that we will discuss is the prescription of effective study skills for students. This application entails the use of the profile's principles as guides to effective ways to study. If a student knew the principles of test–presentation consistency and presentation adequacy, then it would be easier to skip over irrelevant material, to search for essential information, and to organize it better (especially with respect to main ideas—generalities—versus illustrative material—instances—and with respect to knowledge on a remembering level versus on the using level).

It would also be easier for the student to determine whether or not a given presentation is adequate for learning what is necessary to pass the test. Thus a student could ask for examples when the presentation is inadequate in this regard. A student could ask for feedback with helps when this is not provided. One could request clarification as to what constitutes the primary generality versus what is elaboration or illustration. Such a set of study skills would probably make it much easier for a student to acquire the knowledge and behavior that a given set of instructional materials attempts to teach. Additional learning strategies can be found in O'Neil (1978) and O'Neil and Spielberger (1979).

RESEARCH SUPPORT

Over the past 6 years the Instructional Quality Profile and the principles underlying its formulation have been the subject of an intensive research effort. These research activities have involved several research methodologies, including experimental studies, correlation studies, and intervention studies.

Experimental Studies

One of our first major efforts to test the profile's principles was a review of experimental research literature (Merrill, Olsen, & Coldeway, 1976). Most of the studies reviewed were not purposely designed to test the profile's principles, and the vocabulary used by different investigators for the same variables differed considerably. Therefore, it was necessary to study the methods section of each study carefully and to reclassify the variables investigated on the basis of the profile's variables. In the process, many studies were rejected because sources of confounding were discovered. Of the many studies surveyed, 51 were selected as valid tests of one or more of the profile's principles. This review of research literature showed considerable empirical support for most of the principles. There were a few principles that no studies tested, and there were occasionl studies that showed no significant differences. But no studies contradicted any of the principles underlying the profile.

The authors and their asssociates have also devoted considerable time and resources to designing and conducting new experimental studies to test more fully the contribution of each of the profile's variables. A detailed review is beyond the scope of this chapter. Research already completed includes the following. Olsen, Reigeluth, and Merrill (1976), Reigeluth (1977), and Reigeluth and Merrill (1977) investigated test–presentation consistency specifications of presentation forms (shown in Figure 6.12) for the use-a-generality task level. Wilcox, McLachlan, and Merrill (1978), and Wilcox, Richards, and Merrill (1978) investigated the isolation of presentation forms. Merrill and Tennyson (1971a) and Tennyson, Steve, and Boutwell (1975) investigated attention-focusing help for concept tasks. Coldeway and Merrill (1976), Wood, Gilstrap, and Merrill (1978), and Young, Smith, and Merrill (1972) investigated attention-focusing help on practice feedback for concept tasks. Wood, Gilstrap, and Merrill (1978) investigated alternative representations for generalities. Axtell and Merrill (1978) investigated the use of helps for generalities and instances. Merrill and Tennyson (1971b), Tennyson (1973), Tennyson, Steve, and Boutwell (1975), Tennyson, Woolley, and Merrill (1972), and Woolley (1971) investigated instance divergence and matching for concept tasks. Fletcher, Evans, and Merrill (1978) and Norton, Graham, and Merrill (1978) investigated instance divergence. Spiller, Rogers, and Merrill (1978) and Walker and Merrill (1978) investigated presentation form sequence.

In addition, about 25 research studies are in various stages of completion, including studies on presentation form sequence, instance number, generality and instance helps, practice feedback, attention-focusing help, and presentation form isolation.

In no case has any study that we have reviewed or conducted contradicted any of the profile's principles; all studies have either supported them or have shown no significant differences.

Correlation Studies

The purpose of these studies was to determine the degree to which consistency and adequacy indexes—as determined by profile ratings of existing instructional materials—correlate with student performance on the tests that correspond to those materials. The procedure consists of (a) identifying the presentation that corresponds to each test item; (b) rating each presentation using the profile's consistency and adequacy indexes; and (c) collecting test performance data on each test item (these are usually collected from existing sources—past tests). The presentations and their corresponding test items form the pairs for the correlation. Because several indexes are possible, multiple correlation is used.

No studies have been conducted yet on presentation adequacy, but three studies (Wood, Richards, & Merrill, 1976) have been conducted for test–presentation consistency. The first was a college-level statistics course that was taught using a workbook. A multiple correlation showed that test–presentation consistency and test-item complexity together accounted for 50% of the student variance on the test. Consistency was not correlated alone, so we do not know its unadjusted contribution.

The second study involved a Navy course in electronics. The method of presentation was individual study. Test–presentation consistency and test-item complexity accounted for 58% of the student variance on the test.

The third study was a college-level physics course. This course had several components, including discussion sections, video tapes, textbook, and lectures. We analyzed only the textbook. Test-item complexity and consistency accounted for only 2% of the variance on the test.

After the high correlation in the previous studies, this latter result was very disappointing. But after careful analysis we realized that the test items were very different from the statistics and the electronics test items. The physics test items were mostly integrative items rather than items assessing a single principle, procedure, or concept (this distinction was illustrated in Figure 6.2). Furthermore, the methods of scoring for these items were very ambiguous. This has motivated us to extend the profile to a concern for content structure and integration (i.e., ways of organizing instruction on more than one conept, etc.).

The conclusion of these three studies is that the consistency index of the profile in its current version is an effective tool in predicting test performance when the test involves items that measure the use of a single concept, procedure, or principle but is less effective in predicting performance on tests that measure the integration of a set of interrelated ideas.

No correlation studies have been completed using the adequacy indexes or combinations of the consistency and adequacy indexes.

An Intervention Study

The purpose of this study is to see how much a course can be improved by the use of profile principles. The procedure entails (a) selecting a unit from an existing course in which students had demonstrated difficulty; (b) revising the unit using the profile as a guide; and (c) administering the modified materials to a group of students and comparing their performance with the performance of students on the original materials.

An intervention study has been conducted by our associates (Merrill, Wood, Baker, Ellis, & Wulfeck, 1978). It involved an individualized course for Navy enlisted men. The subject matter of the unit selected was pumps. Twelve treatments were designed by varying different aspects of the profile variables. There were 20 students in each treatment. Eight of the treatments were designed to teach at the use-a-generality level and four of the treatments were designed to teach at the remember-an-instance level. The tests measured both ability to classify new instances of pumps—the use level—and ability to identify parts of a previously taught pump—the remember-an-instance level. Those trained with use treatments did significantly better on the use-level test items and significantly worse on the remember-level test items, whereas those trained with the remember treatments did significantly better on the remember-level test items and significantly worse on the use-level test items. This finding verifies the consistency hypothesis of the profile.

Within the eight use-level treatments, three specific presentation adequacy variables were manipulated: (a) the isolation of presentation forms; (b) the use of attention-focusing devices with instance displays; and (c) the use of a divergent set of instances for instance and instance practice displays.

On the use-level test items, the isolation groups performed significantly better than nonisolation groups, the divergent-instance groups performed significantly better than convergent-instance groups, and there were no significant differences between the attention-focusing groups and those which did not receive the attention-focusing material. This provides support for two of the three adequacy hypotheses tested.

Within the four remember-level treatments, one profile variable was manipulated—mnemonic versus no mnemonic—but there were no significant differences.

The conclusion of this study is that when the profile is used as a guide to revise materials in an ongoing instructional situation, performance can be improved over existing materials, and for the use level this improvement takes the specific forms predicted by the profile.

SUMMARY

In "Where Does It Fit?" we discussed the context of of the Instructional Quality Profile with respect to all of the aspects of the quality of instruction. That context is summarized in Figure 6.2.

In "What Does It Do?" we briefly described each of the six areas that must be analyzed in order to determine the quality of the instruction: (a) purpose–objective consistency; (b) objective adequacy; (c) objective–test consistency; (d) test adequacy; (e) test–presentation consistency; and (f) presentation adequacy.

In "How Does It Work?" we described the concepts, principles, and procedures that comprise the Instructional Quality Profile in each of the six areas. The procedures are summarized in Figure 6.13. Of these six areas, the profile probably makes the largest original contribution in Areas 5 and 6: test–presentation consistency and presentation adequacy. The principles of test–presentation consistency are summarized in the test–presentation consistency table (Figure 6.12). the principles of presentation adequacy are summarized in Figure 6.14.

In "Applications" we described five major applications of the principles underlying the profile: (a) diagnosing specific weaknesses in existing instruction; (b) rating the effectiveness of existing instruction; (c) prescribing revisions for existing instruction so as to eliminate those weaknesses; (d) prescribing ways to design more effective new instruction; and (e) prescribing an effective study strategy for students.

Finally, in "Research Support" we indicated that there is broad empirical support for the principles underlying the profile. This support comes from studies utilizing several different types of research methodology, including experimental studies, correlation studies, and an intervention study.

REFERENCES

Axtell, R. H., & Merrill, M. D. *Learner-controlled instructional strategy options: Effects for generality help and instance help on a procedure-using task* (Instructional Research Report No. 79). Provo, Utah: Courseware, Inc., 1978.

Coldeway, N. A., & Merrill, M. D. *Attribute isolation versus correct answer feedback effects on response confidence, latency, and test performance.* (Instructional Science Report No. 52). Provo, Utah: Brigham Young University, Department of Instructional Science, 1976.

Courseware, Inc. *Author training course.* San Diego, Calif.: Author, 1977.

Davies, I. K. *Objectives in curriculum design.* London: McGraw-Hill, 1976.

Ellis, John A., & Wulfeck, Wallace H., II. *Interim training manual for the Instructional Quality Inventory* (NPROC TN 78-5). San Diego, Calif.: Navy Personnel Research and Development Center, 1978.

Fletcher, K., Evans, W. & Merrill, M. D. *Homogeneous versus heterogeneous practice* (Instructional Research Report No. 85). Provo, Utah: Courseware, Inc., 1978.

Gagné, R. M., & Briggs, L. J. *Principles of instructional design.* New York: Holt, Rinehart and Winston, 1974.

Landa, L. N. *Algorithmization in learning and instruction.* Englewood Cliffs, N.J.: Educational Technology Publications, 1974.

Logan, R. S. An instructional systems development approach for learning strategies. In H. F. O'Neil, Jr. (Ed.), *Learning strategies.* New York: Academic Press, 1978.

Mager, R. F. *Preparing instructional objectives.* Belmont, Calif.: Fearon, 1962.

Merrill, M. D., & Boutwell, R. C. Instructional development methodology and research. In F. N. Kerlinger (Ed.), *Review of research in education.* Itasca, Ill.: Peacock Publishers, 1973.

Merrill, M. D., Olsen, J. B., & Coldeway, N. A. *Research support for the instructional strategy diagnostic profile* (Tech. Rep. Series No. 3). Provo, Utah: Courseware, Inc., 1976.

Merrill, M. D., Richards, R. E., Schmidt, R. V., & Wood, N. D. *The instructional strategy diagnostic profile training manual.* San Diego, Calif.: Courseware, Inc., 1977.

Merrill, M. D., & Tennyson, R. D. *Attribute prompting variables in learning classroom concepts* (Dept. of Instructional Research and Development Working Paper No. 28). Provo, Utah: Brigham Young University, 1971. (a)

Merrill, M. D., & Tennyson, R. D. *Concept acquisition and specified errors as a function of relationships between positive and negative instances* (Dept. of Instructional Research and Development Working Paper No. 29). Provo, Utah: Brigham Young University, 1971. (b)

Merrill, M. D., & Tennyson, R. D. *Teaching concepts: An instructional design guide.* Englewood Cliffs, N.J.: Educational Technology Publications, 1977.

Merrill, M. D., & Wood, N. D. *Instructional stategies: A preliminary taxonomy.* Columbus: Ohio State University, 1974. (ERIC Document Reproduction Service No. SE018-771)

Merrill, M. D., Wood, N. D., Baker, M., Ellis, J. A., & Wulfeck, W. H., II. *Empirical validation of selected instructional strategy diagnostic profile prescriptions* (Instructional Research Report No. 65). Provo, Utah: Courseware, Inc., 1978.

Norton, R. F., Graham, S. L., & Merrill, M. D. *The effects of practice-item variety, practice strategy and training mode on performance in a rule finding task* (Instructional Research Report No. 75). Provo, Utah: Courseware, Inc., 1978.

Olsen, J. B., Reigeluth, C. M., & Merrill, M. D. *Sequence of primary presentation forms in teaching coordinate concepts* (Instructional Science Report No. 51). Provo, Utah: Brigham Young University, 1976.

O'Neil, H. F., Jr. (Ed.). *Learning strategies.* New York: Academic Press, 1978.

O'Neil, H. F., Jr., & Spielberger, C. D. (Eds.) *Learning strategies: Issues and procedures.* New York: Academic Press, 1979.

Reigeluth, C. M. *Effects of generalities, examples, and practice: Instructional outcomes for concept-classification, principle-using, and procedure-using tasks.* Unpublished doctoral dissertation, Brigham Young University, 1977.

Reigeluth, C. M., Bunderson, C. V., & Merrill, M. D. What is the design science of instruction? *Journal of Instructional Development,* 1978, *1* (2), 11–16.

Reigeluth, C. M., & Merrill, M. D. *The effects of rules, examples, and practice on instructional effectiveness and appeal* (Instructional Science Report No. 54). Provo, Utah: Brigham Young University, 1977.

Reigeluth, C. M., & Merrill, M. D. *Classes of instructional variables* (Instructional Research Report No. 70). Provo, Utah: Courseware, Inc., 1978. (a)

Reigeluth, C. M., & Merrill, M. D. A knowledge base for improving our methods of instruction. *Educational Psychologist,* 1978, *13,* 57–70. (b)

Reigeluth, C. M., Merrill, M. D., & Bunderson, C. V. The structure of subject-matter content and its instructional design implications. *Instructional Science,* 1978, *7,* 107–126.

Reigeluth, C. M., Merrill, M. D., Wilson, B. G., & Spiller, R. T. The elaboration theory of instruction: A model for structuring instruction. *Educational Communication and Technology Journal,* in press.

Spiller, R. T., Rogers, D. H., & Merrill, M. D. *The effects of sequence manipulation of primary presentation forms on concept acquisition and learning efficiency* (instructional Research Report No. 89). Provo, Utah: Courseware, Inc., 1978.

Simon, H. A. *The sciences of the artificial.* Cambridge, Mass.: MIT Press, 1969.

Tennyson, R. D. Effect of negative instances in concept acquisition using a verbal-learning task. *Journal of Educational Psychology,* 1973, *64,* 247–260.

Tennyson, R. D., Steve, M. W., & Boutwell, R. C. Instance sequence and analysis of instance attribute representation in concept acquisition. *Journal of Educational Psychology,* 1975, *67,* 821–827.

Tennyson, R. D., Woolley, F. R., & Merrill, M. D. Exemplar and non-exemplar variables which produce correct concept classification behavior and specified classification errors. *Journal of Educational Psychology,* 1972, *63,* 144–152.

Walker, R. A., & Merrill, M. D. *Learner control: primary presentation form sequence and number of instances in an efficiency study* (Instructional Research Report No. 78). Provo, Utah: Courseware, Inc., 1978.

Wilcox, W. C., McLachlan, J. D., & Merrill, M. D. *Isolation of generality statements and instances* (Instructional Research Report No. 66). Provo, Utah: Courseware, Inc., 1978.

Wilcox, W. C., Richards, B. F., & Merrill, M. D. Effects of text condensation, field independence, and sex on comprehension of prose material (Instructional Research Report No. 73). Provo, Utah: Courseware, Inc., 1978.

Wood, N. D., Gilstrap, R. M., & Merrill, M. D. *Framework rule representation and elaborated feedback in statistics instruction* (Instructional Research Report No. 62). Provo, Utah: Courseware, Inc., 1978.

Wood, N. D., Richards, R. E., & Merrill, M. D. *Prediction of student performance on rule using tasks from the diagnosis of instructional strategies* (Instructional Science Report No. 53). Provo, Utah: Brigham Young University, 1976.

Woolley, F. R. *Effects of the presence of concept definition, pretraining, concept exemplars and feedback on the instruction of infinite conjunctive concepts* (Department of Instructional Research and Development Working Paper No. 21). Provo, Utah: Brigham Young University, 1971.

Young, J. I., Smith, K. H., & Merrill, M. D. *The effects of review techniques and instance presentation on concept learning tasks* (Department of Instructional Research and Development Working Paper No. 34). Provo, Utah: Brigham Young University, 1972.

7

A Systems Approach to the Evaluation of Training[1]

GARY D. BORICH

In the opinion of this author the failure of many efforts to evaluate training programs stems from a lack of understanding of the programs themselves.[2] I view a training program as a set of hierarchically arranged instructional experiences that interrelate to generate several well-defined terminal outcomes. The purpose of evaluation is to revise, delete, modify, add to, or confirm the efficacy of these experiences.

When viewed from this perspective, the key to understanding how and why a training prog.am brings about the outcomes it does lies in that program's hierarchical structure, or the way in which its components build upon one another to achieve outcomes greater than those that can be expected from any single part. It is the evaluator's understanding (or misunderstanding) of this systematic interrelationship of components that often determines the utility and relevance of the evaluation to training staff. When evaluators fail to base their evaluation designs on a thorough understanding of the purpose and organization of the training, their results and conclusions seldom address the needs that prompted the evaluation. Moreover, since their results and conclusions fail to represent existing

[1] Portions of this work were supported by the Defense Advanced Research Projects Agency, Contract No. MDA-903-76-C-0249. Views and conclusions contained in this document are those of the author and should not be interpreted as necessarily representing the official policies, either expressed or implied, of the Defense Advanced Research Projects Agency or of the United States government.

[2] The term *training program* will refer to any assembly of related activities brought together for the purpose of producing or changing specified behaviors.

Copyright © 1979 by Academic Press, Inc.
All rights of reproduction in any form reserved.
ISBN 0-12-526660-X

conceptions of the program, they cannot provide direction for program revision or modification.

One implication of the literature on training (e.g., IPISP, 1975; Dick & Carey, 1978) is that there is a need for a coherent, integrated approach to program planning, development, and evaluation. It is argued here that planning, development, and evaluation should be component parts of a unitary process, rather than conceptualized as separate and distinct activities. Program planning, especially, should be conducted with an eye toward program development (which it usually is) and program evaluation (which it usually is not). This implication is reflected in a call for the application of a general systems approach to education, which Kaufman (1972) defines as

> a process by which needs are identified, problems selected, requirements for problem solution are identified, solutions are chosen from alternatives, methods and means are obtained and implemented, results are evaluated and required revisions to all or part of the system are made so that the needs are eliminated [p. 2].

Kaufman (1972) suggests that the systems approach to education requires the application of a variety of tools and techniques borrowed from the fields of computer science, cybernetics, engineering, management, and operations research. Following Kaufman's suggestion, this chapter will introduce a specific systems approach for conducting evaluations of training, present a general model for the evaluation of training that incorporates this approach, and illustrate how various stages of the model can be employed to improve the structure and content of a training program. The overall objective of this chapter is to provide a coherent, integrated systems approach to planning, developing and evaluating training programs.[3]

A SYSTEMS VIEW

A systems view of a training program assumes that behavior is generated or changed by specific, discrete instructional activities, and that the interrelationships among these activities build to more general behaviors at program completion. In any large-scale training program some activities can be expected to benefit trainees, some to hinder trainees, and still

---

[3] For further rationale and development of the systems approach to evaluation, see Borich, G. A state of the art assessment of educational evaluation. In H. F. O'Neil, Jr. (Ed.), *State of the art assessment of computer-based instruction.* New York: Academic Press, in press.

others to have no measurable effect upon them. The purpose of evaluation is to assess the instructional activities that comprise the global program in a manner that makes possible the rendering of a judgment as to whether these activities should be revised, deleted, modified, unchanged, or supplemented with additional instructional components.

The role of evaluation from a systems viewpoint is first to break down the training program into its instructional components in order to understand the interrelationship among its parts and then to collect evaluative data from which to judge the adequacy of each part in relation to the whole. Should a program component fail to engender the intended outcome or fail to relate to other program components to produce more comprehensive outcomes, the effectiveness of that component can be called into question. Generally, evaluations of training have placed little emphasis on the interrelationships among program parts and thus have often failed to consider the extent to which program parts interrelate to build successively more complex outcomes.

Underlying the systems viewpoint presented in this chapter is the belief that evaluation cannot be divorced from program definition, that evaluation functions not only during but also before program development, and that the evaluator cannot judge a program's parts without considering the composition of the whole. In the systems approach that follows, the evaluator is viewed not only as an analyzer of data and reporter of program effects, but also as a logician and systems analyst. This perspective differs from typical notions of the role and function of the evaluator. Though traditional representations of the evaluator are not invalid, they often portray the relationship between the evaluator and program planners, designers, and developers as limited and distant. Such a relationship allows the evaluator minimal exposure to the training program in its earliest stages of development and affords him little opportunity to assist planners, designers, and developers in fostering a common conceptualization of program components and their interrelations.

This traditional view of evaluation can be illustrated by arranging the role functions of those involved in program planning, development, and evaluation on a single continuum, as shown in Figure 7.1(a). Traditionally, planning has included two roles: the planner and the designer. Development has involved the roles of developer and formative evaluator. Program evaluation has included both the formative and summative evaluator, the latter being primarily responsible for comparing the training program with a control or alternative program.

Unfortunately, such a continuum of activities and role functions separates planning and development activities from what may be seen as legitimate evaluation activities. This distinction between developer and formative evaluator has prompted some to view the two as opposing

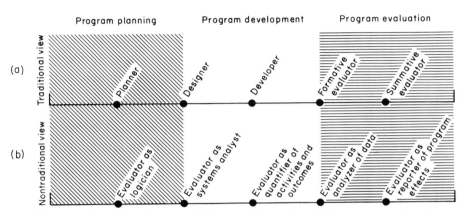

Figure 7.1 (a) Traditional view and (b) nontraditional view of the evaluator during planning, development, and evaluation.

forces, some arguing that the formative evaluator must guard against the influence of the developer, who is likely to be favorably biased toward the program, and others arguing that the developer and formative evaluator must work in close relationship in order to achieve the best mix of evaluation and development.

In practice, this conception of role functions often encourages the emergence of formal boundaries between program planning, program development, and program evaluation. Where one activity ends, the next begins with a different set of tools and techniques. Thus, it is not uncommon to find planners, designers, developers, and evaluators each beginning their work with a different "picture" of what the training is supposed to accomplish. Though the professional boundaries generated by these roles may be inevitable with a compartmentalized view of planning, development, and evaluation, we need not persist in maintaining this conceptualization with the emergence of a systems approach that allows us to link these role functions. Though some insights have been gained into the evaluative process by these highly specialized roles, any further separation of the evaluator from the work of the developer and planner may not be in the best interest of program planning, development, or evaluation.

Figure 7.1(b) presents a second continuum, on which the evaluator is shown contributing to the planning and development process. Here the evaluator, rather than entering the scenario late in the development process, plays an integral role in program planning and development alongside planners and developers. What are the evaluator's functions in this new role?

The emerging view of evaluation depicted in Figure 7.1 (b) is facilitated by the development of techniques and procedures that can be applied throughout the planning, design, development, and evaluation process to define and describe the program, to clarify its purposes and intents, and to foster a common conceptualization of it among project personnel. Ideally, such techniques would provide a basic language to use in articulating the program during all stages of planning, design, development, and evaluation. It also would allow the evaluator to serve as a *logician* and *systems analyst* in order to clarify and focus the work of the planner and designer, as *quantifier of program activities and outcomes* to provide process and outcome data for analysis, as *analyzer of data* to determine program outcomes, and as *reporter of program effects* to communicate results and recommendations.

Traditionally, development and evaluation have been viewed as two distinct roles or functions, related in sequence but not in substance. Formal training in instructional design and development does not always include evaluation concepts and vice versa. Though the notion of formative evaluation links development and evaluation in theory, it has in practice provided only a limited connection between these two activities. Given the importance of developing effective social, behavioral, and human service programs, the time for a closer relationship among evaluation, development, and planning seems at hand.

THE NATURE OF DECOMPOSITION

Structured decomposition is a systems methodology that can be used to interrelate the role functions of planner, designer, developer, and evaluator. It is a simple and straightforward concept, best explained in terms of Bloom's (1956) work *Taxonomy of educational objectives: The classification of educational goals. Handbook 1. Cognitive domain.* One level of Bloom's taxonomy of educational objectives is *analysis,* which Bloom (1956) describes as

> The breakdown of a communication into its constituent elements or parts such that the relative hierarchy of ideas is made clear and/or the relations between ideas expressed are made explicit. Such analyses are intended to clarify the communication, to indicate how the communication is organized, and the way in which it manages to convey its effects, as well as its basis and arrangement [p. 206].

Analysis is the sin qua non of decomposition because it emphasizes the process of breaking down the whole to determine the nature, structure, and sequence of its parts. It is especially suited to helping one understand the complex nature of training programs in which it is often difficult to see the forest for the trees.

Decomposition has six distinct characteristics. First, structured decomposition graphically breaks down the global concept of a training program into its individual parts, called *activities* or *transactions*. Second, it charts the flow of activities from beginning to end of the program, revealing the nature and structure of the experiences to which participants will be exposed. Third, it uncovers constraints upon training activities by indicating sources of influence that affect implementation of particular activities. Fourth, structured decomposition forces the integration of program parts by simultaneously detailing both the instruction to be provided and the behavioral outcomes to be expected. Fifth, it fosters a common conception of the program by providing planners, designers, and evaluators the opportunity to work in teamlike fashion on the decomposition and modeling task. And sixth, structured decomposition builds for planners, designers, and evaluators a working vocabulary with which to describe key concepts in concise semantic and graphic terms for use across the planning, design, development, and evaluation phases of the training program.

Structured decomposition achieves the above objectives by depicting the program hierarchically, from the top down. Program detail is introduced gradually so that substantive detail is integrated into the whole without obscuring the overall intent.

Figure 7.2 presents the decomposition process by showing program activities as boxes and outcomes expected from these activities as lines connecting the boxes. When a training activity is decomposed into subactivities, interfaces among subactivities are shown as arrows. The title of each subactivity along with its interface arrows circumscribes a context in which program planners, designers, developers, and evaluators can work in detailing the precise nature of that subactivity.

In contrast, a typical procedure is to evaluate a program by focusing on its sequence beginning with activities on Day 1 and following through to Day *N*. This practice can unnecessarily confine the evaluator's understanding of the training program to lateral flow. Hierarchically organized instructional activities and outcomes can go unnoticed by the evaluator when using only lateral flow or process models (e.g., Provus, 1971; Stufflebeam, Foley, Gephart, Guba, Hammond, Merriman, & Provus, 1971), no matter how thorough the effort to uncover all training activities and outcomes. In such a case, the problem is often not with the evaluator, who is attempting to describe the program, but with the limited dimensionality of the model used for evaluating it. These traditional evaluation models can be useful guides to program evaluation, but they cannot reveal the nature, sequence, and structure of program content and thus do not serve the same purpose as structured decomposition. Structured decom-

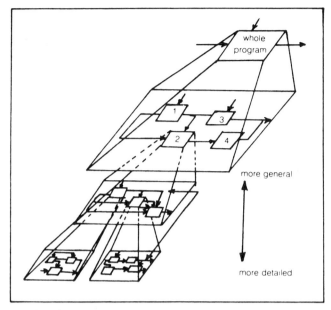

Figure 7.2 Each activity in a model is shown in precise relationship to other activities by means of interconnecting arrows. When an activity is decomposed into subactivities, all interfaces between the subactivities are shown as arrows. The title of each subactivity plus its interfaces defines a well-constrained context for the detailing of that subactivity.

position keeps the global intent of the program in view while gradually introducing substantive detail, using input, output, and constraint data to relate activities at a given level of detail to those at any other level.

Each program activity is depicted in a decomposition model of a program as a box. The interrelationships between program activities are indicated by input, output, and constraint arrows, as shown in the following diagram:

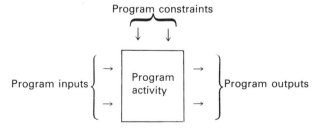

Program activities are "activated," or brought to life, via inputs, constraints, and outputs that lead to or emanate from each activity box.

Inputs, always positioned on the left side of an activity box, represent raw data (e.g., participants, materials, processes) that stimulate the activity into action and are eventually converted to output, or "changed" participants, materials, or processes. Control data, always indicated by arrows at the top of the activity box, indicate how the input may be constrained (e.g., by dollars), regulated (e.g., by policies), or modified (e.g., by trainee's experience and background) to produce the output. And, output data, shown by arrows emanating from the right side of the activity box, indicate the behavioral effect or finished "product" expected as a result of the program activity represented by the box. Structured decomposition diagrams with their activity boxes and input, constraint, and output arrows tell a story about a well-bounded portion of the training program, as is illustrated in Figure 7.3. All input, constraint, and outputs are numerically coded so that specific input, constraint, and output data can be traced from the most general to the most detailed levels of the program.

Application of structured decomposition starts with the most general or abstract description of the training to be planned, developed, and evaluated. If we confine this description to a single "activity" represented by a single box, we can then decompose, or break down, that activity into a number of more detailed activities, each of which symbolizes successively more detailed training activities. Each of these more detailed activities can be further decomposed to amplify information contained in the parent boxes. This top-down approach avoids the complication of considering too many details too soon by introducing substantive detail gradu-

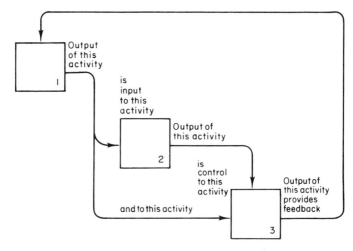

Figure 7.3. Some possible input, control and outcome connections among program activities.

ally, and in meaningful steps, to form an overall picture of the interrelationships among program activities.

Most organizations and agencies communicate planning and design decisions to program developers with a program proposal that describes the planned training and its expected effects. The proposal is often the most formal expression of program intent. Not coincidentally, it is usually the only document available to aid developers and evaluators in selecting and guiding their own activities. Because the proposal must often respond to policy as well as content considerations of the sponsoring agency, it frequently provides only a broad, global description of program components, unified by loose conceptual scaffolding upon which training objectives are supported. Thus, the proposal rarely serves developers and evaluators as a definitive guide to intended activities and expected outcomes. Hence, not only are evaluators uninvolved in the development process, but developers themselves are often unsure of program intents, since planning and design decisions may be poorly communicated from designer to developer. There is a need for a systematic methodology with which to transmit planning and design decisions to developers and to define, focus, and refine program activities and intended outcomes systematically prior to formative evaluation. A systematic methodology for accomplishing this purpose is structured decomposition.

APPLICATION OF
STRUCTURED DECOMPOSITION

The idea that the human mind can understand any amount of complexity as long as it is presented in small, accessible chunks that are linked together to make the whole is the basic assumption of structured decomposition. Since the early 1970s, computer software development specialists have been developing, applying, and improving general but practical approaches to handling complex systems problems. The approach taken in this chapter borrows from the work of Douglas T. Ross (1977), which has become known as the Structured Analysis and Design Technique (SADT)®, one of a family of systems analysis techniques for analyzing and structuring complex problems. These techniques are essentially modeling approaches to problem solving, some of which have a distinct format and purpose requiring the use of "flow charts" for the general purpose of displaying or describing a system and its components and subsystem relationships (see Schoman, 1977, for a comparison of some of these techniques). In the area of computer software technology, the application of decomposition methodology to real-life environments has significantly increased the productivity and effectiveness of teams of specialists involved in software development projects (Ross & Schoman, 1977). The basic ideas of these computer software specialists, however, are applicable to any field in which there is a need to analyze and effectively communicate the interrelationships among activities and outcomes occurring in complex systems or programs.

The structured decomposition approach provides methods for thinking in an organized way about large and/or complex programs, for working as a team with effective division and coordination of efforts and roles, and for communicating planning, development, and evaluation decisions in clear and precise notation.

The following fundamental assumptions underlie the application of structured decomposition to the evaluation of training:

1. Training programs are best studied by building a model that expresses an in-depth understanding of the program, sufficiently precise to serve as the basis for program development.
2. Analysis of any training program should be top-down, modular, hierarchic, and structured.
3. Program activities should be represented by a diagram that shows components, their interfaces, and their place in the hierarchic structure.
4. The model-building technique must represent behaviors to be produced, activities to be provided, and relationships among these behaviors and activities.
5. Decomposition is best accomplished through a team effort involving planners, designers, developers, and evaluators.
6. All planning, design, development, and evaluation decisions should be in writing and available for open review by all team specialists.

Structured decomposition uses a graphic model to define a program. This modeling process may be applied to a variety of training programs, whether or not they are highly structured.

In summary, structured decomposition systematically breaks down a complex training program into its components parts. The process starts with a general or abstract description of the program, which serves as a working model from which successively more detailed portions of the program are conceived. Graphically, this process involves division of a cell representing the overall program into a number of more detailed cells, each symbolizing a major program activity within the parent cell. The extent of analysis within any step of structured decomposition is limited to a small number of program activities, each of which is further broken down in succeeding steps of the process. This approach ensures uniform systematic exposition of successive levels of detail.

Because the complex interrelationships among program activities do not lend themselves to clear and concise expression in prose, structured decomposition utilizes a graphic language designed to expose detail gradually in a controlled manner, to encourage conciseness and precision, to focus attention on the relationships between program activities, and to provide an analysis and design vocabulary for use by program planners, developers, and evaluators.

Structured decomposition is a methodology that can be used by planners, developers, and evaluators for

1. Thinking in a structured way about large and complex programs
2. Communicating planning and design concepts to developers and evaluators in clear and precise notation
3. Documenting program evolution, planning and design history, and related decisions
4. Working as a team with effective division and coordination of effort
5. Managing and guiding the development of a training program
6. Providing strategic concepts for evaluating the results of the planning, designing, and development process

From an adequately constructed decomposition of the program, it should be apparent what the purpose of the program is, what the specific program components and activities are, and what outcomes are expected to result from them.

BEGINNING THE EVALUATION PROCESS: USING THE DECOMPOSITION

From an examination of the decomposition of program activities and outcomes and before the collection of any empirical data, the evaluator often can suggest program modifications on logical grounds. Planners, developers, and evaluators can use the decomposition model to interpret the program's meaning and to bring all parties who have a stake in the program into agreement about its intents and purposes.

The heart of the decomposition is the instructional activities that make up the program. These instructional activities for purposes of this chapter will constitute well-specified units of instruction for which a behavioral outcome is expressed or implied. I will refer to these instructional units as *program transactions*. The evaluator, in particular, uses the decomposition to identify incongruities between program transactions and outcomes—that is, to spot small units of instruction that unrealistically are expected to produce large changes in behavior (e.g., a weekend workshop expected to change racial attitudes, a classroom lecture expected to make one proficient in program evaluation, an assigned reading expected to teach linear algebra). Many times these incongruities, unnoticed with lateral-flow decomposition techniques such as the Program Evaluation and Review Technique (PERT) (Cook, 1966), appear obvious with decomposition methodology. When incongruities are found on the decomposition model, program development is halted until logical relationships between transactions and outcomes are achieved either by redefining behavioral expectations or by revising the nature of the program transactions. Evaluation efforts may be temporarily shifted to redefinition of ambiguous parts of the program and construction of better, more effective transactions and more realistic outcomes.

Several concepts can assist the evaluator in determining the logic of the relationships mapped by the decomposition. These concepts serve to uncover mismatches between program transactions and expected outcomes. To affirm from the decomposition that logical relationships among transactions and outcomes are in evidence, the evaluator classifies each outcome as terminal or enabling and determines the fidelity of each transaction to terminal program outcomes. *Terminal outcomes* are behaviors expected of trainees at program completion; *enabling outcomes* are intervening behaviors prerequisite to subsequent transactions and the attainment of terminal outcomes. Here is how the process works.

Transactions whose outcomes closely approximate the behavioral outcomes expected of trainees at program completion are considered to have high fidelity. For this type of transaction successful completion of the transaction by trainees is expected to lead to a direct improvement in terminal behavior. The transaction may even require the participant to perform the same or similar behaviors that are expected at program completion. In contrast, transactions whose outcomes do not approximate the behaviors expected of trainees at program completion have low fidelity. Successful completion of this type of transaction is expected to lead to enabling behaviors that indirectly link the transaction to terminal outcomes through a more circuitous route.

Figure 7.4 contrasts three conditions of fidelity between program transaction and terminal outcome. In the first instance, the overlap between the behavior produced by the transaction and the type of performance expected at program completion is almost complete. Here, fidelity is high; one may logically expect that if the transaction is successfully completed, performance on the terminal behavior will improve. In the second instance, some fidelity is apparent, but the overlap is not nearly as great as

Figure 7.4 Degrees of fidelity between instructional transaction and terminal outcome.

in the first case. This transaction has medium fidelity. In the third example, only a small portion of the behavior produced by the transaction matches that which is expected at program completion, and thus the transaction has low fidelity with the terminal behavior.

Not surprisingly, high-fidelity transactions are linked to terminal outcomes by relatively few enabling behaviors. Their relationship to the behaviors expected at program completion is direct and uncomplicated by mediating processes.

In contrast lower-fidelity transactions must be connected to terminal outcomes via many mediating or enabling processes and clustered with other transactions before their impact on the terminal performance of program participants can be measured. This relationship is illustrated in Figure 7.5.

Note that at some point along the curve in Figure 7.5, the number of mediating processes required to link a low-fidelity transaction to a terminal behavior may be quite large, even exceeding available resources. This accounts for the curve's shape, moving upward gradually at first but more rapidly where transactions have little or no fidelity with terminal behaviors. Some transactions at extremely low levels of fidelity may not be

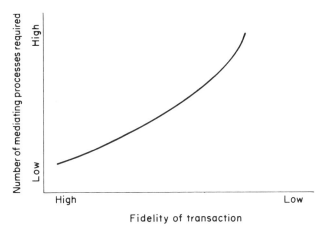

Fidelity of transaction

Figure 7.5 Generalized curve denoting the relative number of mediating processes required for transactions at different levels of fidelity.

cost-effective for this reason. However, both low *and* high-fidelity transactions are important ingredients in program composition, and developers should not favor one over the other without considering the purpose of each.

Typically, low-fidelity transactions comprise orienting or introductory activities, such as reading a chapter in a book, listening to the instructor lecture, or viewing a video cassette. Each by itself is likely to improve a terminal outcome—for example, repair a truck, learn algebra, appreciate the Hispanic culture—only slightly, if at all. Although the fidelity of these transactions to terminal outcomes may be low, they nevertheless may be prerequisite to a sequence of transactions and enabling behaviors that together comprise a significant and necessary portion of the training program. High-fidelity transactions, on the other hand, are directly related to terminal outcomes and may actually require program participants to perform all or a significant portion of the behaviors expected at completion of training. Lower-fidelity transactions commonly comprise more global, orienting, or introductory experiences that are prerequisite to higher-fidelity transactions that approximate the tasks for which training is being provided.

The concepts of high and low fidelity help the evaluator to determine gaps or mismatches between program intents and program transactions and between program transactions and program outcomes. Often planners and developers make "inferential leaps" by espousing certain objectives for training but failing to provide the resources or specifications by which to incorporate the required transactions into the training program at the appropriate level of fidelity. Or transactions can be mismatched to outcomes. For example, (a) low-fidelity transactions are sometimes expected to produce behaviors that approximate terminal outcomes, or (b) high-fidelity transactions are sometimes expected to produce enabling behaviors that may have little or no relation to terminal outcomes. Just the opposite should be apparent from the decomposition. In the second type of mismatch noted above, the cost-effectiveness of the match-up might be questioned. High-fidelity transactions usually are more costly to develop than low-fidelity transactions because their purpose is to produce terminal or performance-type outcomes; thus, a desired intervening or enabling behavior might be obtained in a more efficient and less expensive manner with a low-fidelity transaction. Such mismatches are exposed by decomposition diagrams, since transactions (shown as boxes) and outputs (shown as output arrows) are contiguous.

Table 7.1 illustrates the process of matching transactions and outcomes for maximum fidelity. The answers to this exercise are 4, 3, 2, and 1.

TABLE 7.1.
Matching Hypothetical Transactions and Outcomes for Maximum Fidelity

Choose the most appropriate outcome on the right that has the highest fidelity with each transaction on the left.

Transaction	*Outcome*
____Reading about a concept	1. Evaluation—that is, decision making, appropriately judging or selecting the concept in an ongoing setting
____Writing or completing exercises about the concept	2. Application—that is, using the concept in a situation different from the one in which it was learned
____Practicing the concept in a simulated environment	3. Comprehension—that is, translating the concept into different terms, summarizing it, organizing it differently
____Using the concept in a real-life (performance) setting	4. Knowledge—that is, recognition and recall of facts, defining terms, recalling names

BEHAVIORS, VARIABLES, AND COMPETENCIES

Many of the ambiguous findings of evaluation studies can be traced to poorly defined outcomes. Outcomes can be expressed not only as enabling and terminal behaviors but also as behaviors, variables, and competencies. It is important for evaluators as well as designers and developers of training programs to note the distinction among these concepts.

The term *behavior* involves description of an outcome at its most general level. At this level the meaning of an outcome can be conveyed without it being operationalized but simply by relating it to other behaviors with which we are already familiar. For instance, the outcomes identified in the right-hand column of Table 7.1 are examples of behaviors. These outcomes are defined simply in terms of related or associated concepts—for example, evaluation is defined in terms of decision making, judging, and selecting; knowledge in terms of recognizing, recalling, and defining. Because behaviors like these are described in such general terms, they must be tied to specific variables and competencies in order to be useful to the evaluation process. Variables and competencies, then, are derived from behaviors.

The word *variable* refers to the terms in which a particular behavior is to be observed and recorded. A variable specifies behavior by stating explicitly the way in which the behavior is to be measured. Variables redefine behaviors in terms of the operations that are necessary to observe and measure them. These operations express the behavioral concepts in the form of a measurement, which represents the level of differentiation at which the particular behavior can be reliably observed and distinguished from other behaviors.

Just as general behavioral concepts are used to derive variables, variables are used to determine the next level of behavioral description. *Competencies,* like variables, are characterized by a metric or scale. However, unlike variables, competencies include the specification of a desired quantity of behavior, which is referenced in the metric. Competencies identify a single level of proficiency, or a range of levels, determined through theoretical or empirical processes, at which the trainee is expected to perform. Unlike variables, competencies are either attained or not attained. Hence, it is the level of proficiency that is critical, not—as in the case of variables—simply the separation and differentiation of various degrees of behavior. The process of deriving competencies from behaviors and variables is depicted in Figure 7.6.

In preparing a decomposition model of a training program, it is important to note whether outcomes are expressed in terms of behaviors, variables, or competencies, and whether or not they can be quantified at the competency level.

In the decomposition of a program, the evaluator notes not only the conceptual precision with which outcomes can be translated into com-

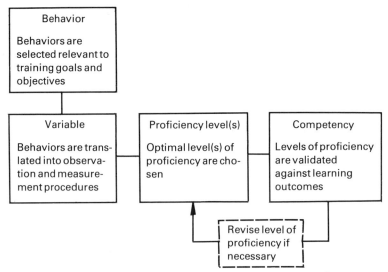

Figure 7.6 The developmental task of deriving competencies.

petencies but also changes in the descriptions of outcomes across levels of the decomposition. The description of outcomes on the decomposition is expected to represent a progression from behaviors at the more general levels of the decomposition to competencies at the more detailed levels.

In addition, low-fidelity transactions are expected to be linked to knowledge or comprehension-type outcomes and high-fidelity transactions to application or performance-type outcomes (Table 7.1). Knowledge outcomes often are the legitimate goals of low-fidelity transactions consisting of early training experiences; application outcomes, on the other hand, are the legitimate goals of high-fidelity transactions involving real-life tasks that the trainee is expected to perform at program completion. These application or performance outcomes provide the basis for summative evaluations of the trainee at program completion.

DECOMPOSITION AND EVALUATION AS A TEAM EFFORT

The decomposition becomes a working document for project personnel to use in discussing the program. It is not intended to be impervious to change and critical assessment. On the contrary, it is meant to serve as an initial definition of the training program and a vehicle by which to reconcile differing viewpoints held by members of the staff. Upon completion of the design phase, members of the team meet and each works through details of the decomposed model, usually prepared by the evaluator but reviewed by team members during development. Here is where the evaluator works as logician and systems analyst, contributing to the work of planners by probing, questioning, and then mapping the evolving conceptual structure of the program.

It is not unusual at staff meetings to learn that each member of the development team has a slightly different interpretation of what the training program is supposed to accomplish. These differences often persist throughout the development phase and into program evaluation, complicating implementation and evaluation decisions. One purpose of the decomposition model is to identify and correct misconceptions among team members before development begins and to resolve inconsistencies and clarify ambiguities that may remain after planning is completed. The decomposition at this stage has four distinct effects:

1. Because its development is a team effort, it forces staff to use a common vocabulary and mode of expression in describing the program.

2. It exposes differing and sometimes contradictory viewpoints of the

program. It is not uncommon—and is in fact healthy at this stage—to have various team members develop competing decomposition models from which a final version is selected.

3. The decomposition model of the program serves as a framework in which to identify mismatches between transactions and intended outcomes (i.e., inferential leaps overlooked in earlier planning efforts). Here logical relationships between transactions and outcomes are a prime consideration.

4. The decomposition model serves as a framework for examining the nature of the outcomes intended. Outcomes that are not stated as operational behaviors are replaced by more conceptually precise and quantifiable outcomes, and if possible, expressed as competencies to be exhibited by trainees, complete with required proficiency levels. Also, the description of outcomes is closely examined to assure that those stated as behaviors at the more general levels of the decomposition are represented as competencies at the more detailed levels of the decomposition.

A SYSTEMS-ORIENTED APPROACH

After revisions in the program structure are made from the initial decomposition, the empirical work of the evaluator begins. This work entails the selection of transactions and groups of transactions from the structured decomposition of the program completed during the planning and design phases. This begins the evaluator's work as quantifier of activities and outcomes for the purpose of providing process and outcome data. A model of the evaluator's task during the planning, development, and evaluation phases is presented in Figure 7.7.[4]

Figure 7.7 represents the evaluator's work in six stages. The first stage, assessing client information needs, involves reviewing program proposals and related documents and interviewing and questioning planners, designers, and developers about the program's objectives and purposes. Here, the evaluator's work is much like that of a logician, examining via nonempirical methods the completeness, accuracy, and internal consistency of program content and structure as recorded by program planning documents and expressed by program personnel. From these data the evaluator, together with planners, designers, and developers, creates a structured decomposition model of the intended training (Stage II)—a model that is continually revised to increase the clarity of training con-

---

[4] The model presented here is intended as a heuristic device to help the evaluator conceptualize his or her functions across the planning, development, and evaluation stages of a project. It is not intended as a sequence of steps that represents the precise way in which an evaluation is to be performed.

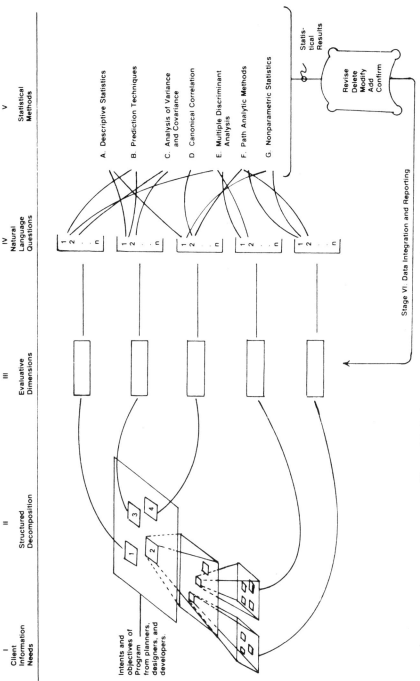

I
Client
Information
Needs

II
Structured
Decomposition

III
Evaluative
Dimensions

IV
Natural
Language
Questions

V
Statistical
Methods

A. Descriptive Statistics

B. Prediction Techniques

C. Analysis of Variance
   and Covariance

D Canonical Correlation

E. Multiple Discriminant
   Analysis

F. Path Analytic Methods

G. Nonparametric Statistics

Statis-
tical
Results

Revise
Delete
Modify
Add
Confirm

Intents and
objectives of
Program
from planners,
designers, and
developers.

Stage VI. Data Integration and Reporting

Figure 7.7 A six-stage model for program evaluation.

cepts, to eliminate inferential leaps, and to resolve differences in viewpoint that may exist among members of the development team. This begins the evaluator's work as systems analyst, setting forth with systems methodology the content and structure of the program delineated in Stage I.

The second stage is the decomposition itself. This stage becomes the foundation for all subsequent activities of the evaluator. Until the structured decomposition model of the training program is completed, the evaluator's work is mostly qualitative and nonempirical in nature. However, completion of the decomposition model is a cue to the evaluator to begin the quantitative empirical process of assessing the intended impact of the training and its components. The decomposition serves as a reference for the evaluator as he begins synthesizing "evaluative dimensions."

The evaluator arrives at the evaluative dimensions by working through the parts of the decomposed model. The first and most general part can be referred to as the subsystem diagram. Subsystems are referenced on the decomposition model as the first diagram after an initial single box description of the program has been written. Subsystems represent the initial breakdown of the global program into its primary components. Figure 7.8 illustrates three subsystems of a program to train regular classroom teachers in the practice of mainstreaming.[5] This decomposition diagram provides an example of three general transactions, each representing a subsystem of the program. Detailing of these subsystems reveals greater specificity of each of the three instructional activities identified and the outcomes they are expected to produce. These detail diagrams translate general outcomes at higher levels into more specific outcomes at lower levels. This model, edited for purposes of this chapter, is shown here without the benefit of still further detail.

The most specific part in a structured decomposition model is the transaction. Transactions represent activities, or boxes, within diagrams. They are always interrelated by inputs, controls, and outputs both within and between diagrams at successive levels of detail. Since a diagram contains a set of homogeneous transactions at a single level of detail, the purposes of these transactions can be easily grouped under a single generic classification. This generic purpose, or dimension, may be defined with the title that defines the diagram itself. For example, in Figure 7.8, there are three subsytems and, therefore, three evaluative dimensions:

[5] Mainstreaming is the practice of integrating cognitively, emotionally, and physically handicapped school children into regular classrooms. This practice is now mandated by law. For an example related to training in the military, see SofTech, Inc., *Task 3 Report: The Army Training and Evaluation System* (Item No. 0002AC). Waltham, Massachusetts: SofTech, Inc., 1976.

"instill values and attitudes," "teach human relations," and "provide teaching strategies"—which are decomposed into still more specific evaluation dimensions. Evaluative dimensions help the evaluator reduce the important concepts in a large and complex training program to a manageable number that capture the full flavor of the program. Nothing is lost in the formation of evaluative dimensions, since smaller, more detailed portions of the program are tucked within more general dimensions that can be selected for evaluation when further levels of detail are not desired.

A priori formulation of evaluative dimensions is critical to the meaningful evaluation of training. The conceptualization of these dimensions provides the following advantages:

1. In projects containing voluminous data of varying importance, evaluative dimensions can focus activities and identify data that are most relevant to the questions being asked. Evaluative dimensions provide criteria for setting priorities among the data and ensure that evaluation activities will not get bogged down in irrelevant detail. By guiding the evaluation effort, these dimensions bring a conceptual handle and framework to program intents and objectives.

2. The construction of evaluative dimensions also ensures that subsequent evaluation activities will be congruent with the information needs of the client organization. To be effective, evaluative dimensions must reflect what the client wants to know. Therefore, the development of evaluative dimensions is a critical component of the overall evaluation, because such dimensions link the client's priorities to the available data in a meaningful manner. In short, these dimensions ensure that the most relevant questions will be answered.

To be sure that these dimensions reflect appropriate informational needs and to obtain critical feedback on the evaluation plan, the evaluator submits the evaluative dimensions to the development team before collecting and analyzing data. This interaction can and often does yield conceptual insights about what sponsoring agencies want to know about the training program, thus allowing the evaluator to become more in tune with sponsor intents and objectives for applying the evaluation findings.

Since evaluative dimensions necessarily group transactions into a single, more parsimonious configuration, evaluative dimensions often contain slices of the training structure that can be meaningfully evaluated. Thus, in Stage IV (Figure 7.7), the evaluator uses the evaluative dimensions to compose natural-language questions (questions expressed in everyday, common-sense terms) that can provide practical information to those who will use the evaluation results. Natural-language questions are user-oriented, geared to those who must act on the results of the evalua-

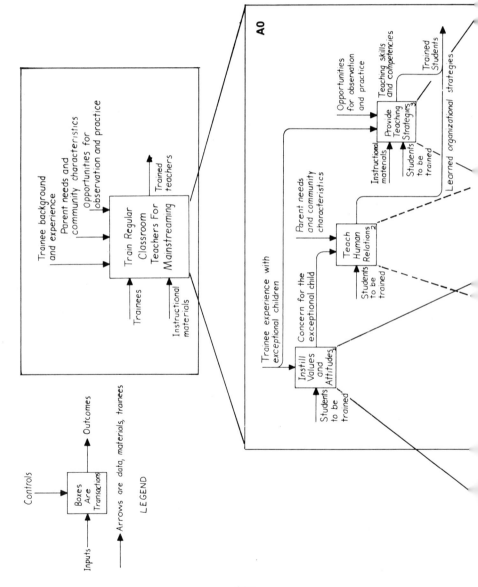

226

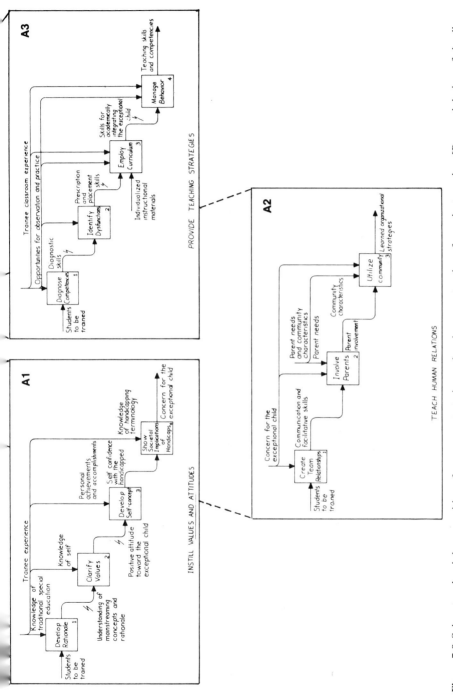

Figure 7.8 Subsystem level decomposition of a program to train regular classroom teachers for mainstreaming. [Prepared during a federally funded program to train preservice teachers to teach handicapped children in a traditional classroom.]

227

tion. They should have strong intuitive appeal to those who will implement and revise the training and a direct bearing on decisions that will be made in subsequent applications of the training program. The posing of natural-language questions with program staff constitutes the evaluator's role as a quantifier of activities and outcomes.

After constructing and ordering natural-language questions from evaluative dimensions, the evaluator chooses in Stage V one or more statistical methods to answer these questions. Here is where the evaluator fulfills his role as analyzer of data. The methods employed at this stage range from descriptive statistics, which might identify trends using simple graphs, to more sophisticated techniques, which might pinpoint causal relationships between specific transactions and intended outcomes or differences between alternative versions of the same transaction. The evaluator need not have a thorough understanding of the internal workings of many of the statistical tools he uses, but does need to have knowledge of the types of questions to which they apply and the training to accurately interpret their results. Many sophisticated techniques employing advanced mathematics that were inaccessible to the evaluator in the past can now be implemented with computer programs.

The seven statistical methods indicated in Stage V are groupings or sets of procedures—as opposed to individual procedures—that can be applied to a wide variety of natural-language questions. As the connections between Stages IV and V indicate, more than one statistical technique can, and whenever possible should, be applied to each natural-language question to cross-validate the findings relevant to that question. This procedure guarantees convergent validation of any conclusions drawn and enhances the credibility of the evaluator's report.

A. *Descriptive Statistics.* This group includes measures of central tendency and variability (mean, standard deviation, estimates of variance, and various graphing techniques) that can reveal trends in the behavior of program participants. A question that might be addressed by this group of statistics is, Does use of the prescribed training materials vary by instructors?

B. *Prediction Techniques.* This grouping consists of single and multiple regression techniques. These are used to show the relationship between variables. For example, is an instructor's use of program materials associated with the amount of experience in using similar materials? That is, is degree of use predictable on the basis of length of experience with similar materials?

C. *Analysis of Variance and Covariance.* This grouping consists of single and multiple classification comparisons. These techniques permit statistical analyses of the interactions between any two or more variables.

For example, is degree of implementation of program materials highest when the instructor is familiar with the materials and is teaching a small number of students, and lowest when these conditions are reversed?

D. *Canonical Correlation.* This technique is the generalization of multiple regression to any number of dependent and independent variables. It identifies common variance in any two sets of variables and is used to study the underlying relations between these variables. Its most common applications have been to input–output analyses and cost-benefit analysis. For example, input variables might be (*a*) degree of student preparation; (*b*) degree of student motivation; and (*c*) extent to which students use prescribed materials; and output variables might involve various measures of trainee performance, such as attitudes and cognitive understandings. Canonical correlations can identify various relationships between the two sets of variables and specify the contribution of each variable to the overall relationship.

E. *Discriminant Analysis.* This technique is similar to regression analysis. It can be used to identify those variables that are most critical to the performance of trainees assigned to groups—for example, on the basis of whether or not the trainee attained the desired level of proficiency. It can be effectively used to determine what variables best discriminate groups of trainees on variables such as attitude, knowledge, and ability to execute specific behaviors. Solutions could indicate, for example, the personality, prior training, attitude, and experience variables that account for group differences.

F. *Path Analysis.* This technique is used to hypothesize and test relationships among selected variables. It is applied primarily to determine causal relationships among variables that are hypothesized on the basis of some theory of the interrelationships among program variables. For example, it might be hypothesized that the extent to which a trainee learns specific behaviors is dictated by previous experience and to a lesser degree by attitudes and cognitive understandings. Path analysis can indicate whether such relationships between variables and outcomes are causal or spurious and whether some relationships are created by intervening or moderating variables.

G. *Nonparametric Statistics.* This grouping includes techniques such as chi-square (χ^2) and the sign test, which are employed when data fail to meet the assumptions required by the parametric methods already described.[6]

The five foregoing stages tie available data to client information needs

---

[6] All of these techniques are treated in most intermediate statistics texts in the social and behavioral sciences. Their relationship to the data derived from decomposition models are further described in various working papers by the author to be incorporated in Borich, G.,

in a logically consistent manner. This model maximizes the information yield of an evaluative study, since each stage is built upon the preceding stage and all partners in the development process participate in formulating the evaluative dimensions and natural-language questions from which the data collection is planned. Involvment of the development team at various stages of program implementation ensures that evaluation activities will address relevant issues and provide additional data that may have been overlooked in earlier formulations of the program.

In Stage VI, the evaluator reports conclusions about each evaluative dimension based on results of the statistical analysis. As noted by the feedback loop in Figure 7.7, conclusions are posed in terms of the original evaluative dimensions, thereby giving statistical results continuity and an intuitive, common-sense appeal. The report is organized according to the evaluative dimensions (major headings) and the natural-language questions (minor headings). Here the evaluator completes his role as reporter of program effects.

The evaluator's final task is to make recommendations to the program development team concerning the efficiency of the various training components. The answers to natural-language questions often have implications for specific transactions. Consequently, evaluator recommendations are made at the transaction level whenever data permit. These recommendations, which are directed to the development team, reference specific aspects of the training program for which data have been collected. They advise developers to revise, delete, modify, add, or maintain given subsystems and transactions. Developers then proceed with the program changes for which personnel and fiscal resources are available. Finally, the structured decomposition model is revised to reflect the changes that are made to communicate the training program accurately in final form to all those who have a stake in it.

CONCLUSION

This chapter has attempted to provide an integrated approach to program planning, development, and evaluation. The major strengths of this approach lies in its stance with regard to how training programs should be planned, and its attempt to apply technical innovations from other disciplines. The approach represents an excursion into "uncharted territory" and as such will be open to revision and refinement as weaknesses evidence themselves through applications in a variety of contexts.

---

and Jemelka, R. *A systems approach to planning and evaluation.* New York: Academic Press, in preparation.

Application of this approach requires open-mindedness and nondefensiveness on the part of the program developer or administrator who has ultimate responsibility for the planning, design, development, and evaluation of an instructional program. If the developer has inflexibly decided on program composition and "already knows" what the evaluation results will be, this would not be the approach of choice. Nor should this approach be used if there is not a commitment to developing a thorough, well-planned program to meet some established instructional need. If, on the other hand, the developer wants to determine optimal program composition and is willing to use negative evaluation results to revise, delete, modify, or add to program components to achieve ultimate program success, the approach is heartily recommended.

ACKNOWLEDGMENTS

The author would like to thank the staff of SofTech, Inc. in Waltham, Massachusetts—particularly John Brackett and Reuben Jones—for their support in developing many of the ideas presented in this chapter during a joint DARPA–TRADOC project. The author would also like to thank Ron Jemelka for contributing some of his own ideas to this chapter.

REFERENCES

Bloom, B. S. (Ed.). *Taxonomy of educational objectives: The classification of educational goals. Handbook 1. Cognitive domain.* New York: David McKay, 1956.

Borich, G. D. A state of the art assessment of educational evaluation. In H. F. O'Neil, Jr. (Ed.), *State of the art assessment of computer-based instruction.* New York: Academic Press, in press.

Borich, G. D., & Jemelka, R. *A systems approach to program planning and evaluation.* New York: Academic Press, in preparation.

Cook, D. L. *Program evaluation and review technique: Applications in education.* Washington: U.S. Government Printing Office, 1966.

Dick, W., & Carey, L. *The systematic design of instruction.* Glenview, Ill.: Scott, Foresman, and Co., 1978.

IPISP. *Interservice Procedures for Instructional System Development.* Ft. Monroe, Va. U.S. Army Training and Doctrine Command, Pamphlet 350-30, August, 1975.

Kaufman, R. A. *Educational system planning.* Englewood Cliffs, N.J.: Prentice-Hall, 1972.

Provus, M. M. *Discrepancy evaluation for educational program improvement and assessment.* Berkeley, Calif.: McCutchan, 1971.

Ross, D. T. Structured analysis (SA): A language for communicating ideas. *IEEE Transactions on Software Engineering,* January 1977, *SE-3* (1), 16–34.

Ross, D. T., & Schoman, K. E. Structured analysis for requirements definition. *IEEE Transactions on Software Engineering,* January 1977, *SE-3* (1), 6–15.

Schoman, K. E. *Interface of SADT and PERT (and Mark III).* Waltham, Mass.: SofTech, Inc., 1977.

SofTech, Inc., *Task 3 report: The Army training and evaluation system.* (Item No. 0002 AC). Waltham, Mass.: SofTech, Inc., 1976.

Stufflebeam, D. I., Foley, W. J., Gephart, W. J., Guba, E. G., Hammond, R. I., Merriman, H. O., & Provus, M. M. *Educational evaluation and decision making.* Itasca, Ill.: Peacock, 1971.

8

A Cost-Effectiveness Specification[1]

ROBERT J. SEIDEL and
HAROLD WAGNER

In this chapter we will describe our recent effort to develop a cost-effectiveness specification for the Defense Advanced Research Projects Agency. Following a brief description of the project's background, we will discuss the iterative approach used to develop, evaluate, and refine the specifications.

The purpose of our project was to develop and implement a set of procedures that would lead to an evaluation methodology for computer-based training. The specific goal was to provide a set of standard tools to evaluate the cost-effectiveness of such computer-based training systems. The purpose of the cost-effectiveness specification was to facilitate the purchase, monitoring, and evaluation of computer-based training systems. The format of a specification was chosen because it provides a precise and detailed set of items and parameters to use for assessment purposes. It provides a standardized structure through which training system costs can be derived and communicated. Although it was designed with a military training focus, the specification is oriented toward an instruction (including civilian) that is administered, aided, or managed by computer. The only restrictions on its generality are some of the formal guidelines and assumptions (e.g., inflation factors, personnel cost burdens) that were derived from Department of Defense doctrine.

[1] Preparation of this chapter was supported in part by the Defense Advanced Research Projects Agency under contract number MDA903-76C-0210. Views and conclusions contained in this document are those of the authors and should not be interpreted as necessarily representing the official policies, either expressed or implied, of the Defense Advanced Research Projects Agency or of the United States government.

PROCEDURES FOR INSTRUCTIONAL
SYSTEMS DEVELOPMENT

233

Copyright © 1979 by Academic Press, Inc.
All rights of reproduction in any form reserved.
ISBN 0-12-526660-X

BACKGROUND

Computer-based training has been implemented in order to provide solutions to training problems such as limited financial resources, a student population of heterogeneous abilities, and the demand for increasing skills. Prior to any wide-scale implementation of computer-based training, a need must be met to provide specifications for appropriate evaluation designs and tools. Through the use of a common framework for evaluation, it should be possible to make more meaningful and efficient use of resources for evaluating advanced technology instructional systems.

Cost-effectiveness methods constitute one set of evaluative techniques. Application of these methods to the evaluation of training technology is fraught with conceptual and methodological difficulties. These difficulties were highlighted in a recent computer-based instruction conference. Scanlon (1974) asserted—with no argument from the other participants— that virtually no data exist on the cost-effectiveness of computer-based instruction. He tentatively suggested that adding such costs would be offset by lowered clerical and associated staff requirements. However, he was unaware ". . . of any literature which might support or refute . . ." this suggestion. The lack of standardized costing procedures and accepted effectiveness criteria contributes to this lack of cost-effectiveness data.

Two other statements emphasize the difficulties in this area.

> Cost figures for military instructional expenditure are virtually impossible to obtain . . . a lack of uniformity of cost recording practices accounts at least partly for this difficulty as far as the Department of the Army Schools are concerned [Kopstein & Seidel, 1967, p. 8].

> During the past year's study, it became evident that course level costing data presently available are frequently incomplete and inconsistent [Greenberg, 1977, p. 12].

The importance of these two quotes is that they came from two different periods of time. The first one is from a paper written in 1967 by Kopstein and Seidel. The second quote came from a paper written by Greenberg (1977) 10 years later, which discussed efforts by the Department of Defense to increase training efficiency. The point is that there was and still is interest in the establishment of costing standards within and across the services.

A simple number purporting to be a cost-effectiveness ratio hides more than it reveals about the overall value of an educational program. This is because the requirements of a program for resources are multidimensional and time-variant; the same may be said for indicators of effectiveness.

The views of economists are important in this area. They can show how training can be measured in economic terms as a production function and what relationships there are between inputs and outputs that are useful in defining instructional productivity. However, the value of their contribution will depend on the clarity with which these terms can be defined operationally.

Any cost-effectiveness analysis of instruction must clarify the following parameters at least: development costs, operating costs, cumulative costs of hardware–software and course materials, cost per hour for development and for student access to materials, minimum and maximum number of students served by the delivery system.

The above factors must all be considered in the analysis of conventional, computer-based, or any other instructional delivery system. Other factors must also be considered, such as costs for integrating computer-based instruction into an existing training installation, skill levels required to implement the system, time distribution of staff and students in alternative environments, effects on attrition (dropout) rates, space requirements, effects on other resource requirements.

On the effectiveness side, measures and criteria must be clarified: long- versus short-term criteria, end-of-course versus on-the-job requirements, appropriate achievement data. Some of these items are currently being addressed in the Computerized Training System project by the Army and in the Advanced Instructional System by the Air Force (Longo, Gatldis, & Whitehouse, 1974; Yasutake, 1974). These efforts highlight the need for developing a common language and descriptive conventions.

To accomplish the measurement of the above cost-and-effectiveness parameters, an endeavor to develop a cost-effectiveness specification must design a coherent data structure, specify clear-cut collection procedures, and provide a feedback capability for modifying the approach as required.

The complexity of the problem was noted by Barro and Levien (1972) in their appraisal of the computer as an emerging technology for education and training. They stressed the fact that cost-effectiveness of instructional computing would vary by application and thus by institutions having differing applications requirements and different instructional alternatives. Therefore, they concluded that it would be inappropriate to evaluate the cost-effectiveness of instructional computer use on a national basis. We would simply stress that their conclusion was due, at least in part, to not having a common or clean data base to attempt any project, program, or regional—much less national—cost-effectiveness evaluation. Specifications are thus needed for cost-effectiveness parameters that can be applied to the evaluation of computer-based training. It was this need that our effort attempted to meet.

APPROACH

Because of the lack of commonalities in training–evaluation nomenclature, evaluation methods and criteria, and cost-effectiveness parameters in the armed services, it was decided to separate cost-effectiveness into two components for the feasibility of attacking the problem. Also, we focused our study on computer-based training within a formal school environment rather than in a field unit. This was to lessen our ambiguity regarding the costs of the system when it was being used for training purposes—a distinction that is often blurred in an operational field unit.

Costing

The first step was to perform a search of the literature with respect to the state of the art in cost-effectiveness evaluation of computer-based training systems, and currently available tools in economics, accounting, management, and education that might be adapted. The information gathered in this step permitted us to determine the magnitude of the effort required to provide costing specifications.

The next step was to select experts in the fields that impinge on the study of training cost-effectiveness (i.e., economics, accounting, training program auditing, instructional computing) to assist us in our project. One criterion for selection was experience in using cost-effectiveness methods within the Department of Defense training community. Thus, we decided to hold a working "mini-conference" of such costing experts in order to establish agreed-upon criteria and methods for measuring costs across the services.

As a result of our review, we focused on a limited number of models that might be appropriate for military costing. Our review focused on five such costing approaches. One of these is already in computerized form currently being refined by Braby, Henry, Parrish, & Swope (1975) at the Training Analysis and Evaluation Group, U.S. Navy, Orlando, Florida. Johnson and Neal, and their associates at the Training and Doctrine Command Systems Analysis Activity, were chosen to participate in our conference and represent the Army's approach in their Cost and Training Effectiveness Analysis (TRASANA Handbook, 1976). This model provides the cost-effectiveness requirements for all new Army training systems. A second Army approach toward cost-effectiveness in advanced training technology is represented in a model developed by Wilkinson (1973) of the University of Georgia, which is being adapted by the Army's Computerized Training System project at Ft. Eustis and Ft. Gordon (Operational Test Plan, 1975). The Air Force approach is typified by the

Method of Designing Instructional Alternatives (MODIA) Cost Model developed by Hess and Kantar (1976) of the Rand Corporation (see also Carpenter-Huffman, 1977a, 1977b, 1977c).

A working mini-conference of costing experts (representatives of the groups cited above) was held, the results of which were synthesized into a preliminary costing model. A report describing this costing model was then completed (Seidel, Wagner, & Kastner, 1976).

This preliminary design for a costing specification was distributed to the consultants[2] who contributed to its development. They were asked to critique and refine the costing specification before it was field-tested. A second mini-conference with the costing experts was then held to discuss their findings and recommendations. Much effort was spent during these two conferences just to agree upon common terminology or data structure. We felt justified in separating cost from effectiveness, since much ambiguity was eliminated before we attempted the effectiveness model.

Following the second mini-conference, the costing specification was refined. The classification scheme and data structure derived from the second mini-conference was termed a Training Cost Breakdown Structure. The use of a cost breakdown structure emerged from the field of weapon systems procurement. This type of structure permits one to allocate costs to the functional components of a system throughout its life cycle. Although we could not directly adopt a specific cost breakdown structure, we were able to adapt and tailor this concept to our needs. The structure included in the refined specification is reported in Seidel, Wagner, & Hargan (1976). Next, it was presented to several members of the staff at the Air Training Command (Randolph Air Force Base) for review.[3] We also applied this specification at that time within the Human Resources Research Organization (HumRRO) to a computer-based train-

---

[2] A group of experts in costing of training systems provided the authors with valuable guidance and information that are incorporated in this specification. Opinions in this chapter do not necessarily represent those of our consultants: Richard Braby, Training Analysis and Evaluation Group, U.S. Navy, Orlando, Florida; Charles Gant, Air Force Human Resources Laboratory, Lowry Air Force Base, Colorado; John Germas, Army Research Institute, Arlington, Virginia; Ronald Hess, Rand Corporation, Washington, D.C.; Douglas Johnson, TRADOC Systems Analysis Activity, U.S. Army, White Sands, New Mexico; William Swope, Training Analysis and Evlauation Group, U.S. Navy, Orlando, Florida; Stuart Wells, San Jose State University, California; and Gene Wilkinson, University of Georgia.

[3] The assistance of J. B. Gilbreath, Gary Hoff, Perry Main, Donald Meyers, L. C. Scott, and Wayne Shore was greatly appreciated. The revised specification does not necessarily reflect their views.

ing system being developed for the United States Postal Service (Wagner, Trexler, Hillelsohn, & Seidel, 1978).

As a result of this review and HumRRO application, substantial changes were made in the costing specification. For example, much more emphasis was placed on identifying specific instructional preparation costs than had been the case. The revised data structure (Training Cost Breakdown Structure) to be used in the cost-effectiveness specification is shown in Appendix 1. In addition, there was a considerable change in the format of the documents that make up the specification (e.g., personnel cost worksheets were added to aid in calculating these costs).

Effectiveness

In the next stage of our project we studied the effectiveness dimensions to be covered by the specification. A literature review was performed to identify and categorize the dimensions and measures that are appropriate for evaluating the effectiveness of training programs. As a result of this review, HumRRO staff prepared procedures for classifying and reporting effectiveness data.

The term *training effectiveness* refers to the specific effects that training has on the students who receive instruction. These effects are usually measured in terms of the time it took students to reach given training goals–objectives and/or according to the levels of achievement reached. Training effectiveness data should be collected to determine the degree to which a training course or system achieves its established goals. This can be done only by evaluating the graduates of the training program.

In the ideal case, the effectiveness of a training program should be evaluated from the viewpoint of long-term as well as short-term criteria. However, many intervening factors and events, as well as attitude changes, can take place and effect the long-term measures, totally unrelated to the course of instruction. Since it is usually impractical to account for these intervening factors, the validity of long-term measures decreases the longer these measures are separated in time from the training that is being evaluated. Therefore, the training effectiveness of a course should be assessed immediately upon completion of that course. Tests administered at the time are the most direct and relatively unconfounded measures of training effectiveness.

End-of-course measures to be used for evaluating training effectiveness are defined and presented in Appendix 2. In addition, procedures and forms were developed and included in the specification to record and summarize within-course effectiveness data. These formats and guidance were then integrated with the refined costing specification. An outline of the resulting specification follows.

Cost-Effectiveness Specification

The approach in using this specification involves accumulating cost-effectiveness data during each phase of a computer-based training system's life cycle. The cost-effectiveness specification is divided into three volumes, each representing a different phase of the life cycle. These life cycle phases are *development, procurement,* and *operation and maintenance*. The three phases are of variable lengths depending upon each specific system. Although the three phases in fact may overlap, for purposes of consistent calculation we assumed that they occur sequentially. The development phase can take up to 6 years, the procurement phase 1 year, and the operation and maintenance phase 8 years. Although procurement can take more then 1 year, we assumed that all procurement activities occur within the year following development of a tested prototype system. In this way, we could assume a relatively instantaneous implementation of systems as they entered the operation and maintenance phase. By not showing the more realistic, phased approach of procurement, we felt that it would be easier to identify clearly the operational costs of the systems (especially if more than one copy of the system was involved). Definitions related to the phases follow.

Development-phase activities are related to the design and production of a tested, prototype computer-based training system. Development-phase activities include applied research, engineering design, analysis, development, test, evaluation, and management related to a specific computer-based training system.

Procurement-phase activities are related to the production, purchase, and installation of the operational computer-based training system. Included in these activities are fabrication, communication, reproduction, packaging and shipping, instructional preparation, etc. Procurement activities are necessary to transform or copy the tested, prototype system into a fully operational system consisting of the hardware, software, facilities, training, and support necessary to initiate operations.

Operation-and-maintenance-phase activities are related to the daily operation and maintenance of the computer-based training system over its projected life after its official acceptance. Operation and maintenance activities include replacement training for site personnel, administration, instructional delivery, etc.

In each phase, **one** individual should be given the responsibility for gathering the data and performing the analysis required by the specification. This is the only approach that permits data collection consistent with the guidance and formats provided in the specification.

Each volume of the specification (Seidel & Wagner, 1977) is composed of several parts. These will now be listed and described.

- *Part A. System Description.* A form is presented in which individuals who use the specification are to be identified, and general characteristics of the computer-based training system are to be described.
- *Part B. General Costing Assumptions and Definitions.* A discussion of the assumptions that underlie the costing approach taken in the specification is presented. In addition, definitions of terms and guidelines related to costing are provided.
- *Part C. Computer-based Training System Elements: Definitions and Costs.* Costing information is to be entered for each element of the computer-based training system. The elements are categorized and hierarchically arranged in a training cost breakdown structure. Definitions of all system elements are provided with examples of how these items are to be costed. To assist the user in identifying personnel costs, personnel cost worksheets accompany this part of the specification.
- *Part D. Training Cost Breakdown Structure.* In this part of the specification, the training cost breakdown structure is used for entering summary cost data. In Volumes I and III, the training cost breakdown structure is presented in matrix form so that yearly costs can be specified. (In the procurement phase, Volume II, all costs are presented as having been spent in 1 year.)
- *Part E. Training Effectiveness Assumptions and Definitions.* Guidance, definitions, and procedures are provided by which the effectiveness of the computer-based training system can be measured. A general discussion of evaluation and effectiveness is followed by definitions of terms. Effectiveness measures are described and procedures recommended for acquiring this information.
- *Part F. Within-course Training Effectiveness Data.* Instructions and recording forms are provided for entering training effectiveness data for each major course section. Additional forms are provided for weighting and summarizing these data for the entire course. Such summary data are **not** to be used in evaluating the cost-effectiveness of the system unless end-of-course information is unavailable.
- *Part G. End-of-course Training Effectiveness Data.* Instructions and recording forms are provided for entering data on training effectiveness for the course as a whole.

Cost-Effectiveness Analysis

The last accomplishment in our effort to create and apply the specification was the development of guidance on performing the cost-effectiveness analysis. Guidance is provided on how to use the data to calculate and interpret the cost-effectiveness ratios and other indexes by which to evaluate and compare alternative training systems. This guidance is found in the following two sections of the specification:

• *Part H. Cost-Effectiveness Analysis Guidance.* The approach to be taken in analyzing the cost-effectiveness of computer-based training systems is described. The assumptions that underlie this approach are discussed and general guidance is presented for interpreting and applying the findings.

• *Part I. Cost-Effectiveness Analysis Calculations.* Instructions and worksheets are provided for calculating the cost-effectiveness ratios that can be used to evaluate a computer-based training system.

The examples that follow are formulas for two efficiency indexes that are provided in the cost-effectiveness specification. These indexes are appropriate for evaluating the cost-effectiveness of computer-based training systems provided that *graduation* signifies attainment of the training requirements established as effectiveness criteria.

EXAMPLES

$$(1) \text{ Graduation cost} = \frac{\text{Total operation and maintenance costs}}{\text{Total number of graduates}}$$

This index provides the ratio of total dollars spent to produce **one** graduate of the course(s) supported by the system.

$$(2) \text{ Hourly cost of instruction} = \frac{\text{Total operation and maintenance costs}}{\text{Total number of instructional hours}}$$

This index provides the ratio of total dollars spent for each student hour in the course(s) supported by the system.

The first index is a good measure of productivity, since it takes attrition into consideration, through distribution of all costs to only those who graduate. With the second index, it is still necessary to know the number of graduates before there can be a meaningful evaluation of training system effectiveness. In a recent report by the Department of Defense on the efficiency and effectiveness of military training (Military Manpower Training Report, 1977), there is a considered and detailed discussion of the appropriate effectiveness or efficiency measures to use when evaluating military training. One of the measures that is suggested in this report is the cost per graduate. If there are established criteria for graduation, then the number of graduates provides a useful gauge of training output. To the extent that established graduation criteria actually measure training effectiveness, then the costs required to produce that graduate can be used as a measure of training efficiency.

If cost-effectiveness indexes are to be calculated during the development phase, it should be clearly specified that each index is **projected** based upon **estimated** costs, graduates, and/or instructional hours. Comparative cost-effectiveness analysis can be validly performed only when the training systems being compared are in their operation-and-maintenance phase. However, since decisions are often required in earlier stages, projected cost-effectiveness analyses are performed during the development phase. These projections should occur when the prototype system has reached its operational test stage. At that time, the Operation and Maintenance Volume (III) can be used for entering data and making computations. It should be noted that such projections are often erroneous, since the hardware–software base of the system is still undergoing validation and debugging. Training effectiveness data, therefore, can be unduly influenced during the development phase by factors that would not be present in the operational system.

Yet, no matter when comparisons are made of alternative training systems, or of media within a course, cost-effectiveness evaluation is meaningful only if training objectives, content, testing conditions, and criteria are equivalent. The effectiveness of a computer-based training system can be attributed to its instructional technology only if the effectiveness measures are tied to those portions of the course that are supported by this technology. Otherwise, no conclusions can be drawn regarding the cost-effectiveness of that technology.

The decision maker needs to calculate the cost-effectiveness ratio of a system by (a) fixing operating costs and evaluating the system on its training effectiveness (e.g., achievement scores, number of objectives mastered, etc.); **or** (b) fixing level of effectiveness and evaluating the system on how much it costs to attain this level in an operational environment. If both costs and effectiveness levels are allowed to vary together, difficulties arise in determining the value of any additional benefits (Doughty, Stern, & Thompson, 1976).

The decision maker also needs to establish *criteria* for evaluating the cost-effectiveness of a system. These criteria should be based on the training requirements imposed on the system. In setting the criteria, the decision maker should determine the relative importance of each measure in assessing the overall effectiveness of the training system. In this way, decisions can be based on those factors that are "relevant" to the needs for which the system was designed. The cost-effectiveness of a computer-based system may also be determined by its relative efficiency in aiding in the development and dissemination of primary and auxiliary training materials. This is perfectly acceptable as long as it is clear to the decision maker that these evaluation criteria are to be applied independent of whether or not the system is used for training. Many computer-managed instruction systems, for example, could be evaluated solely in terms of their relative adequacy for developing materials, scheduling equipment usage, and record keeping. However, if training **effectiveness** is of primary importance, such efficiency indexes should not be substituted for achievement measures.

FINDINGS

A need exists· to verify the costing and effectiveness dimensions and criteria employed in the current specification (as described above) by applying it at various computer-based training sites in the services. The current Army field test of the Computerized Training System, Ft. Gordon, Georgia, has just been completed (Seidel, Rosenblatt, Wagner, Schulz, & Hunter, 1978). At the time of our field test, cost data had already been collected based upon the cost model in the Operational Test Plan (1975). Although we intended to apply our specification to all the Computerized Training System cost data, this was not possible. In most cases, we were not able to reorganize and analyze these data within the framework of our specification. Rather, the cost categories developed for the Computerized Training System were used. Whenever possible, guidelines from our specification (e.g., adjustments for inflation, determining personnel costs) were adhered to in calculating costs.

We were unable to make any valid cost projections of the Computerized Training System, assuming the system was to be replicated, because of the lack of sufficient operational cost data. On the other hand, we did describe a way to assess the value of the system for computer-managed instruction by recommending a criterion different from that identified in the Operational Test Plan. That model used hourly instruction costs as the key index, but the model was designed for evaluating the cost-effectiveness of a computer-assisted instruction system. However, with the change to a computer-managed instruction system, a different cost-effectiveness index is more useful (e.g., cost per graduate). Our field test confirmed the inappropriateness of trying to retrofit a cost-effectiveness model on data collected using a model designed for another purpose.

Thus, our cost-effectiveness specification has still to be field-tested at an appropriate site. It is expected that the next application will be in the

Air Force (possibly the Advanced Instructional System at Lowry Air Force Base, or a PLATO site). It is important, once a site is selected, that at least one staff person be located at the training base during the data collection period. As pointed out earlier, one individual should be given the responsibility for collecting the data needed for the specification. In the planned verification study, this individual would contribute to the revision of the specification by giving particular attention to those parameters for which no data exist, or which are not meaningful to training site personnel.

Procedures for identifying and rating the relative importance of training effectiveness dimensions will be evaluated. Those measures or procedures that are disputed will be noted, as will any alternative recommended by the training site cadre.

It is hoped that as a result of the planned on-site study, changes will be made to the specification to ensure its applicability throughout the Department of Defense and the civilian sector. If there is too great a difference in the procedures, terminology, or information sources between the services to adopt one specification, then consideration will be given to the development of separate service-specific versions.

APPENDIX 1: TRAINING COST BREAKDOWN STRUCTURE DEFINITIONS

Development Phase

Equipment

Included in this category are all the components of equipment related to a computer-based training system (e.g., the computer and its associated auxiliary memory requirements, terminals, carrels, auxiliary audiovisual devices). Also included are local interface hardware, telephone lines, special lines, satellites, receivers, power-generating equipment, associated test and checkout equipment, etc. Maintenance costs, derived from factors such as mean time before failure and mean time or cost to repair, should be included in the costs of every piece of equipment maintained.

1. Computer(s)
2. Terminal(s)
3. Auxiliary audiovisual devices
4. Auxiliary memory
5. Local interfaces
6. Telephone lines
7. Special lines
8. Satellites
9. Receivers
10. Power-generating equipment

11. Carrels
12. Other Equipment

Facilities

Included in this category are all the physical facilities required for housing the equipment components, administrators, and users of the computer-based training system. This category includes classrooms, laboratories, large group instruction spaces, officers, individual learning spaces, libraries and other information resource centers, etc. Units should be specified as to the number of square feet required to house all components of the computer-based training system.

1. Classrooms
2. Laboratories
3. Large Group instruction spaces
4. Offices
5. Individual learning spaces
6. Libraries and other information resource centers
7. Other facilities

Software

This category of the computer-based training system includes systems programming support, general applications programs, diagnostic and checkout software, utility programs, etc.

1. Systems programs
2. General applications programs
3. Diagnostic–test programs
4. Utility programs
5. Other computer programs

Instructional Systems Development Activities

This category includes the costs incurred during the process of developing the instruction. The activities covered in this category are described in Instructional Systems Development (ISD) Phases I, II, and III (analyze, design, and develop). However, for purposes of this specification, this category does not include the costs of actually preparing the test items and instructional materials (see following category).

1. Analyze (Phase I)
2. Design (Phase II)
3. Develop (Phase III)
4. Other instructional systems development (ISD) activities

Instructional Methods–Materials

Included here are all forms of instructional methods, materials, and tests in the computer-based training program. All print and mediated instruction is included, as well as specific-applications computer programs when appropriate. Printed materials would include such items as training manuals, instructor guides, printouts, books, and programmed texts. Other mediated forms of instruction include film, audio, audiovisual, video, and computer displays, etc. Indicate the estimated number of course hours for each element of instruction developed.

1. Audio instruction
2. Audiovisual instruction
3. Film–text–visual instruction
4. Lecture–demonstration
5. Group discussion–seminar
6. Performance–practice
7. Tutoring (peer or other)
8. Printed text–visual
9. Computer-administered instructional materials
    a. Drill and practice
    b. Simulation
    c. Games
    d. Tutorial
    e. Problem solving
    f. Inquiry
    g. Specific applications programs
    h. Other computer-administered instructional materials
10. Other instructional methods–materials
11. Tests
    a. Paper-and-pencil
    b. Performance tests

System Management–Test

This category includes costs of the technical and business management effort expended in the process of developing an integrated and tested computer-based system prototype. It includes systems integration–engineering, program–project management and operational test component costs.

1. System integration–engineering
2. Program management
3. Operational test
4. Other direct management costs

Other Direct Costs

This category contains elements that are not covered in other categories. Costs related to travel, supplies, consultants, contracts and subcontracts, etc., not identified otherwise are represented here.

1. Supplies
2. Travel
3. Consultants
4. Contracts–subcontracts
5. Other direct costs

Procurement Phase

This phase includes the same categories as the development phase, with the following exceptions:

Instructional Preparation

This category includes all training costs necessary for initial site personnel to acquire sufficient skills to operate, maintain, and support the computer-based training system. Included are the costs of training initial site personnel cadre as well as their pay and allowances during the period in which they receive training.

1. Training of initial site personnel cadre
2. Site personnel pay and allowances
3. Other instructional preparation costs

Acceptance Test–Management

This category includes costs of the technical and business management effort expended in the process of producing, purchasing, and installing the tested, operational computer-based training system. It includes costs associated with program management, acceptance testing, engineering changes, site checkout–activation, etc.

1. Program–project management
2. Acceptance test
3. Engineering changes
4. Site checkout–activation
5. Other direct management costs

Operation and Maintenance Phase

Categories are the same as in the development phase, with the following exceptions:

Equipment

Included in this category are all the components of equipment related to a computer-based training system (e.g., the computer and its associated auxiliary memory requirements, terminals, carrels, auxiliary audiovisual devices). Also included are local interface hardware, telephone lines, special lines, satellites, receivers, power-generating equipment, associated test and checkout equipment, etc. Replacement spares and repair test equipment are included in the operation and maintenance phase. Maintenance costs, derived from factors such as mean time before failure and mean time or cost to repair, should be included in the costs of every piece of equipment maintained. A possible formula to use for each type of equipment is this: *Number of times each unit fails or needs servicing per year times the average cost to service–repair each unit times the number of units equals total unit maintenance cost per year.*

12. Replacement spares and repair test equipment
13. Other equipment

Instructional Systems Development Activities

This category includes the costs incurred during the process of implementing and validating. The activities covered in this category are described in ISD Phases IV and V (implement and control). However, for purposes of this specification, this category does not include the costs of actually revising the test items and instructional materials (see Instructional Methods–Materials).

1. Implement (Phase IV)
   a. Replacement training of site personnel
   b. Instructor pay and allowances
   c. Student pay and allowances
2. Control (Phase V)
3. Other instructional systems development (ISD) activities

System Management

This category includes the management effort costs expended in the process of operating, maintaining, and supporting the operational computer-based training system. It includes costs associated with program management, etc.

1. Program–project management
2. Other direct management costs

APPENDIX 2: END-OF-COURSE MEASURES FOR EVALUATING TRAINING EFFECTIVENESS

Time Measures

1. *Training Time.* This measure represents the time actually spent in learning the subject matter and practicing the skills to be acquired. It does not contain time devoted to nonacademic subjects, in- and out-processing, and other activities unrelated to the instruction. Training time should include any self-study, remedial, or recycle time, even if these times are not officially prescribed.

2. *Testing Time.* This measure represents the time spent in taking *criterion* tests. It includes all the time spent in taking tests that are *graded*—tests that determine whether a student has attained the training objectives of the course. Testing time does not include time spent in skill practice, practical exercises, or quizzes that are part of the instruction. That time is included under a training time measure.

3. *Course Time to Criterion.* This measure refers to the total number of hours, days, weeks, or other time units a trainee spends in a given course in order to reach mastery of the required objectives. It represents the sum of training time and testing time—see below.

Achievement Measures

These measures either reflect trainee achievement of within-course enabling objectives or assess end-of-course proficiency. In order for this kind of assessment to be possible, the objectives must be explicitly stated and translated into performance or behavioral terms. Examples of such achievement measures would be scores on criterion-referenced tests related to objectives, or gain scores taking into account the initial proficiency level of each trainee. Additional scores that can be used to describe a trainee's level of achievement are number of objectives mastered, skill level attained, etc. All of these would be objective-based achievement scores. Normative (norm-referenced) test scores, or a student's class standing, are achievement scores that are used when comparing each trainee's performance with that of the class as a whole. If achievement scores are used to compare the effectiveness of different training programs, a considerable effort should be undertaken to identify the differences that exist in training objectives and/or trainee population characteristics.

1. *Accuracy Scores.* Accuracy scores indicate the level of achievement reached within certain tolerances on specific scales. Such scores can be described in terms of the number of positive instances (correct items) or the number of errors made on a given scale.

2. *Speed Scores.* This term refers to the rate of acceptable task performance. If time or speed of performance is the standard for certain training objectives, then a measure of training effectiveness must reflect this criterion. If a task must be performed in a given time, a possible effectiveness measure to use could be the number of trainees who perform acceptably in that time. Another speed score could be the number of steps or activities in a task that are completed by a certain percentage of trainees by a given time. In either case, the scores used to measure training effectiveness must reflect the training objectives and criteria.

3. *Gain Scores.* These scores refer to the difference between scores on a pretest taken prior to a course of instruction and scores on an equivalent posttest following a given course of instruction. The gain (difference between pre- and posttests) is said to be the measure of effectiveness. One weakness in this type of measure stems from the fact that the absolute amount that can be gained by a trainee is a function of his initial level in the skill being measured. Therefore, it is not a sufficient measure unless trainees enter the program with relatively low levels of the skill for which they are being trained.

4. *Mastery Scores.* Generally, this term means achievement of all requirements to exhibit expertise in a given course of instruction. In practical terms, it is often used to mean achievement of the required number of objectives at a minimally acceptable level of performance. If instructional decisions are made on a "go–no-go" basis (achievement or not) per course objective, then mastery is defined as meeting the required number of "go" decisions in order to complete the course.

Other Effectiveness Measures

1. *Student Attitudes.* These are subjective, indirect measures of training effectiveness. They are designed to elicit the opinions of trainees regarding their positive or negative feelings about the course, method of instruction, or other related matters. On the other hand, they can be valuable indicators of the emotional states of trainees, instructors, or others. These measures can point to possible training problems and provide reasons for a given level of proficiency measured in the course.

2. *Ratings.* Ratings are indirect, subjective measures of effectiveness. Though ratings have the advantage of being easily obtained, they often have low reliability and validity. As ratings and *indirect* measures of productivity or performance they are less valid than direct performance measures. It is often difficult to obtain consistent ratings over time from the same individual, and from several raters at the same time (interrater reliability) without training the raters.

3. *Attrition Rates.* This measure refers to the percentage of trainees who fail to meet the within-course or end-of-course criteria and, thus, are dropped from the training program. It also includes those students who voluntarily leave the training program for reasons other than academic failure.

4. *Recycles (Washbacks).* This term refers to the number or percentage of students who are forced to go through all or a portion of a course more than once because of failure to achieve that course section's required objectives in a specified amount of time. These trainees are then recycled through the instruction and given an opportunity to take the criterion tests(s) again.

5. *Absentee Rates.* This measure refers to the average percentage of trainees who are not present for training on any given day for each course.

6. *Other measures.*

REFERENCES

Barro, S. M., & Levien, R. E. Framework for decision. In R. E. Levien (Ed.), *The emerging technology: Instructional uses of the computer in higher education.* New York: McGraw-Hill, 1972.

Baraby, R., Henry, J. M., Parrish, W. F., & Swope, W. M. *A technique for choosing cost-effective instructional delivery systems* (TAEG Report No. 16). Orlando, Fla.: Training Analysis and Evaluation Group, April 1975.

Carpenter-Huffman, P. *MODIA: Vol 1. Overview of a tool for planning the use of Air Force training resources.* Santa Monica, Calif.: Rand Corporation, March 1977. (a)

Carpenter-Huffman, P. *MODIA: Vol 2. Options for course design.* Santa Monica, Calif.: Rand Corporation, April 1977. (b)

Carpenter-Huffman, P., Fujisaki, M., & Pyles, R. *MODIA: Vol 3. Operation and design of the user interface.* Santa Monica, Calif.: Rand Corporation, September 1977. (c)

Doughty. P. L., Stern, H. W., & Thompson, C. *Guidelines for cost-effectiveness analysis for Navy training and education* (Special Report 76). San Diego, Calif.: Navy Personnel Research and Development Center, June 1976.

Greenberg, I. M. DoD's efforts to increase training efficiency. *Commanders Digest,* July 7, 1977, *20*(12).

Hess, R. W., & Kantar, P. *MODIA: The cost model.* Santa Monica, Calif.: Rand Corporation, June 1976.

Kopstein, F. F., & Seidel, R. J. *Computer-administered instruction versus traditionally administered instruction: Economics* (Professional Paper 31-67). Alexandria, Va.: Human Resources Research Organization, June 1967.

Longo, A. A., Gaddis, J. T., & Whitehouse, B. *Preliminary evaluation plan for U.S. Army Computerized Training System* (CTS-TR-74-1). F. Monmouth, N.J.: Office of the Product Manager, U.S. Army Signal Center and School, January 1974.

Military manpower training report for FY 1978. Washington, D.C.: Department of Defense, March 1977.

Operational Test Plan: Prototype Computerized Training System, Project ABACUS. Ft. Eustis, Va.: Evaluation and Studies Office, U.S. Army Training Support Activity, September 1975.

Scanlon, R. An examination of the short-range potential of computer-managed instruction. In H. E. Mitzel (Ed.), *Conference proceedings* (November 6–8, 1974). University Park, Pa.: The Pennsylvania State University, 1974.

Seidel, R. J., Rosenblatt, R., Wagner, H., Schulz, R., & Hunter, B. *Evaluation of a prototype Computerized Training System (CTS) in support of self-pacing and management of instruction* (FR-ED-78-110). Alexandria, Va.: Human Resources Research Organization, August 1978.

Seidel, R. J., & Wagner, H. *Cost-effectiveness specification for computer-based training systems* (Executive Summary: Vol. I, Development: Vol. II, Procurement: Vol. III, Operation and Maintenance). Alexandria, Va.: Human Resources Research Organization, September 1977.

Seidel, R. J., Wagner, H., & Hargan, C. *Development of a DARPA cost specification for computer-based training systems* (SR-ED-76-40). Alexandria, Va.: Human Resources Research Organization, September 1976.

Seidel, R. J., Wagner, H., & Kastner, C. *Towards the development of DARPA costing specifications for computer-based training systems* (SR-ED-76-29). Alexandria, Va.: Human Resources Research Organization, June 1976.

TRASANA Handbook. Cost and training effectiveness analysis handbook. White Sands Missile Range, N.M.: U.S. Army TRADOC Systems Analysis Activity, July 1976.

Wagner, H., Trexler, R. C., Hillelsohn, M. J., & Seidel, R. J. *Automated instructional development system: Validation study* (RP-ED-78-6). Alexandria, Va.: Human Resources Research Organization, March 1978.

Wilkinson, G. L. Cost evaluation of instructional strategies. *AVCR*, 1973, *21*(1).

Yasutake, J. Y. An examination of the short-range potential of computer-managed instruction. In H. E. Mitzel (Ed.), *Conference proceedings* (November 6–8, 1974). University Park, Pa.: The Pennsylvania State University, 1974.

9

Toward an Intelligent Computer Tutor[1]

DONALD R. GENTNER

For the past few years I have been involved in a research effort that is basically aimed toward understanding how information is represented in the mind, how those representations are changed in the process of learning, and how they are used in the process of teaching. Along with several others in the Center for Human Information Processing, University of California, San Diego, I have been building computer models of learners and teachers, primarily as a tool to force us to specify clearly our theories about the representation of information and how those representations are modified during learning. In this chapter I will first discuss my general image of an intelligent computer tutor, and then illustrate parts of that by discussing a specific system that I have been working on, the FLOW tutor system. The FLOW tutor system is an intelligent computer tutor that gives advice to students who are learning a simple computer language called FLOW.

[1] This research was supported by the Office of Naval Research, Personnel and Training Research Programs and the Advanced Research Projects Agency, and was monitored by ONR under Contract N00014-76-C-0628, NR 154-387, under terms of ARPA Order No. 2284. Views and conclusions contained in this chapter are those of the author, and should not be interpreted as necessarily representing the official policies, either expressed or implied, of the Advanced Research Projects Agency, the Office of Naval Research, or the United States government.

253

Copyright © 1979 by Academic Press, Inc.
All rights of reproduction in any form reserved.
ISBN 0-12-526660-X

THE INTELLIGENT TUTOR

Abilities of an Intelligent Tutor

What can an intelligent tutor do? As a psychologist, I try to understand people, and to do that I have attempted to simulate them with computer systems. In the following discussion I will consider the abilities that are required of a human tutor or an intelligent computer-based tutorial system.

An intelligent tutor must be able to perform a number of tasks. A tutor must be able to generate instructional material: to present the subject matter, ask questions of the student, give examples, and give explanations to the student. A tutor must be able to answer free-form questions from the student. The tutor must be able to evaluate the student's responses or behavior. And as one of the more difficult tasks, the tutor must be able to diagnose student errors, or "bugs." It is relatively easy to tell when a student is making an error; the more difficult task for the tutor is to determine the underlying misconceptions responsible for that error. And once the source of the error has been found, the tutor has to figure out the most efficient way to correct the student's misunderstanding. Finally, intelligent tutors must themselves be able to learn. On one level, the tutor must be able to learn and teach new topic matters. And at the microlevel, the tutor must be aware of the student's progress or lack of progress, and adapt the instructional techniques to that particular student.

Underlying Skill Areas

What skills must a tutor have in order to exhibit these abilities? In this section I will discuss the underlying skill areas that form the basis for the abilities of an intelligent human or computer tutor.

Subject Matter

The tutor must be competent in the subject matter. In order for an intelligent system to be able to adapt to the student, it must have more than just a textbook inside. The tutor must have the subject matter represented in a structured data base, which it can access in many ways. It must be able to access the data base to discuss the topic with the student and answer questions. If the topic area involves problem solving (e.g., computer programming), the tutor must be able to use information in the data base to find solutions for the problems. In the case of computer programming, the tutor itself would have to understand computer programming at a level that would enable it to solve the sort of problems the student must solve. It is clear that if the tutor is going to be able to explain to the student how a problem should be solved, all this information cannot be explicitly preprogrammed, once you allow the student to have freeform interaction with the tutor. The tutor must be able to generate responses on-line from a general-knowledge data base.

Teaching Strategy

The second thing the tutor needs is a teaching strategy. In a conventional computer-assisted instruction system that is easily built in with the frames and the branching between frames. Once you go to a more intelligent system, the teaching strategy itself must be a part of the data base, so that the tutor can alter its strategy depending upon the needs of the student.

Natural Language

The next underlying skill is so basic that it is easily overlooked. The tutor should be able to communicate with the student in a natural language, such as English. The tutor needs a natural language capability to interact efficiently with the student; in most cases it is the most direct way of communicating. Ideally this would be a verbal interaction, but that is probably impractical in any present-day computer-based system. At the least, an intelligent tutor should be able to carry on a natural-language conversation with the student through a computer terminal display and keyboard.

World Knowledge

World knowledge (what is generally known as common sense) is an important part of natural-language skill. That is, a good tutor must know more than just the subject matter. You can think of the stereotype of a very narrow person who really understands computer programming but cannot talk to anyone else—that type of person would not make a good tutor. The fact is that in order to speak with other people about computer programming, you need a large body of knowledge that is shared with the other person. Some of the shared knowledge is more specific to computers, such as how to use a typewriter keyboard, whereas other knowledge is very general, such as the length of typical pauses in human speech.

The central importance of world knowledge is not at all obvious, and this has been a big trap for artificial intelligence and cognitive psychology.

In many areas, we did not even understand where the difficulties were. In our normal, everyday interactions, we use such a wide range of knowledge so automatically that we are seldom even aware of its role. One only becomes aware of it when programming computer systems to perform these tasks. Since initially a computer completely lacks this shared world knowledge, we are forced to determine the required knowledge and explicitly build it into the system. From the standpoint of a cognitive psychologist, this requirement to be completely explicit about all the information needed to perform a task is one of the major reasons for building these computer systems.

I find that the problems I am aware of at the beginning when building these systems usually turn out to be the easy ones. I know what they are and often have an idea of how to solve them. Where I get into difficulties (and I think this is the general experience in artificial intelligence) is with issues that initially I did not even realize were going to be problems. And these unexpected problems often involve world knowledge.

Let me give an example of a world-knowledge issue that might not initially appear to be related to computer programming. We are now building a computer model of a person who is learning to use a computer text editor. A learner must be able to do a great deal of inference, because the general rules are often not stated explicitly in the typical instructional materials. This is especially true with "discovery" learning, where the students are usually given only specific examples and are expected to derive the general principles on their own. Most students have no difficulty with making these simple inferences. But our computer model of a learner had great difficulty in inferring how events are causally related. You might think that a simple rule would be sufficient, such as, "The effect must come after the cause." But how long after? What is a reasonable time interval between the cause and its effect? Of all the events that occur after some cause, which ones do you associate with that particular cause?

For example, imagine that we are in a room together, and I push a book off the table, and it hits the floor. You would have no difficulty in understanding that the book hit the floor because I pushed it off the table. Things were happening all around the room at that time, and yet you automatically made the connection between pushing the book and the book's hitting the floor. If, at the same time that I pushed the book, the second hand on the wall clock passed 3, you normally would not make any association between the second hand and the book's hitting the floor. That ability to draw causal connections between events is an example of a skill based on the general world knowledge that people use continually, although they are often unaware of it. To function intelligently, a tutor must have and use this type of knowedge.

Model of the Student

It is probably apparent by now that the skills required by an intelligent tutor are closely interrelated. These interrelations are basic to the power of the tutor, although they make it difficult to talk about or analyze the separate skills. Modeling the student is closely intertwined with skills involving teaching strategy, natural language, and world knowledge.

You cannot effectively communicate with or teach another person unless you are able to model that person. That is, you have to have in your own mind a model of the person you are communicating with or teaching. It is the model of the other person that you actually communicate with. For example, if you were describing your work to a child, a stranger at a bus stop, or a professional colleague, you would choose different words based on the different models you form of these people. The models of other people include information such as their overall knowledge, their recent replies, the types of inferences they should be able to make, and what they are hoping to gain from the interaction. Many of the communication problems of artificial intelligence systems can be traced to a poor ability to model the other person.

Higher-level Goal Structures

The final underlying area I will describe is that of higher-level goals. Something is necessary to tie together all the skills and activities of the tutor. By higher-level goals I mean goals that describe what the interaction is all about: The tutor is trying to communicate a body of information to the student; the tutor wants the student to learn the material; if the student is having difficulties, the tutor wants to find the underlying misconceptions and deal with them. These goals are intertwined into a structure that gives overall guidance to the tutor's entire interaction with the student. Learners also have comparable high-level goal structures that guide the interaction from their side. Students bring a lot of structure into learning situations. They are not only paying attention to individual sentences; they are also aware that they are in a school, or that their job depends upon learning this material. They are aware of the role of the teacher, that certain statements of the teacher are relevant to the topic, whereas others are irrelevant and can be safely ignored. Students know that their task is to make up general principles out of the specific examples presented by the teacher. This sort of higher-level goal structure seems to override all our activities, including learning and teaching.

Learning To Teach

I have already discussed many aspects of an intelligent tutor. Now I will briefly consider learning on the part of the tutor: An intelligent tutor must be able to learn new material in preparing to teach a different course; a good tutor must also modify the teaching strategy to adapt to individual students. Human tutors normally learn and adapt quite well, of course, but once again there are complexities that might not be apparent at first. Think of what a tutor must do in preparing to teach a particular topic. You might think that a tutor could just read a book on the topic and then would be ready to teach, but this is not the case. First of all, just at the simple level of the subject matter, it takes a month or years to become competent to teach a new topic matter, depending upon how difficult it is and how far removed it is from the tutor's current knowledge. But more importantly, even before that, there are 20 or 30 years of learning that start when the tutor is born. This includes learning in school: learning language, academic subjects, and a great deal of general cultural background information. Even more learning goes on outside of school, in areas such as social interaction, world knowledge, and modeling the listener. Topics such as these have to be learned, and probably the knowledge acquired outside school is more important for being a teacher than that learned inside school.

The point I am making here is that there is a great deal of knowledge that an intelligent tutor must have, in addition to the subject matter knowledge, if the tutor is going to be successful or even function well.

Conclusion

What are the implications of all this? The general approach in artificial intelligence and cognitive psychology has been that at first we just charged ahead and said we were going to solve all of these problems. Then we realized how deep the problems were and developed a different approach: to take limited pieces of the world, explore those in depth, see in detail what the problems are, and attempt to solve these problems in the restricted domain. The systems described by John Brown (1978) are good examples of this approach. They take what at first might appear to be a limited area, such as subtraction, explore the relevant issues in depth, and try to get an intelligent tutorial system working there. One system will capture some aspects of these problems, and another system will capture other aspects. But the basic approach is to try to work on the important issues in a limited domain and then, as our understanding builds, to enlarge the system's areas of competence until we arrive at something approximating an intelligent human tutor.

AN EXAMPLE: THE FLOW TUTOR SYSTEM

I will illustrate some of the abilities that an intelligent tutor must have by describing the FLOW tutor system. It is a computer-based tutor to teach a very simple computer language called FLOW. The language has a structure similar to that of BASIC, with a total of about 15 instructions in the language. FLOW is essentially a string manipulation language; it has a single variable and no arithmetic functions. A typical college student with no previous computer experience can learn FLOW and become fairly competent in one or two hours. It takes a few hours more to master the language. That gives you a rough idea of the complexity of the task. It is an effective experimental tool for us, because an hour or two is a good length for an experiment. FLOW is complicated enough that it challenges a college student who has had no computer programming experience, and yet it is approachable—it is not like trying to teach BASIC or another real-world computer language.

Experimental Environment

We have studied the learning of FLOW in many different instructional environments (Gentner & Norman, 1977). The instructional arrangement shown in Figure 9.1 depicts my image of the FLOW tutor system. On the right, a student is shown in top view, sitting at a terminal that is connected to a minicomputer. The FLOW language runs on this minicomputer. The student has an instruction booklet that contains general discussions of computers and computer languages, a description of the FLOW language, examples to type in and try out, and problems to work on. In principle the student could go through the whole booklet without help, and occasionally we find students who can.

We tried to make the instructional booklet fairly complete, although if you look at it carefully, you find that many details have been left out, as is the case in almost any instructional material. So a student can just work at the terminal and try to solve the problems. The minicomputer executes the student's FLOW programs and thus provides the student with feedback. The system also provides a line-at-a-time execution mode to help the student debug the program. Thus a student could, in principle, go through the entire FLOW course without any help from the tutor. Most

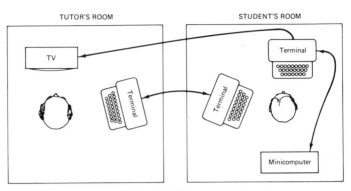

Figure 9.1 The FLOW experimental setup.

students, however, have considerable difficulty. Sometimes they are
aware of their problems immediately, and other times they are not aware
of their problems as they develop, and only later do they get in trouble. So
we have a provision for help, and we have worked with tutors in many
different experimental arrangements.

Figure 9.1 shows an arrangement that we have often used with a human
tutor. We have a tutor in another room who is sitting in front of a CRT
terminal that displays a copy of everything appearing on the student's
terminal. The student and tutor can send messages back and forth on a
pair of interconnected terminals. We chose this arrangement because we
were interested in eventually simulating this human tutor with a
computer-based system, and so we have eliminated much of the communication that normally goes on between the student and the tutor. In
particular, human tutors often pay attention to body language and all sorts
of little signals from the students that we had no hope of capturing in the
computer simulation. So we restricted the information the tutor gets to
just what appears on the student's terminal. Now, in fact, human tutors
can handle this situation fairly well, and with experience they get quite
proficient at providing help to the student.

At the next conceptual step we make a major modification in this
arrangement: We replace the human tutor with a computer-based system.
And this is the system I will be describing in the rest of the chapter. Every
time the student presses a key, the minicomputer sends that information
over to our computer tutor. In our computer system I have almost completely ignored the natural-language-understanding aspects of the
student–tutor interaction. The student's messages to the tutor are restricted to four things: help, yes, no, and OK. And although the tutor's
messages to the student appear to be natural English, the sentences are
actually assembled from previously prepared segments. The FLOW tutor

lacks any serious natural-language capabilities. I wanted to avoid the whole natural-language problem. The next chapter by Burton and Brown addresses this problem in some detail.

Of course, the lack of natural-language communication makes the task of the FLOW tutor much more difficult at times. Often a human tutor will want to ask a student questions such as "What are you trying to do now?" or "What is the function of this section of the program?" The FLOW tutor system cannot ask such questions because it would not be able to interpret the student's natural language replies. In addition, if students could ask questions of the tutor, the students could often easily clarify their misunderstandings and deal more directly with known problems.

The Tutor's Task

The main focus of the FLOW tutor project is to discover how a tutor perceives, diagnoses, and resolves the student's difficulties. The problem of correctly diagnosing a student's problems is a particularly interesting and challenging one, and one that is closely related to that of instructional designers who are trying to evaluate the student while the student is working on the instructional materials.

Figure 9.2 gives an example of the sort of information that the tutor sees. Presumably this information does not make much sense to you, for very interesting reasons. First, let me interpret the information for you. The time, in seconds, since the beginning of the session is shown in the left column. The right column gives the corresponding key presses made by the student. So, for example, the first line indicates that the student pressed the "0" key 1386 seconds after the start of the session. In this case the student has typed the sequence 0, 3, 3, I, etc. Now why does this not make sense to you, even after I have explained it? It does not make sense because you do not know the higher-level context in which this is

Time	Keypress
1386	0
1387	3
1387	3
1390	I
1393	:
1396	RUBOUT
1397	RUBOUT
1400	I
1400	*
1404	0
1404	5
1405	0
1418	L
1434	R

Figure 9.2 Information received by the tutor.

embedded. You do not know where the student is in the instruction booklet. In fact you do not even know very much about the instruction booklet! You know very little about the FLOW language. You do not know what sort of problem the student could be working on, what sort of difficulties the student has had recently, or what commands in the language the student has mastered. You do not know what topics are about to be introduced or which ones have already been covered. The tutor must have all this higher-level knowledge in order to be able to interpret the student's key presses. This is one of the major focuses of my research: What sort of higher-level context do you have to have in order to understand what the student is doing and why the student is doing it?

Operation of the Tutor

The FLOW tutor system uses two basic modes of human information processing: *conceptually guided* processing (often called top-down processing), and *data-driven* processing (often called bottom-up processing). Conceptually guided processing is based on higher-level prior knowledge from which expectations are derived. Although this is normally an efficient strategy, gaps in the higher-level knowledge or improper reasoning could lead to serious errors. To overcome this problem, it appears that the human information system allows itself to be interrupted, to be driven by the occurrences of important data, even when its primary attention has been directed elsewhere. This latter mode is data-driven processing. Conceptually guided and data-driven processing are sometimes overused concepts these days, but they divide the operations effectively and in fact describe how the system generally works. The reason I say "generally" is that though conceptually guided and data-driven processing are relatively clear in isolation, their interaction can be quite complex. What makes the FLOW tutor system both interesting and difficult is that the system uses a combination of both conceptually guided and data-driven processing much of the time, and the interaction of the two processes turns out to be both an exciting area and one that is threaded with difficulties.

The FLOW tutor has a great deal of information in its data base: information about the instruction booklet, including the contents of the various paragraphs, how long the paragraphs are, what all the examples are, and programming problems. The tutor uses this information in conjunction with conceptually guided processing in four ways.

First, at the highest level the tutor follows the student through the instruction booklet. The goal of the tutor is to get the student through the instruction booklet and have the student acquire all of the concepts that are contained there. Second, the tutor predicts the student's behavior. As the tutor follows the student through the instruction booklet, it allows time for the student to read. It keeps track of the student's reading speed, and from the length of the passage estimates a reasonable maximum and minimum time for reading. If students do not use the minimum time, the tutor assumes the passage was not read. If students go over the maximum time, they are assumed to be having difficulty. The tutor checks example programs as the student enters them.

Third, the tutor uses conceptually guided processing to solve the programming problems. The statement of the problems in the tutor's data base is in fact very close to what the student gets. It is essentially a functional description of what the program should do. When the student tries to solve a programming problem, the tutor also solves it. The programming problems in the FLOW instruction booklet are quite simple. The final problem that the student gets is to write a program that will examine an input word and print "YES" if that word contains one or more "E"'s and print "NO" otherwise. That is the most complicated problem the student has, and the FLOW tutor is able to solve these problems, essentially by expanding the functional description of the problem. The tutor solves the problem itself and then looks at its own solution of the problem and predicts that the student is going to do the same thing. If the student's key presses match the predictions, the tutor assumes that the student is in fact solving the problem in the same way and is making good progress.

Fourth, the tutor uses conceptually guided processing to interpret what otherwise would be very ambiguous behaviour on the part of the student. For example, the student could press a "D" key and that could mean a variety of things in different contexts—it could be part of a DISPLAY statement, a DISPLAY VARIABLE statement, a character string, or an illegal key typed in error. But if the tutor has already predicted that for solving this part of the problem the student needs a DISPLAY statement that requires a "D" and the student presses a "D" key, the tutor figures that it is part of a DISPLAY statement. The student may be doing something completely different, but that is what the tutor figures, and thus it is able to interpret ambiguous student behavior. Obviously the tutor can get into problems with conceptually guided processing. This approach works well most of the time, as long as everything is going along well. It is a most efficient way to understand what is going on, but sometimes you can be badly misled.

What we need is a way to recover when conceptually guided processing leads us down the wrong path. That role is filled by data-driven processing, which comes in when something unexpected happens—when things are not going according to the tutor's predictions from the top level. This gives us a way to deal with unexpected student behavior. There are two important types of unexpected student behavior. The first is an alternate correct response. Even though the FLOW problems are quite simple, there are many correct ways of solving them, and so the tutor must be able to understand what the student is doing and see whether it is also a reasonable way to attack the problem. The second sort of unexpected response you can get is an actual error, and often it is initially difficult for the computer tutor to distinguish between these two. In some cases the tutor will have to wait until the student types in additional material before the tutor can interpret what the student is doing. In either case, data-driven processing operates by starting with the lowest-level concepts, such as the student's key presses, and building up to higher-level structures that the tutor can eventually recognize.

The Concept of Schemata

Structure of Schemata

The data base that the tutor uses is based on the concept of schemata, or prototypes (Bobrow, Kaplan, Kay, Norman, Thompson, & Winograd, 1977; Minsky, 1975). That is, we have structures that represent the various concepts involved in programming at all levels. At the highest level are concepts like the teaching goals and the instruction booklet, and at the lowest level are schemata for individual key presses or time passing. Figure 9.3 shows some relatively low-level schemata for two statements in the FLOW language. The statements themselves, two DISPLAY-QUOTED-STRING statements, are shown in the top left of the figure. When the computer executes the first statement, it displays the word "BILLY" on the screen. The general schema for a DISPLAY-QUOTED-STRING statement is shown in the lower left. It has a series of

```
020 DISPLAY "BILLY"              *DISPLAY-QUOTED-STRING-1786
                                    schema DISPLAY-QUOTED-STRING
030 DISPLAY "JEAN"                  statement-number 020
                                    value BILLY
                                    status OBSERVED
                                    host *DISPLAY-1853
                                    element *D-1796
                                    element *QUOTED-STRING-1805

DISPLAY-QUOTED-STRING            *DISPLAY-QUOTED-STRING-1932
   statement-number EMPTY            schema DISPLAY-QUOTED-STRING
   value EMPTY                       statement-number 030
   specialist DISPLAYQSER            value JEAN
   phost DISPLAY                     status OBSERVED
   instance *DISPLAY-QUOTED-STRING-1786    host *DISPLAY-1911
   instance *DISPLAY-QUOTED-STRING-1932    element *D-1937
                                    element *QUOTED-STRING-1941
```

Figure 9.3 FLOW statements with their corresponding schema and instances.

slots that will be filled in for any particular instance of a DISPLAY-QUOTED-STRING statement. The schema has a couple of instances, which are shown on the right side of the figure. The instance at top right corresponds to statement 020. Here the schema slot is filled in by DISPLAY-QUOTED-STRING, referring back to the original schema. Following that we have two argument slots that distinguish all the individual instances of a DISPLAY-QUOTED-STRING schema. This particular instance has a statement number of 020 and a value of BILLY. The second instance, at lower right, has a statement number of 030 and a value of JEAN. The two argument slots are all that distinguish the various instances of a DISPLAY-QUOTED-STRING schema. To give an example in another realm, you could imagine a schema for a table with several arguments: You might have the material that it is made from, the number of legs, and so forth. The different values of these arguments could then be used to distinguish between various tables. Note that two actual tables might be considered the same or different, depending on the specific arguments chosen.

Hierarchy of Schemata

All these instances of schemata in the FLOW tutor system are part of a large hierarchy, which ranges from high-level information about goals, the instructional booklet, and the whole instructional strategy, to key presses at the bottom level. The host and element slots on the instances shown in Figure 9.3 refer to the higher- and lower-level instances in this hierarchy. The host refers to a higher-level instance—an instance of displaying something—and the elements refer to the lower-level instances, which make up this instance. Here an instance of display forms the higher level, and the lower-level elements are instances of D and quoted-string schemata.

Figure 9.4 shows these higher- and lower-level instances. First there is an instance of a display schema, which was the host of the DISPLAY-QUOTED-STRING instance in Figure 9.3. You will notice that this has as its element the previous DISPLAY-QUOTED-STRING instance. Figure 9.4 also shows the lower-level elements of the DISPLAY-QUOTED-STRING instance: a D instance and a quoted string instance. The D instance is at the bottom level of the hierarchy. A key press is the lowest level of analysis used by the FLOW tutor, and the D instance therefore does not have any elements. On the other hand, a quoted string is further broken down into a couple of quotes and a character string.

The FLOW tutor uses this multilevel hierarchy in many ways. It gives the tutor a representation of the same information at a whole succession of different levels of abstraction. That is very useful for the tutor in terms

```
*DISPLAY-1911                        *QUOTED-STRING-1941
  schema DISPLAY                       schema QUOTED-STRING
  after *DISPLAY-1853                  value JEAN
  value JEAN                           status OBSERVED
  status OBSERVED                      host DISPLAY-QUOTED-STRING-1932
  host *DISPLAY-SEQUENCE-1842          element *QUOTE-1946
  element *DISPLAY-QUOTED-STRING-1932  element *CHARACTER-STRING-1951
                                       element *QUOTE-1955
*D-1937
  schema D
  time-observed 00857
  status OBSERVED
  host *DISPLAY-QUOTED-STRING-1932
```

Figure 9.4 The hierarchy of instances.

of being able to understand what the student is doing. For example, there are many different programs that can be a correct solution to a given problem. But if you compare two programs, at the bottom level they are very different: They contain different key presses and different statements. But as you start to look at the higher-level schemata that describe these programs, eventually you get up to the schemata that describe the function of the program, and here two programs that might appear to be completely different can have the same functions. And so at that higher level the tutor is able to recognize that these in fact are functionally the same program, and the student's program can be an acceptable alternate solution. As another example of the use of the hierarchical structure of schemata, the tutor often must determine the level at which to give advice to the student. In some cases, if the student is having a simple difficulty (for example, with typing a quote, which requires that the quote key and shift key be pressed at the same time), the tutor should simply tell the student to hold down the shift key and press the quote key. At other times, the tutor should structure its advice at a very high level—saying, for example, "Your program should have a loop at this point." Having this multilevel description of the same problem, ranging from high-level functions through subfunctions and all the way down to key presses, offers the tutor a wide range of choices of explanations to give. The difficulty here, of course, is to decide on the appropriate level for that particular student.

How Schemata Work

Finally, I would like to say a little about how all these schemata interact. The FLOW tutor system is a distributed intelligence system. That is, all these schemata are essentially independent and they just take care of themselves; they want to "fulfill" themselves. The only central coordination in the system is an agenda. The agenda is a list of incomplete schemata waiting to find their parts. When an instance of a schema wants to schedule another instance for attention, it puts the instance in the agenda. There is a specialist procedure associated with each schema, and when an instance's turn comes up on the agenda, the corresponding specialist is invoked. The job of the specialist is to try to complete the instance. It looks at the instance and checks to see whether all its elements have been found. If not, it goes off and tries to find some of these parts. Once it has found all the parts, the instance may already be part of some higher-level instance if it has been predicted from the top. In that case the instance just goes back and says, "OK, I'm all here, you can take over now," and the specialist for that higher-level instance checks to see whether all its parts are present, and so on. In the other case, where data-driven processing is involved, an instance may fill itself out and say, "OK, I'm all here," but it is an orphan: It does not have any higher instance that predicted it. Then the job of that instance is to find out what it could be a part of. In that way these instances can start to build themselves up from the bottom into some recognizable form, which may be, for instance, a program that was expected. That is the way in which an alternate correct solution would be recognized.

On the other hand, a structure might build itself up until it was recognized as an error. Since the tutor that I am modeling is meant to be an experienced tutor, it has, stated often in very general terms, many ideas about the typical problems that students have. As the student starts typing in something unexpected, the corresponding instances might build themselves up until finally they recognize that they are part of some error schema. If the error schema is able to find all of its components, which typically include a pause on the part of the student, it then sends off a message of advice to the student.

So the intelligence of the system is distributed among all these schemata, and the hope is that, as with all these distributed systems, the individual small bits of intelligence spread throughout the system will add up to some reasonable overall intelligence.

Giving Advice to the Student

A fundamental issue needs to be addressed at this point. To what extent should the tutor diagnose the students' difficulties and give advice rather than providing the students with a system that allows them to do their own diagnosis? Let us assume that to solve a given problem that we have presented to the student, there are one or a few reasonable algorithms that the student is expected to use. The tutor is trying to build a model of a student's solving this problem or perhaps of the student's erroneous attempts to solve the problem. The tutor must detect these erroneous attempts and give advice to the student before it is too late. This is of course a very challenging task, but this approach, where the burden of diagnosing errors is entirely on the tutor, is only one extreme of a learning environment. The other extreme is to give the students the conceptual and debugging tools to trace through the algorithm and effectively diagnose their own problems.

The FLOW tutor uses both these approaches. One of the commands in the FLOW system is "WALK," which allows the student to step through the program, one statement at a time. Since FLOW is such a simple programming language, it is possible to display all the essential information needed to determine how a program is functioning or malfunctioning. There is only one variable in FLOW, and this variable is displayed continuously along with the input text, the program statements, and any output generated by the program. A moving pointer indicates the program statement about to be executed.

Sometimes the tutor uses the WALK command to avoid giving a diagnosis. That is, when it cannot figure out what the student's difficulty is, it might say, "Try WALKing your program," and hope that the student figures out what the problem is. But, at other times, it asks the student to WALK a program just to encourage the use of the WALK command, particularly if the student has RUN an incorrect program but not yet WALKed it. So there is an interesting trade-off here, especially in an interactive environment like programming, where students have ample opportunities to find their own problems and solve them.

Whether the tutor should actively give advice to the students or give the students the opportunity and facilities to find their own errors also depends on the specific problem that the student is having. This is related to the earlier discussion of the appropriate level of advice to be given to the student. If students cannot figure out how to type a quote because they do not realize that you have to hold down the shift key, there is no point in letting them explore that; just tell them. But if the students do not understand what a jump statement in the program is doing, then it is very helpful to let them WALK through the program on their own and see how the control is getting transferred among the statements in the program. Encouraging students to diagnose the errors in their own procedural skills turns out to be helpful, not only from the standpoint of the immediate problem, but also because it is a good way to lead them to begin to reflect on the meaning of the procedural skill they have been taught.

Another point to keep in mind is that, at least in the early stages of learning computer programming, there can be an enormous frustration factor. I think part of that originates when students have errors in their programs that do not show up right away, and they go on without realizing their misconceptions. They may even have done all the problems correctly up to this point, or have made small mistakes that they did not recognize. Then by the time they realize they have made errors, they are in deep trouble: They have got several misconceptions at once and the misconceptions interact. Often in these early stages of learning, students do not realize when they are having difficulties. When using human tutors, we find it is very helpful to intervene as soon as the tutors have the slightest indication that something is really wrong, and we are trying to get the computer tutor to do that too. In any event, no intervention strategy will be ideal for all situations. The task of the tutor is to choose the strategy that will best aid the student at that particular time.

Extensions to the FLOW Tutor

Although the FLOW tutor system is designed as a theoretical tool to investigate the cognitive processes that underlie tutoring, I will briefly describe some topics related to extending the system to tutor another computer language such as BASIC. Although its structure is similar to that of FLOW, BASIC is a real-world computer language and has a much wider range of features and applications. A complete beginner can learn to use FLOW in a couple of hours, whereas it requires hundreds of hours to become competent in BASIC. Most of the fundamental programming concepts found in BASIC are also present in FLOW, however, and much of the FLOW tutor should transfer over directly to a new computer language.

The most serious ɔroblems would result from the more complex programs that are possible in BASIC. The FLOW tutor expands the functional specification of the problem into a multilevel description of the program that is used to interpret the student's program and generate advice based on a comparison with the student's program at the appropriate level. With more complex programming problems, such as those encountered in a typical BASIC course, the tutor would have great difficulty in either solving the problems itself or interpreting the student's solutions. At its present level of development, a system similar to the FLOW tutor would only be able to cope with a restricted domain of problems. This is generally true of automated tutoring systems. For instance, Mark Miller and Ira Goldstein (1977) have built a system that models program planning and debugging in the LOGO language, but only for a limited range of simple picture programs.

Evaluation

Computer-based tutorial systems, such as the FLOW tutor, can be evaluated according to their fidelity as a simulation of a human tutor and their function as a tutor. Though no formal evaluation of the FLOW tutor system has been carried out as yet, I will briefly describe some of the topics to consider in conducting such an evaluation. The fidelity of the simulation is of interest to us as cognitive psychologists. The computer system implements a theory of human information processing, and the match between the performance of the system and that of human tutors in similar circumstances is a measure of the worth of our theory. The primary external behavior of interest is the advice given to the student. We can ask how closely the advice generated by the computer system compares with the advice given by human tutors. We should also look at the internal details of the computer system. Do the internal states and conceptual structures of the computer correspond to those of humans (as indicated, for instance, when tutors are asked to "think out loud")? How well do the computer and human correspond in terms of their ease in interpreting a given event, or in terms of the errors that they make?

Evaluation of the computer system as a tutor would also be based on the quality of advice given to the student. How do students perform in the course with a computer tutor, as compared with a human tutor or no tutor? A few practical considerations are also important. What is the cost of the required computer facilities? Is the tutor able to perform fast enough to keep up with the student? How easy is it to adapt the tutor to new subject material?

CONCLUSION

I believe substantial progress is being made toward the intertwined goals of understanding how human tutors function and building a computer-based system that can give intelligent tutorial aid to a student. Existing computer tutors, such as the FLOW tutor system described in this chapter, are able to perform reasonably, and occasionally brilliantly, in restricted environments. Additional studies in these restricted environments will enable us to compare different approaches to constructing tutorial systems, and will clarify the problems that need to be solved before we can build more comprehensive systems. When we better understand how knowledge interacts with processing on a limited scale, we can turn our attention to the problems of integrating very large and diverse knowledge bases.

Our studies with the FLOW tutor system have been primarily concerned with the representation of the subject matter, the tutor's teaching strategy, and the tutor's model of the student. Other research currently in progress in our laboratory focuses on how the student's general world knowledge and initial subject matter knowledge interact with the instructional material as the student's understanding of the subject matter is formed and modified during learning. These studies, and related work in other laboratories, will add to our knowledge about the fundamental processes involved in human learning, thought, and performance. They will form the basis for the eventual development of practical, computer-based tutorial systems that can give students individualized, insightful, and intelligent help in learning a wide variety of materials.

ACKNOWLEDGMENTS

Donald A. Norman and Mark R. Wallen made important contributions to the work described in this chapter, and Olga Ramirez made many helpful comments on the manuscript.

REFERENCES

Bobrow, D. G., Kaplan, R. M., Kay, M., Norman, D. A., Thompson, H., & Winograd, T. GUS, a frame-driven dialog system. *Artificial Intelligence,* 1977, *8,* 155–173.

Brown, J. S., Collins, A., & Harris, G. Artificial Intelligence and Learning Strategies. In O'Neil, H. F., Jr. (Ed.), *Learning strategies.* New York: Academic Press, 1978.

Gentner, D. R., & Norman, D. A. *The FLOW tutor: Schemas for tutoring* (Tech. Rep. 7702). La Jolla: University of California, San Diego, Center for Human Information Processing, 1977.

Miller, M. L., & Goldstein, I. P. Structured planning and debugging. *Proceedings of the 5th Joint International Conference on Artificial Intelligence,* 1977, *2,* 773–779.

Minsky, M. A framework for representing knowledge. In P. H. Winston (Ed.), *The psychology of computer vision.* New York: McGraw-Hill, 1975.

Toward a Natural-Language Capability for Computer-Assisted Instruction[1]

RICHARD R. BURTON and
JOHN SEELY BROWN

THE NATURE AND REQUIREMENTS OF A NATURAL-LANGUAGE SYSTEM

This is a period of dramatic advances in computer technology that should change the way computers are employed in instruction. Technological advances will decrease the cost of computer hardware to the extent that each student will have available computational resources that are currently restricted to a few elite users. Traditional computer-assisted instruction (CAI) paradigms were developed under the assumption that computational power is a scarce resource, and these paradigms are, for the most part, incapable of exploiting the latest technological advances. To use the increased computational power effectively requires a reevaluation of the role of the computer in instructional paradigms, and, in turn, a reevaluation of the authoring aids needed to facilitate efficient development in this medium.

[1] This research was supported in part by the Defense Advanced Research Projects Agency, Air Force Human Resources Laboratory, Army Research Institute for Behavioral and Social Sciences, and Naval Personnel Research and Development Center under contract number MDA903-76-C-0108. Views and conclusions contained in this document are those of the author and should not be interpreted as necessarily representing the official policies, either expressed or implied, of these agencies or of the United States government.

Copyright © 1979 by Academic Press, Inc.
All rights of reproduction in any form reserved.
ISBN 0-12-526660-X

The type of instructional system that we see emerging has specific knowledge and problem-solving expertise that is used to aid students. First, as a source of information, it can answer their questions, evaluate their theories, and critique their solution paths. Second, as a tutorial mechanism, it can form models of both the students' states of knowledge and their reasoning strategies. These structural models are used both to identify fundamental misconceptions and to determine when and how to provide remediation, heuristic recommendations ("hints"), or further instruction.

In general, we are not focusing on techniques for teaching factual, textbook knowledge. Computer-assisted instruction systems that do not use the knowledge they contain (as a textbook does not use the knowledge it contains) can competently handle this task and are inherently cheaper for it. Instead, we are focusing on techniques for teaching *procedural knowledge* and *reasoning strategies* that are learned when students must use their factual knowledge in hands-on laboratory or problem-solving tasks. While the students are getting a chance to exercise their knowledge, the "intelligent" instructional systems that we are considering here attempt to mimic the capabilities of a laboratory instructor. The system works on a one-to-one basis with students, carefully diagnosing what they know, how they reason, and what kinds of deficiencies exist in their ability to apply factual knowledge. The system then uses this inferred knowledge of the students together with its knowledge of pedagogy to determine how best to advance their learning.

Although we are still a long way from attaining this goal, we have developed an organization for intelligent instructional systems (described in Brown, 1977) that appears fruitful. Our methodology for developing this organization (and the theory underlying it) has been to explore parts of the overall organization in *paradigmatic systems*. A paradigmatic system is an easily modified prototype system constructed over a carefully chosen domain of knowledge. This methodology allows experimentation with some aspect of the overall system by simplifying other aspects. We have developed systems for such domains as electronic trouble-shooting—SOPHIE (Brown, Burton, & Bell, 1975; Brown, Rubinstein, & Burton, 1976); arithmetic drill and practice—WEST (Burton & Brown, 1976, 1978); elementary algebra (Brown, Burton, & Bell, 1975); and procedural skills in arithmetic—BUGGY (Brown & Burton, 1978). In addition, systems of similar spirit are being developed by Carr and Goldstein (1977).

One of the major stumbling blocks for an intelligent instructional system is the lack of a natural means of communication between the student and the computer. This chapter addresses the problems of using natural language (English) as the communication language for advanced computer-based instructional systems. The instructional environment places requirements on a natural-language understanding system that exceed the capabilities of all existing systems. These requirements include (*a*) efficiency; (*b*) habitability; (*c*) tutorial capability; and (*d*) the ability to exist with ambiguity. However, there are major leverage points within the instructional environment that allow these requirements to be met. In the remainder of this section, we will elaborate on these requirements.

A primary requirement for a natural-language processor, in an instructional situation, is *efficiency*. Imagine the following setting: The student is at a terminal actively working on a problem. The student decides that another piece of information is needed to advance the solution, so a query is formulated. Having finished typing the question, the student will wait for the system to give an answer before continuing to work on the solution. During the time it takes the system to understand the query and generate an answer, the student is apt to forget pertinent information and lose interest. Psychological experiments have shown that response delays longer than 2 seconds have serious effects on the performance of complex tasks via terminals (Miller, 1968). In these 2 seconds the system must understand the query; deduce, infer, look up, or calculate the answer; and generate a response. Another adverse effect of poor response time is that more of the student's searching for the answer is done internally (i.e., without using the system). This decreases the amount of information the tutoring system receives and increases the amount of induction that must be performed, making the problem of figuring out what the student is doing much harder (e.g., students will not "show their work" when solving a problem; they will just present the answer).

The second requirement for a natural-language processor is *habitability*. Any natural-language system written in the foreseeable future is not going to be able to understand all of natural language. What a good natural-language interface must do is characterize and understand a usable subset of the language. Watt (1968) defines a "habitable" sublanguage as "one in which its users can express themselves without straying over the language boundaries into unallowed sentences [p. 338]." Very intuitively, for a system to be habitable it must, among other things, allow the user to make local or minor modifications to an accepted sentence and get another accepted sentence. Exactly how much modification constitutes a minor change has never been specified. Some examples may provide more insight into this notion.

1. *Is anything wrong?*
2. *Is there anything wrong?*

3. *Is there something wrong?*
4. *Is there anything wrong with Section 3?*
5. *Does it look to you as if Section 3 could have a problem?*

If a natural-language processor accepts Sentence 1, it should also accept the modifications given in Sentences 2 and 3. Sentence 4 presents a minor syntactic extension that may have major repercussions in the semantics but that should also be accepted. Sentence 5 is an example of a possible paraphrase of Sentence 4 that is beyond the intended notion of habitability. Based on the acceptance of Sentences 1–4, the user has no reason to expect that Sentence 5 will be handled.

Any sub-language that does not maintain a high degree of habitability is apt to be worse than no natural-language capability at all because, in addition to the problem one is seeking information about, the student is faced, sporadically, with the problem of getting the system to understand a query. This second problem can be disastrous both because it occurs seemingly at random and because it is ill-defined.

In an informal experiment to test the habitability of a system, the authors asked a group of four students to write down as many ways as possible of asking a particular question. The original idea was to determine how many of the various paraphrasings would be accepted by the prototype systems we were testing. The students each came up with one phrasing very quickly but had tremendous difficulty thinking of any others, even though three of the first phrasings were different! This experience demonstrates the lack of the student's ability to do "linguistic" problem solving and points out the importance of accepting the student's first phrasing.

An equally important aspect of the habitability problem is multisentence (or dialogue) phenomena. When students use a system that exhibits "intelligence" through its inference capabilities, they quickly start to assume that the system must also be intelligent in its conversational abilities as well. For example, they will frequently delete parts of their statements that they feel are obvious, given the context of the preceding statements. Often they are totally unaware of such deletions and show surprise and/or anger when the system fails to utilize contextual information as clearly as they (subconsciously) do. The use of context manifests itself in the use of such linguistic phenomena as pronominalizations, anaphoric deletions, and ellipses. The following sequence of questions exemplifies these problems:

6. *What is the population of Los Angeles?*
7. *What is it for San Francisco?*
8. *What about San Diego?*

The third requirement for a natural-language processor is that it be *self-tutoring* (i.e., that it should teach the students about its capabilities). As the students use the system, they should begin to feel the range and limitations of the sub-language. When the students use a sentence that the system cannot understand, they should receive feedback that will enable them to determine why it cannot. There are at least two kinds of feedback. The simplest (and most often seen) merely provides some indication of what parts of the sentence caused the problem (e.g., unknown word or phrase). A more useful kind of feedback goes on to provide a response based on those parts of the sentence that did make sense and then indicate (or give examples of) possibly related, acceptable sentences. It may even be advantageous to have the system recognize common unacceptable sentences and in response to them, explain why they are not in the sub-language. (See the fifth section, on experiences with SOPHIE, for further discussion of this point.)

The fourth requirement for a natural-language system is that it be aware of *ambiguity*. Natural language gains a good deal of flexibility and power by not forcing every meaning into a different surface structure. This means that the program that interprets natural language sentences must be aware that more than one interpretation is possible. For example, when asked

9. *Was John believed to have been shot by Fred?*

one of the most potentially disastrous responses is "Yes." The user may not be sure whether Fred did the shooting or the believing or both. More likely, the user, being unaware of any ambiguity, assumes an interpretation that may be different than the system's. If the system's interpretation is different, the user thinks he has received the answer to his query when in fact he has received the answer to a completely independent query. Either of the following is a much better response:

10. *Yes, it is believed that Fred shot John.*
11. *Yes, Fred believes that John was shot.*

The system need not necessarily have tremendous disambiguation skills, but it must be aware that misinterpretations are possible and inform the user of its interpretation. In those cases where the system makes a mistake the results may be annoying but should not be catastrophic.

This chapter presents the development of a technique that we have named *semantic grammars* for building natural-language processors that satisfy the above requirements. The next section presents a dialogue from the "intelligent" CAI system SOPHIE that we used to refine and demonstrate this technique. This dialogue provides concrete examples of the kinds of linguistic capabilities that can be achieved using semantic grammars. The third section describes semantic grammar as it first evolved in SOPHIE, and points out how it allows semantic information to be used to handle dialogue constructs and to allow the directed ignoring of words in the input. The fourth section discusses the limitations that were encountered in the evolution of semantic grammars in SOPHIE as the range of sentences was increased and how these might be overcome by using a different formalism—augmented transition networks (ATN). This section also reports on the conversion of the SOPHIE semantic grammar to an ATN, and the extensions to the ATN formalism that were necessary to maintain the solutions presented in the previous section. It also includes comparison timings between the two versions of the natural-language processor. The fifth section describes experiences we have had with SOPHIE and presents techniques developed to handle problems in the area of nonunderstood sentences. The sixth section suggests directions for future work.

DIALOGUE FROM SOPHIE

Before delving into the structural aspects and technical details of the semantic grammar technique, we would first like to provide a concrete example of the dialogues it has supported. This section presents an annotated dialogue of a student using the "Intelligent" CAI system SOPHIE.[2] SOPHIE was developed to explore the use of artificial intelligence techniques in providing tutorial feedback to students engaged in problem-solving activities. The particular problem-solving activity that SOPHIE is concerned with is the troubleshooting of a malfunctioning piece of electronic equipment. SOPHIE models the piece of equipment and answers the student's requests for measurements and other information to aid in debugging the equipment. More important, throughout the problem-solving session, SOPHIE can evaluate the logical consistency of a student's hypothesis or generate hypotheses that are consistent with the behavior the student has thus far observed.[3] In the dialogue, the student's typing is underlined. Even though the dialogue deals with electronic jargon, the linguistic issues it exemplifies occur in all domains. The

---

[2] The dialogue is intended to demonstrate SOPHIE's linguistic capabilities and, though it touches upon the major features of SOPHIE, it is not meant to exhibit the logical or deductive capabilities of the system.

[3] The reader is encouraged to see Brown and Burton (1975) for further examples and descriptions of SOPHIE's tutorial and inferential capabilities.

annotations (below the dialogue) attempt to point out these problems and should be understandable to the non-electronics-oriented reader.

WELCOME TO SOPHIE—A SIMULATED ELECTRONICS LABORATORY.
> The circuit (Figure 10.1) is based on the Heathkit IP-28 power supply. The IP-28 is a reasonably sophisticated power supply with both current-limiting and voltage-limiting behavior. These two interrelated feedback loops make troubleshooting this circuit nontrivial.

≫INSERT A FAULT
> The Student tells SOPHIE to make one of the components in the circuit bad. SOPHIE randomly selects a fault, inserts it into a model of the instrument, and tells the student how the front panel controls are presently set.

THE INSTRUMENT HAS A FAULT AND ITS PRESENT CONTROL SETTINGS ARE:

CC	1.0	CURRENT CONTROL—FROM .0 (MIN CURRENT) TO 1.0
CR	HIGH	CURRENT RANGE SWITCH, HIGH=1 AMP, LOW=.1 AMP
LOAD	1000	LOAD RESISTANCE IN OHMS
VC	1.0	VOLTAGE CONTROL—FROM .0 (MIN VOLTAGE) TO 1.0
VR	HIGH	VOLTAGE RANGE SWITCH, HIGH=30, LOW=10 VOLTS

≫WHAT IS THE OUTPT?
OUTPT ⇒ OUTPUT
THE OUTPUT VOLTAGE IS 1.2 VOLTS.
> SOPHIE corrects the student's typing mistake.
> Notice that the output was disambiguated as the output voltage.

IF YOU ARE NOT SURE WHETHER A VALUE IS CORRECT, YOU CAN ASK "IS THAT VALUE CORRECT?"
> The system points out a feature that the student may not otherwise be aware of. Correct here means what it is in a working instrument.

≫IS THAT RIGHT?
IN A WORKING CIRCUIT THE OUTPUT VOLTAGE IS 30.1 VOLTS.
THAT VALUE IS INCORRECT.
> SOPHIE permits reference to previous objects in the dialogue. Here, That refers to the value of the previous measurement.

≫WHAT IS THE VOLTAGE BETWEEN THE CURRENT LIMITING TRANSISTOR
. . . AND THE CONSTANT CURRENT SOURCE?
THE VOLTAGE AT N4 IS 2.48 VOLTS.
> This is an example of some of the complexities that arise in even limited domains. Although the syntax of the sentence is voltage between x and y, it really means voltage at z with respect to ground where z is the point between x and y. The output routines rephrase the input in a simpler form (i.e., between x and y reduces to N4) so that the user knows the system's interpretation and has an easier way of referring to that location.

≫WHAT IS IT BETWEEN THERE AND THE BASE OF Q6?
THE VOLTAGE BETWEEN N4 AND N5 IS 1.28 VOLTS.
> Here it refers to the voltage and there refers to N4. Also notice that

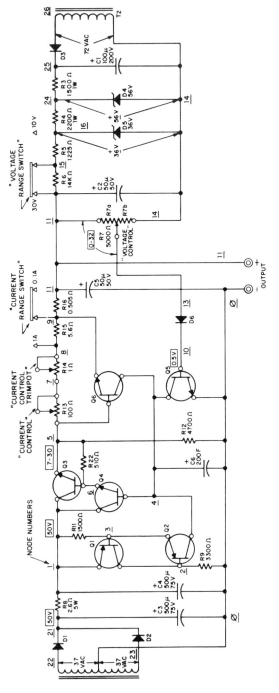

Figure 10.1 Circuit schematic of the power supply.

280

between has to be treated differently—that is, two nodes are explicit now.

≫IS THERE ANY RIPPLE IN THE VOLTAGE AT THE BASE OF Q4?
I'M SORRY, I DO NOT HANDLE AC CHARACTERISTICS.

SOPHIE recognizes that the student is moving into an area that it is unable to handle. This is currently done by keyword recognition (e.g., ripple) but points out a technique that should be incorporated in other aspects of the system as well.

≫WHAT IS THE BASE CURRENT OF Q3?
THE BASE CURRENT OF Q3 IS 12 MICROAMPS.

The following collection of sentences demonstrates the conciseness and flexibility of the dialogue mechanism. After introducing a context in a complete sentence, the student can easily and naturally ask related questions.

≫THRU THE EMITTER?
THE EMITTER CURRENT OF Q3 IS −.26 MILLIAMPS.

This type of sentence fragment, which we will refer to as an ellipsis, occurs frequently in dialogues. Rather than specifying a complete thought, an ellipsis gives only that piece of the thought that contrasts an earlier thought. Notice that the referent cannot be determined on syntactic grounds (as is possible with the ellipsis "the emitter current"); yet this is the sort of statement a student might make if the last answer had caused a slight shifting of his thinking.

≫Q4
THE EMITTER CURRENT OF Q4 IS −.26 MILLIAMPS.

In this case, the student is changing his attention to a different transistor. There is ambiguity as to whether he wanted the base current, the emitter current, or both. SOPHIE picks the most recent one and gives its interpretation as a complete sentence.

≫IF C2 WERE LEAKY, WHAT WOULD THE VOLTAGE ACROSS IT BE?
As this sentence shows, the referent to it can occur earlier in the same sentence.

IS IT OKAY IF I USE 10000 FOR THE LEAKAGE RESISTANCE OF C2?
> YES
IF THE LEAKAGE RESISTANCE OF C2 WERE 10000
UNDER THE PRESENT SETTINGS, THE VOLTAGE ACROSS C2 WOULD BE 26.3 VOLTS.
IN A WORKING CIRCUIT IT IS 28.9 VOLTS.

≫IF Q6 HAS AN OPEN EMITTER AND A SHORTED BAE COLLECTOR JUNCTION WHAT HAPPENS TO THE VOLTAGE BETWEEN ITS BASE AND THE JUNCTION OF THE VOLTGE LIMITING SECTION AND THE VOLTAGE REFERENCE SOURCE?
BAE ⇒ BASE
VOLTGE ⇒ VOLTAGE

Several examples of the use of conjunction. Imagine the student's frustration if forced to type this query over because of spelling mistakes.

UNDER THE SETTINGS:
CC=9, CR=LOW, LOAD=10, VC=1.0, VR=LOW.
THE VOLTAGE BETWEEN N5 AND N13 WOULD BE 8.94 VOLTS.
IN A WORKING CIRCUIT IT IS 9.57 VOLTS.

≫WHAT IS THE CURRENT THRU THE CC WHEN THE VC IS SET TO 1.0?
WITH THE VOLTAGE CONTROL NOW SET AT 1.0
THE CURRENT THRU THE CURRENT CONTROL IS 30 MILLIAMPS.
    CC and VC are abbreviations. The controls are also "parts" that can be
    used in measurements.
≫WHAT IS IT WITH IT SET TO .8?
WITH THE VOLTAGE CONTROL NOW SET AT .8
THE CURRENT THRU THE CURRENT CONTROL IS 24 MILLIAMPS.
    Here the system must correctly instantiate two occurrences of it. The
    referent to the second it could be either CC or VC, since these are both
    controls.

SEMANTIC GRAMMAR

Introduction

In the first section we described the requirements for a natural-language
processor in a learning environment. Briefly, they are efficiency and
friendliness over the class of sentences that arise in a dialogue situation.
The major leverage points we have that allow us to satisfy these requirements are (*a*) limited domain; (*b*) limited activities within that domain; and
(*c*) known conceptualizations of the domain. In other words, we know the
problem area, the type of problem the students are trying to solve, and the
way they should be thinking about the problem in order to solve it. What
we are then faced with is taking advantage of these constraints in order to
provide an effective communication channel.

Notice that all of these constraints relate to concepts underlying the
student's activities. In SOPHIE, the concepts include voltage, current,
parts, transistors, terminals, faults, particular parts, hypotheses, controls,
settings of controls, and so on. The dependency relationships between
concepts include things such as these: Voltage can be measured at terminals, parts can be faulted, and controls can be set. The student, in
formulating a query or statement, is requesting information or stating a
belief about one of these relationships (e.g., *What is the voltage at the
collector of transistor Q5?* or *I think resistor R9 is open.*)

It occurred to us that the best way to characterize the statements used
for this task was in terms of the concepts themselves as opposed to the
traditional syntactic structures. The language can be described by a set of
grammar rules that characterize, for each concept or relationship, all of
the ways of expressing it in terms of other constituent concepts. For
example, the concept of a measurement requires a quantity to be measured and something against which to measure it. A measurement is

typically expressed by giving the quantity followed by a preposition, followed by the thing that specifies where to measure (e.g., *voltage across capacitor C2, current thru diode D1*). These phrasings are captured in this grammar rule (this is not actually a rule from the grammar but is merely intended to be suggestive):

<MEASUREMENT> := <MEASURABLE/QUANTITY> <PREP> <PART>

The concept of a measurement can, in turn, be used as part of other concepts—for example, to request a measurement (*What is the voltage across capacitor C2?*) or to check a measurement (*Is the current thru divide D1 correct?*) We call this type of grammar a *semantic grammar* because the relationships it tries to characterize are semantic and conceptual as well as syntactic.

Semantic grammars have two advantages over traditional syntactic grammars. They allow semantic constraints to be used to make predictions during the parsing process, and they provide a useful characterization of those sentences that the system should try to handle. The predictive aspect is important for four reasons:

1. It reduces the number of alternatives that must be checked at a given time.
2. It reduces the amount of syntactic (grammatical) ambiguity.
3. It allows recognition of ellipsed or deleted phrases.
4. It permits the parser to skip words at controlled places in the input (i.e., it enables a reasonable specification of control).

These points will be discussed in detail in a later section.

The characterization aspect is important for two reasons:

1. It provides a handle on the problem of constructing a habitable sublanguage. The system knows how to deal with a particular set of tasks over a particular set of objects. The sublanguage can be partitioned by tasks to accept all straightforward ways of expressing those tasks, but does not need to worry about others.
2. It allows a reduction in the number of sentences that must be accepted by the language while still maintaining habitability. There may be syntactic constructs that are used frequently with one concept (task) but seldom with another. For example, relative clauses may be useful in explaining the reasons for performing an experimental test but are an awkward (though possible) way of requesting a measurement. By separating the processing along semantic grounds, one may gain efficiency by not having to accept the awkward phrasing.

Representation of Meaning

Since natural-language communication is the transmission of concepts via phrases, the "meaning" of a phrase is its correspondent in the conceptual space. The entities in SOPHIE's conceptual space are objects, relationships between objects, and procedures for dealing with objects. The meaning of a phrase can be a simple data object (e.g., *current limiting transistor*) or a complex data object (e.g., *C5 open; Voltage at Node 1*). The meaning of a question is a call to a procedure that knows how to determine the answer. The meaning of a command is a call to a procedure that performs the specified action. (Declarative statements are treated as requests because the pragmatics of the situation imply that the student is asking for verification of his statement. For example, *I think C2 is shorted* is taken to be a request to have the hypothesis *C2 is shorted* critiqued.) For example, the procedural specialist DOFAULT knows how to fault the circuit and is used to represent the meaning of commands to fault the circuit (e.g., *Open R9; Suppose C2 shorts and R9 opens*). The argument that DOFAULT needs in order to perform its task is an instance of the concept of faults that specifies the particular changes to be made (e.g., *R9 being open*). These same concepts of particular faults also serve as arguments to two other specialists: HYPTEST, which determines the consistency of a fault with respect to the present context (e.g., *Could R9 be open*) and SEEFAULT, which checks the actual status of the circuit (e.g., *Is R9 open?*).

Result of the Parsing

Basing the grammar on conceptual entities allows the semantic interpretation (the determination of the concept underlying a phrase) to proceed in parallel with the parsing. Since each of the nonterminal categories in the grammar is based on a semantic unit, each grammar rule can specify the semantic description of a phrase that it recognizes in much the same way that a syntactic grammar specifies a syntactic description. The construction portion of the rules is procedural. Each rule has the freedom to decide how the semantic descriptions, returned by the constituent items of that rule, are to be put together to form the correct "meaning."

For example, the meaning of the phrase *Q5* is the data base object Q5. The meaning of the phrase *the collector of Q5* is (COLLECTOR Q-5), where COLLECTOR is a function that returns the data base item that is the collector of the given transistor.

The rule for <MEASUREMENT> expresses all of the ways that the

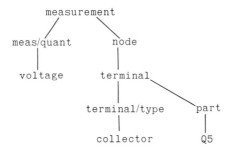

Figure 10.2 Control structure for the <measurement> rule.

student can give a measurable quantity and also supply its required arguments. The structure that results from <MEASUREMENT> is a function call to the function MEASURE that supplies the quantity being measured and other arguments specifying where to measure it. Thus the meaning of the phrase *the voltage at the collector of Q5* is (MEASURE VOLTAGE (COLLECTOR Q5)), which was generated from the control structure (see Figure 10.2).

The grammar rule for <MEASUREMENT> also accepts "meaningless" phrases such as *the power dissipation of Node 4.* In addition, it accepts some meaningful phrases such as *the resistance between Node 3 and Node 14,* which SOPHIE does not calculate. This results from generalizing together concepts that are not treated identically in the surface structure. In this case, *voltage, current, resistance,* and *power dissipation* were generalized to the concept of a measurable quantity. The advantage of allowing the grammar to accept more statements and having the argument checking done by the procedural specialists is that the semantic routines provide the feedback as to why a sentence cannot be interpreted or "understood." It also keeps the grammar from being cluttered with special rules for blocking meaningless phrases. Carried to the limit, the generalization strategy would return the grammar to being "syntactic" again (e.g., all data objects are "noun phrases"). The trick is to leave semantics in the grammar when it is beneficial—to stop extraneous parsings early, or to tighten the range of a referent for an ellipsis or deletion. This is obviously a task-specific trade-off. (Bobrow and Brown [1975] describe an interesting paradigm from which to consider this trade-off.)

The relationship between a phrase and its meaning is usually straightforward. However, it is not limited to simple embedding. Consider the phrases *the base emitter of Q5 shorted* and *the base of Q5 shorted to the emitter.* The thing which is "shorted" in both of these phrases is the "base emitter junction of Q5." The rule that recognizes both of these phrases, <PART/FAULT/SPEC>, can handle the first phrase by invoking its constituent concepts of <JUNCTION> (*base emitter of Q5*) and <FAULT/TYPE> (*shorted*) and combine their results. In the second phrase, however, it must construct the proper junction from the separate occurrences of the two terminals involved.

This discussion has been presented as if the concepts were defined a priori by the capabilities of the system. Actually, for the system to remain at all habitable, the concepts are discovered in the interplay between expanding the corpus of sentences the system can handle and adding capabilities to the system. When a particular English construct is difficult to handle, it is probably an indication that the concept it is trying to express has not been recognized properly by the system. In our example *the base of Q5 is shorted to the emitter*, the relationship between the phrase and its meaning is awkward because the present concept of shorting requires a part or a junction. The example is getting at a concept of shorting, in which any two terminals can be shorted together (e.g., *the positive terminal of R9 is shorted to the anode of D6*). This is a viable conceptual view of shorting, but its implementation requires allowing arbitrary changes in the topology of the circuit, which is beyond the efficiency limitations of SOPHIE's simulator. Thus, the system we were working with led us to define the concept in too limited a way.

Use of Semantic Information during Parsing

Prediction

Having described the notion of a semantic grammar, we will now describe the ways in which it allows semantic information to be used in the understanding process. One use of semantic grammars is to predict the possible alternatives that must be checked at a given point. Consider, for example, the phrase *the voltage at xxx*. After the word *at* is reached in the top-down, left-to-right parse, the grammar rule corresponding to the concept *measurement* can predict very specifically the conceptual nature of *xxx*: It must be a phrase that directly or indirectly specifies a location in the circuit. For example, *xxx* could be *the junctions of the current limiting section and the voltage reference source* but cannot be *3 ohms*.

Semantic grammars also have the effect of reducing the amount of grammatical ambiguity. In the phrase *the voltage at xxx*, the prepositional phrase *at xxx* will be associated with the noun *voltage* without considering any alternative parses that associate it somewhere higher in the tree.

Predictive information is also used to aid in the determination of referents for pronouns. If the above phrase were *the voltage at it*, the grammar would be able to restrict the class of possible referents to locations.

By taking advantage of the available sentence contexts to predict the semantic class of possible referents, the referent-determination process is greatly simplified. For example:

   1a. *Set the voltage control to .8?*
   1b. *What is the current thru R9?*
   1c. *What is it with it set to .9?*

In 1c, the grammar is able to recognize that the first *it* refers to a measurement that the student would like retaken under slightly different conditions. The grammar can also decide that the second *it* refers to either a potentiometer or to the load resistance (i.e., one of those things that can be set). The referent for the first *it* is the measurement taken in 1b, *the current thru R9*. The referent for the second *it* is *the voltage control*, which is an instance of a potentiometer. The context mechanism that selects the referents will be discussed later.

Simple Deletion

The semantic grammar is also used to recognize simple deletions. The grammar rule for each conceptual entity knows the nature of that entity's constituent concepts. When a rule cannot find a constituent concept, it can either

   a. fail (if the missing concept is considered to be obligatory in the surface structure representation) or,
   b. hypothesize that a deletion has occurred and continue.

For example, the concept of a TERMINAL has as one of its realizations the constituent concepts of a TERMINAL-TYPE and a PART. When its grammar rule finds only the phrase *the collector*, it uses this information to posit that a part has been deleted (i.e., TERMINAL-TYPE gets instantiated to *the collector* but nothing gets instantiated to PART). The natural-language processor then uses the dependencies between the constituent concepts to determine that the deleted PART must be a TRANSISTOR. The "meaning" of this phrase is then *the collector of some transistor*. **Which** transistor is determined when the meaning is evaluated in the present dialogue context. In particular, the semantic form returned is the function PREF and the classes of possible referents; in our example the form would be (COLLECTOR (PREF (TRANSISTOR))).

Ellipsis

Another use of the semantic grammar allows the processor to recognize elliptic utterances. These are utterances that do not express complete thoughts—a completely specified question or command—but only give differences between the intended thought and an earlier one.[4] For example, 2b, 2c, and 2d are elliptic utterances.

2a. *What is the voltage at Node 5?*
2b. *At Node 1?*
2c. *And Node 2?*
2d. *What about between nodes 7 and 8?*

Ellipses can begin with introductory phrases such as *and* in 2c or *what about* in 2d; however this is not required, as can be seen in 2b. Part of the ellipsis rule is given in Figure 10.3.

```
<ELLIPSIS> := [<ELLIPSIS/INTRODUCER>] <REQUEST/PIECE> !
              [<ELLIPSIS/INTRODUCER>] if <PART/FAULT/SPEC>
<REQUEST/PIECE> := [<PREP>] <NODE> !
                  [<PREP>] <PART> !
                  between <NODE> and <NODE> !
                  [<PREP>] <JUNCTION> !
                  etc.
```

Figure 10.3 Ellipsis rule.

The grammar rule identifies which concept or class of concepts is possible from the context available in the elliptic utterance.

Though the parser is usually able to determine the intended concepts from the context available in an elliptic utterance, this is not always the case. Consider the following two sequences of statements.

3a. *What is the voltage at Node 5?*
3b. *10?*

4a. *What is the output voltage if the load is 100?*
4b. *10?*

In 3b, *10* refers to Node 10, whereas in 4b it refers to a load of 10. The problem this presents to the parser is that the concepts underlying these two elliptic utterances have nothing in common except their surface realizations. The parser, which operates from conceptual entities, does not have a concept that includes both of these interpretations. One solution would be to have the parser find all parses (concepts) and then choose between them on the basis of context. Unfortunately, this would mean that time is wasted looking for more than one parse for the large percentage of sentences in which it is not necessary to do so. A better solution

---

[4] The standard use of the word *ellipsis* refers to any deletion. Rather than invent a new word, we shall use the restricted meaning here.

would be to allow structure among the concepts, so that the parser would recognize *10* as a member of the concept *number*. Then the routines that find the referent would know that numbers can be either node numbers or values. This type of recognition could profitably be performed by a bottom-up approach to parsing. However, its advantages over the present scheme are not enough to justify the expense incurred by a bottom-up parse to find all possible well-formed constituents. At present, the parser assumes one interpretation, and a message is printed to the student indicating the assumed interpretation. If it is wrong, the student must supply more context in his request. In fact, *10?* is taken as a load specification and if the student meant the node he would have to use *at 10, N10,* or *Node 10.* Later we will discuss the mechanism that determines to which complete thought an ellipsis refers.

Using Context to Determine Referents

Pronouns and Deletions

Once the parser has determined the existence and class (or set of classes) of a pronoun or deleted object, the context mechanism is invoked to determine the proper referent. This mechanism has a history of student interactions during the current session that contains, for each interaction, the parse (meaning) of the student's statement and the response calculated by the system. This list provides the range of possible referents and is searched in reverse order to find an object of the proper semantic class (or one of the proper classes). To aid in the search, the context mechanism knows how each of the procedural specialists appearing in a parse uses its arguments. For example, the specialist MEASURE has a first argument that must be a quantity and a second argument that must be a part, a junction, a section, a terminal, or a node. Thus when the context mechanism is looking for a referent that can be either a PART or a JUNCTION, it will look at the second argument of a call to MEASURE but not the first. Using the information about the specialists, the context mechanism looks in the present parse and then in the next most recent parse, etc., until an object from one of the specified classes is found.

The significance of using the specialist to filter the search instead of just keeping a list of previously mentioned objects is that it avoids misinterpretations due to object–concept ambiguity. As an example, consider the following sequence from the sample dialogue in the previous section:

5. *What is the current thru the CC when the VC is 1.0?*
6. *What is it when it is .8?*

Sentence 5 will be recognized by the following rules from the semantic grammar:

```
$1) <REQUEST> := <SIMPLE/REQUEST> when <SETTING/CHANGE>
$2) <SIMPLE/REQUEST> := what is <MEASUREMENT>
$3) <MEASUREMENT> := <MEAS/QUANT> <PREP> <PART>
$4) <SETTING/CHANGE> := <CONTROL> is <CONTROL/VALUE>
$5) <CONTROL> := VC
```

with a resulting semantic form of:

```
(RESETCONTROL (STQ VC 1.0)
              (MEASURE CURRENT CC))
```

RESETCONTROL is a function whose first argument specifies a change to one of the controls and whose second argument consists of a form to be evaluated in the resulting instrument context. STQ is used to change the setting of one of the controls. The first argument to MEASURE gives the quantity to be measured. The second specifies where it is to be measured. To recognize Sentence 6, the application of Rules $2 and $5 are changed. There is an alternative rule for <SIMPLE/REQUEST> that looks for those anaphora (i.e., *that, it,* and *one*) that refer to a measurement. These phrases, such as *it, that result,* or *the value,* are recognized by the nonterminal <MEASUREMENT/PRONOUN>. The alternative to $2 that would be used to parse (6) is

```
<SIMPLE/REQUEST> := what is <MEASUREMENT/PRONOUN>.
```

The semantics of <MEASUREMENT/PRONOUN> indicate that an entire measurement has been deleted. The alternative to Rule $5,

```
<CONTROL> := it,
```

recognizes *it* as an acceptable way to specify a control. The resulting semantic form for Sentence 6 is

```
(RESETCONTROL (STQ (PREF '(CONTROL)) .8)
              (PREF '(MEASUREMENT)))
```

The function PREF searches back through the context of previous semantic forms to find the most recent mention of a member of one of the classes. In the above example, it will find the control VC but not CC because the character imposed on the arguments of MEASURE is that of a "part," not a "control." The presently recognized classes for deletions are PART, TRANSISTOR, FAULT, CONTROL, POT, SWITCH, DIODE, MEASUREMENT, and QUANTITY. (The members of the classes are derived from the semantic network associated with a circuit.)

Referents for Ellipses

If the problem of pronoun resolution is looked upon as finding a previously mentioned object for a currently specified use, then the problem of ellipsis can be thought of as finding a previously mentioned use for a currently specified object. For example,

7. *What is the base current of Q4?*
8. *In Q5?*

The given object is *Q5*, and the earlier function is *base current*. For a given elliptic phrase, the semantic grammar identifies the concept (or class of concepts) involved. In 7, since Q5 is recognized by the nonterminal <TRANSISTOR/SPEC>, the class would be TRANSISTOR. The context mechanism then searches for a specialist in a previous parse that accepted the given class as an argument. When one is found, the new phrase is placed in the proper argument position and the modified parse is used as the meaning of the ellipsis.

Limitations to the Context Mechanism

The method of semantic classification (to determine reference) is very efficient and works well over our domain. It definitely does not solve all the problems of reference. Charniak (1972) has pointed out the substantial problems of reference in a domain as seemingly simple as children's stories. One of his examples demonstrates how much world knowledge may be required to determine a referent: "Janet and Penny went to the store to get presents for Jack. Janet said 'I will get Jack a top.' 'Don't get Jack a top,' said Penny. 'He has a top. He will make you take *it* back [p. 7]'."

Charniak argues that to understand to which of the two tops "it" refers requires knowing about presents, stores and what they will take back, etc. Even in domains where it may be possible to capture all of the necessary knowledge, classification may still lead to ambiguities. For example, consider the following:

9. *What is the voltage at Node 5 if the load is 100?*
10. *Node 6?*
11. *7?*

In Statement 11 the user means Node 7. In Statement 10, he has reinforced the use of ellipsis as referring to node number. (For example, when Statement 10 is left out, Statement 11 is much more awkward.) On the other hand, if Statement 11 had been *1000* or if Statement 10 had been *10?*, things would be more problematic. When Statement 11 is *1000*, we can infer that the user means a load of 1000 because there is no Node 1000. If Statement 10 had been *10?*, there would be genuine ambiguity slightly favoring the interpretation as a load because that was the last number mentioned. The major limitation of the current technique, which must be overcome in order to tackle significantly more complicated domains, is its inability to return more than one possible referent. It considers each one individually until it finds one that is satisfactory. The amount of work involved in employing a technique that allows comparing referents has not been justified by our experience.

Fuzziness

Having the grammar centered around semantic categories allows the parser to be sloppy about the actual words it finds in the statement. Having a concept in mind, and being willing to ignore words to find it, is the essence of keyword parsing schemes. It is effective in those cases where the words that have been skipped either are redundant or specify gradations of an idea that are not distinguished by the system. For example, in the sentence, *Insert a very hard fault*, *very* would be ignored; this is effective because the system does not have any further structure over the class of hard faults. In the sentence, *What is the voltage across resistor R8?* *resistor* can be ignored because it is implied by *R8*. (The first of these examples could be handled by making *very* a noise word (i.e., deleting it from all sentences). *Resistor*, however, is not a noise word in all cases (e.g., *What is the current through the current sensing resistor?*) and hence cannot be deleted.

One advantage that a procedural encoding of the grammar (discussed later) has over pattern-matching schemes in the implementation of fuzziness is its ability to control exactly where words can be ignored. This provides the ability to blend pattern-matching parsing of those concepts that are amenable to it with the structural parsing required by more complex concepts. The amount of fuzziness—how many, if any, words in a row can be ignored—is controlled in two ways. First, whenever a grammar rule is invoked, the calling rule has the option of limiting the number of words that can be skipped. Second, each rule can decide which of its constituent pieces or words are required and how tightly controlled the search for them should be. In SOPHIE, the normal mode of operation of the parser is tight in the beginning of a sentence, but fuzzier after it has made sense out of something.

Fuzziness has two other advantages worth mentioning briefly. It reduces the size of the dictionary because all known noise words do not have to be included. In those cases where the skipped words are meaningful, the misunderstanding may provide some clues to the user that allow him to restate his query.

Preprocessing

Before a statement is parsed, a preprocessor performs three operations. The first expands abbreviations, deletes known noise words, and canonicalizes similar words to a common form. The second is a cursory spelling correction. The third is a reduction of compound words.

Spelling correction is attempted on any word of the input string that the system does not recognize. The spelling correction algorithm[5] takes the possibly misspelled word and a list of correctly spelled words and determines which, if any, of the correct words is close to the misspelled word (using a metric determined by number of transpositions, doubled letters, dropped letters, etc.). During the initial preprocessing, the list of correct words is very small (approximately a dozen) and is limited to very commonly misspelled words and/or words that are critical to the understanding of a sentence. The list is kept small so that the time spent attempting spelling correction, prior to attempting a parse, is kept to a minimum. Remember that the parser has the ability to ignore words in the input string, so we do not want to spend a lot of time correcting a word that will not be needed in understanding the statement. But notice that certain words can be critical to the correct understanding of a statement. For example, suppose that the phrase *the base emitter current of Q3* were incorrectly typed as *the bse emitter current of Q3*. If *bse* were not recognized as being *base,* the parser would ignore it and misunderstand the phrase as *the emitter current of Q3,* a perfectly acceptable but much different concept.[6] Because of this problem, words like *base,* which if ignored have been found to lead to misunderstandings, are considered critical, and their spelling is corrected before any parse is attempted. Other words that are misspelled are not corrected until the second attempt at spelling correction that is done after a statement fails to parse.

Compound words are single concepts that appear in the surface structure as a fixed series of more than one word. Their reduction is very important to the efficient operation of the parser. For example, in the

---

[5] The spelling correction routines are provided by INTERLISP and were developed by Teitelman for use in the DWIM facility (Teitelman, 1969, 1974).

[6] To minimize the consequences of such misinterpretation, the system always responds with an answer that indicates what question it is answering, rather than just giving the numeric answer.

question, *What is the voltage range switch setting?*, *voltage range switch* is rewritten as the single item *VR*. If not rewritten, *voltage* would be mistaken as the beginning of a measurement (as in *What is the voltage at N4?*) and an attempt would have to be made to parse *range switch setting* as a place to measure voltage. Of course, after this failed, the correct parse could still be found, but reducing compound words helps to avoid search. In addition, the reduction of compound words simplifies the grammar rules by allowing them to work with larger conceptual units. In this sense, the preprocessing can be viewed as a preliminary bottom-up parse that recognizes local, multiword concepts.

Implementation

Once the dependencies between semantic concepts have been expressed in the Backus–Naur Form (BNF), each rule in the grammar is encoded (by hand) as a procedure in the programming language LISP. This encoding process imparts to the grammar a top-down control structure, specifies the order of application of the various alternatives of each rule, and defines the process of pattern matching each rule. The resulting collection of LISP functions constitutes a goal-oriented parser in a fashion similar to SHRDLU (Winograd, 1973), but without the backtracking ability of PROGRAMMER.

As has been argued elsewhere (Winograd, 1973; Woods, 1970), encoding the grammars as procedures—including the notion of process in the grammar—has advantages over using traditional phrase structure grammar representations. Four of these advantages are

1. The ability to collapse common parts of a grammar rule while still maintaining the perspicuity of the grammar
2. The ability to collapse similar rules by passing arguments (as with SENDR)
3. The ease of interfacing other types of knowledge (in SOPHIE, primarily the semantic network) into the parsing process
4. The ability to build and save arbitrary structures during the parsing process. (This ability is sometimes provided by allowing augments on phrase structure rules.)

In addition to the advantages it shares with other procedural representations, the LISP encoding has the computational advantage of being compilable directly into efficient machine code. The LISP implementation is efficient because the notion of process it contains (one process doing recursive descent) is close to that supported by physical machines, whereas those of ATN and PROGRAMMER are nondeterministic and hence not directly translatable into present architecture. (See Burton [1976] for a description of how it is possible to minimize this mismatch.)

In terms of efficiency, the LISP implementation of the semantic grammar succeeds admirably. The grammar written in the INTERLISP dialect of LISP (Teitelman, 1974) can be block-compiled. Using this technique, the complete parser takes about 5K of storage and parses a typical student statement consisting of 8 to 12 words in around 150 milliseconds!

A NEW FORMALISM—SEMANTIC AUGMENTED TRANSITION NETWORKS

Using the techniques described in the previous section, a natural-language processor capable of supporting the dialogue presented in the second section and requiring less than 200 milliseconds cpu time per question was constructed. In addition, these same techniques were used to build a processor for NLS-SCHOLAR (Grignetti, Gould, Hausmann, Bell, Harris, & Passafiume, 1974; Grignetti, Hausmann, & Gould, 1975) (built by K. Larkin), and an interface to an experimental laboratory for exploring mathematics using attribute blocks (Brown & Burton, 1978). In the construction of these varying systems, the notion of semantic grammar proved to be useful. The LISP implementation, however, was found to be a bit unwieldy. Although expressing the grammar as programs is efficient and allows complete freedom to explore new extensions, the technique is lacking in perspicuity. This lack of perspicuity has three major drawbacks: (*a*) the difficulty encountered when trying to modify or extend the grammar; (*b*) the problem of trying to communicate the extent of the grammar to either a user or a colleague; (*c*) the problem of trying to reimplement the grammar on a machine that does not support LISP. These difficulties have been partially overcome by using a second, parallel representation of the grammar in a specification language similar to the Backus–Naur Form, which is the representation we have been presenting throughout this report. This, however, requires supporting two different representations of the same information and does not really solve problems *a* or *c*. The solution to this problem is a better formalism for expressing and thinking about semantic grammars. This section discusses such a formalism.

Augmented Transition Networks (ATN)

Some years ago, Chomsky (1957) introduced the notion that the processes of language generation and language recognition could be viewed in terms of a machine. One of the simplest of such models is the finite state machine. It starts off in its initial state looking at the first symbol, or word, of its input sentence and then moves from state to state as it gobbles up the remaining input symbols. The sentence is **accepted** if the machine stops in one of its final states after having processed the entire input string; otherwise the sentence is **rejected**. A convenient way of representing a finite state machine is as a transition graph, in which the states correspond to the nodes of the graph and the transitions between states correspond to its arcs. Each arc is labeled with a symbol whose appearance in the input can cause the given transition.

In an augmented transition network, the notion of a transition graph has been modified in three ways: (a) the addition of a recursion mechanism that allows the labels on the arcs to be nonterminal symbols that correspond to networks; (b) the addition of arbitrary conditions on the arcs that must be satisfied in order for an arc to be followed; (c) the inclusion of a set of structure-building actions on the arcs, together with a set of named registers for holding partially built structures. (This discussion follows closely a similar discussion in Woods [1970], to which the reader is referred. A reader familiar with the augmented transition network formalism may wish to skip to the section "Advantages to the Augmented Transition Network Formalism.") Figure 10.4 is a specification of a language for representing augmented transition networks. The specification is given in the form of an extended, context-free grammar in which alternative ways of forming a constituent are represented on separate lines and the symbol + is used to indicate arbitrarily repeatable constituents. (+ is used to mean 0 or more occurrences. Though the accepted usage of + is 1 or more, the accepted symbol for 0 or more, *, has not been used to avoid confusion with the use of the symbol * in the augmented transition network formalism.) The nonterminal symbols are lowercase English descriptions enclosed in angle brackets. All other symbols, except +, are terminals. Nonterminals not given in Figure 10.4 have names intended to be self-explanatory.

The first element of each arc is a word indicating the type of arc. For arcs of type CAT, WRD, and PUSH, the arc type together with the second element corresponds to the label on an arc of a state transition graph. The third element is an additional test. A CAT (category) arc can be followed if the current input symbol is a member of the lexical category named on the arc and if the test on the arc is satisfied. A PUSH (network call) arc causes a recursive invocation of a lower level network beginning at the state indicated, if the test is satisfied. The WRD (word) arc can be followed if the current input symbol is the word named on the arc and if the test is satisfied. The TST (test) arc can be followed if the test is

```
<transition network> := (<arc set><arc set>+)
<arc set> := (<state> <arc>+)
<arc> := (CAT <category name> <test> <action>+ <term act>)
        (WRD <word> <test> <action>+ <term act>)
        (PUSH <state> <test> <action>+ <term act>)
        (TST <arbitrary label> <test> <action>+ <term act>)
        (POP <form> <test>)
        (VIR <constituent name> <test> <action>+ <term act>)
        (JUMP <state><test><action>+)
<action> := (SETR <register> <form>)
           (SENDR < register><form >)
           (LIFTR <register> <form>)
           (HOLD <constituent name> <form>)
           (SETF <feature> <form>)
<term act> := (TO <state>)
<form> :=(GETR <register>)
        LEX
        *
        (GETF <form> <feature>)
        (BUILDQ <fragment> <register>+)
        (LIST <form>+)
        (APPEND <form> <form>)
        (QUOTE <arbitrary structure>)
```

Figure 10.4 A language for representing ATNs.

satisfied (the label is ignored). The VIR arc (virtual arc) can be followed if a constituent of the named type has been placed on the hold list by a previous HOLD action and the constituent satisfies the test. In all of these arcs, the actions are structure-building actions, and the terminal action specifies the state to which control is passed as a result of the transition. After CAT, WRD, and TST arcs, the input is advanced; after VIR and PUSH arcs it is not. The JUMP arc can be followed whenever its test is satisfied, control being passed to the state specified in the second element of the arc without advancing the input. The POP (return from network) arc indicates the conditions under which the state is to be considered a final state and the form of the constituent to be returned.

The actions, forms, and tests on an arc may be arbitrary functions of the register contents. Figure 10.4 presents a useful set that illustrates major features of the ATN. The first three actions specified in Figure 10.4 cause the contents of the indicated register to be set to the value of the indicated form. SETR (set register) causes this to be done at the current level of computation, SENDR (send register) at the next lower level of embedding, so that information can be sent down during a PUSH, and LIFTR (lift register) at the next higher level of computation, so that additional information can be returned to higher levels. The HOLD action places a form on the HOLD list to be used at a later place in the computation by a VIR arc. SETF (set feature) provides a means of setting a feature of the constituent being built.

GETR (get register value) is a function whose value is the contents of the named register. LEX (lexical item) is a form whose value is the current input symbol. The asterisk (*) is a form whose value depends on the context of its use:

1. In the actions of a CAT arc, the value of * is the root form of the current input word.
2. In the actions of a PUSH arc, it is the value of the lower computation.
3. In the actions following a VIR arc, the value of it is the constituent removed from the HOLD list.

GETF is a function that determines the value of a specified feature of the indicated form (which is usually *). BUILDQ is a general structure-building form that places the values of the given registers into a specified tree fragment. Specifically, it replaces each occurrence of + in the tree fragment with the contents of one of the registers (the first register replacing the first occurrence of +, the second register the second, etc.). In addition, BUILDQ replaces occurrences of * by the value of the form *. The remaining three forms make a list out of the specified arguments (LIST), append two lists together to make a single list (APPEND), and produce as a value the (unevaluated) arbitrary form (QUOTE).

Advantages of ATN Formalism

The augmented transition network (ATN) formalism was seriously considered at the beginning of the SOPHIE project but rejected as being too slow. In the course of developing the LISP grammar, it became clear that the primary reason for a significant difference in speed between an ATN grammar and a LISP grammar is due to the fact that processing the augmented transition network (ATN) is an interpreted process, whereas LISP is compilable and therefore the time problem could be overcome by building an ATN compiler. During the period of evolution of SOPHIE's grammar, an ATN compiler was constructed (see Burton, 1976). In the next section we will discuss the advantages we hoped to gain by using the ATN formalism.

These advantages fall into three general areas: (a) conciseness; (b) conceptual effectiveness; and (c) available facilities. By conciseness we mean that writing a grammar as an ATN takes fewer characters than LISP. The ATN formalism gains conciseness by not requiring the specification of details in the parsing process at the same level required in LISP. Most of these differences stem from the fact that the ATN assumes it has a machine whose operations are designed for parsing, whereas LISP assumes it has a lambda calculus machine. For example, a lambda calculus machine assumes a function has one value. A function call to look for an occurrence at a nonterminal while parsing (in ATN formalism, a PUSH) must return at least two values: the structure of the constituent found, and the place in the input where the parsing stopped. A good deal of complexity is added to the LISP rules in order to maintain the free variable that has to be introduced to return the structure of the constituent. Other examples of unnecessary details include the binding of local variables and the specification of control structure as ANDs and ORs.

The conciseness of the ATN results in a grammar that is easier to change, easier to write and debug, and easier to understand, and hence provide for better communication. We realize that conciseness does not necessarily lead to these results (APL being a counter example in computer languages, mathematics in general being another); however, this is not a problem. The correspondence between the grammar rules in LISP and ATN is very close. The concepts that were expressed as LISP code can be expressed in nearly the same way as ATN but in fewer symbols.

The second area of improvement deals with conceptual effectiveness. Loosely defined, conceptual effectiveness is the degree to which a language encourages one to think about problems in the right way. One example of conceptual effectiveness can be seen by considering the implementation of case-structured rules. (See Bruce [1975] for a discussion of case systems.) In a typical case-structure rule, the verb expresses the function (or relation name) and the subject, and the object and prepositional phrases express the arguments of the function or relation. Let us assume for the purpose of this discussion that we are looking at four different cases (agent, location, means, and time) of the verb GO—*John went to the store by car at 10 o'clock.* In a phrase structure rule-oriented formalism one would be encouraged to write:

```
<statement> :=<actor> <action/verb> <location> <means> <time>
```

Since the last three cases can appear in any order, one must also write five other rules:

```
<statement> :=<actor> <action/verb> <location> <time> <means>
    ⋮
```

In an ATN one is inclined toward a graph (see Figure 10.5) that expresses more clearly the case structure of the rule. There is no reason why in the

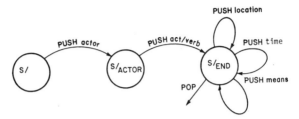

Figure 10.5 A case structure ATN rule.

LISP version of the grammar one could not write loops that are exactly analogous to the ATN (the ATN compiler, after all, produces such code!). However, a rule-oriented formalism does not encourage one to think this way. An alternative rule implementation is

```
<action>:=<actor><action/verb><action1>
<action1>:=<action1><time>
<action1>:= <action1><location>
<action1>:= <action1><means>
```

This is easier (shorter) to write but it has the disadvantage of being left-recursive. To implement it, one is forced to write the LISP equivalent of the augmented transition network that creates a difference between the rule representation and the actual implementation. This method also has the disadvantage of introducing the nonterminal <action1> into the grammar.

Another conceptual advantage of the ATN framework is that it encourages the postponing of decisions about a sentence until a differential point is reached, thereby allowing potentially different paths to stay together. In the rule-oriented SOPHIE grammar there are top-level rules for <set>, a command to change one of the control settings, and <modify>, a command to fault the instrument in some way. Sentence 1 is a <set> and Sentence 2 is a <modify>.

1. *Suppose the current control is high.*
2. *Suppose the current control is shorted.*

The two parse paths for these sentences should be the same for the first five words, but they are separated immediately by the rules <set> and <modify>. An ATN encourages structuring the grammar so that the decision between <set> and <modify> is postponed so that the paths remain together. It could be argued that the fact that this example occurred in SOPHIE's grammar is a complaint against top-down parsing or semantic grammars, or just our particular instantiation of a semantic grammar. We suspect the latter but argue that rule representations encourage this type of behavior.

Another conceptual aid provided by ATNs is their method of handling ambiguity. Our LISP implementation uses a recursive descent technique (which can alternatively be viewed as allowing only one process). This requires that any decision between two choices be made correctly because there is no way to try out the other choice **after** the decision is made. At choice points, a rule can, of course, "look ahead" and gain information on which to base the decision, similar to the "wait-and-see" strategy used by Marcus (1975), but there is no way to back up and remake a decision once it has returned.

The effects of this can be most easily seen by considering the lexical aspects of the parsing. A prepass collapses compound words, expands abbreviations, etc. This allows the grammar to be much simpler because it can look for units like *voltage–control* instead of having to decode the noun phrase *voltage control*. Unfortunately, without the ability to handle ambiguity, this rewriting can be done only on words that have no other possible meaning. So, for example, when the grammar is extended to handle

3. *Does the voltage control the current limiting section?*

the compound *voltage–control* would have to be removed from the prepass rules and included in the grammar. This reduces the amount of bottom-up processing that can be done and results in a slower parse. It also makes compound rules difficult to write because all possible uses of the individual words must be considered to avoid errors. Another example is the use of the letter "C" as an abbreviation. Depending on context, it could possibly mean either current, collector, or capacitor. Without allowing ambiguity in the input, it could not be allowed as an abbreviation unless explicitly recognized by the grammar.

The third general area in which ATNs have an advantage is in the available facilities to deal with complex linguistic phenomena. Though our grammar has not yet expanded to the point of requiring any of the facilities, the availability of such facilities cannot be ignored as an argument favoring one approach over another. A primary example is the general mechanism for dealing with coordination in English described in Woods (1973).

Conversion to Semantic ATN

For the reasons discussed above, the SOPHIE semantic grammar was rewritten in the ATN formalism. We wish to stress here that the rewriting was a process of **changing form** only. The content of the grammar remained the same. Since a large part of the knowledge encoded by the grammar continues to be semantic in nature, we call the resulting grammar a *semantic ATN*.

Figure 10.6 presents the graphic ATN representation of semantic grammar nonterminal, which recognizes the straightforward way of expressing a terminal of a part in the circuit—the base of Q5, the anode of it, the collector. It also shows a simple example of how the recognition of anaphoric deletions can be captured in ATN formalism. By the state TERMINAL/TYPE, both the determiner and the terminal type—base, anode—have been found. The first arc that leaves TERMINAL/TYPE accepts the preposition that begins the specification of the part. The second arc (JUMP arc) corresponds to hypothesizing that the specification of the part has been deleted, as in *The base is open.* The action on the arc builds a place-holding form that identifies the deletion and specifies (from information associated with the terminal type that was found) the classes of objects that can fill the deletion. The method for determining the referent of the deletion remains the same as described in the third section.

The SOPHIE semantic ATN is compiled using the general ATN compiling system described in Burton (1976). The SOPHIE grammar provides the compiling system with a good contrast to the LUNAR grammar (Woods, Kaplan & Nash-Webber, 1972) (that was used as a test during development of the compiler), since it does not use many of the potential features. In addition, a bench mark, of sorts, was available from the LISP implementation of the grammar that could be used to determine the computational cost of using the ATN formalism.

There were two modifications made to the compiling system to improve its efficiency for the SOPHIE application. In the SOPHIE grammar, a large number of the arcs check for the occurrence of particular words. When there is more than one arc leaving a state, the ATN formalism requires that all of these arcs be tried, even if more than one of these is a WRD (word) arc and an earlier WRD arc has succeeded. This is especially costly, since the taking of an arc requires the creation of a configuration (data structure) to try the remaining arcs. In those cases when the grammar writer knows that none of the other arcs can succeed, this should be avoided. As a solution to this problem, the GROUP arc type was added. The GROUP arc allows a set of contiguous arcs to be designated as

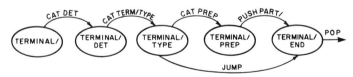

Figure 10.6 A semantic ATN that recognizes deletion.

mutually exclusive. The form of the GROUP arc is (GROUP arc1 arc2 . . . arcn). The arcs are tried, one at a time, until the conditions on one of the arcs are met. This arc is then taken, and the remaining arcs in the GROUP are forgotten—not tried. If a PUSH arc is included in the GROUP, it will be taken if its test is true, and the remaining arcs will not be tried even if the PUSHed-for constituent is not found. For example, consider the following grammar state:

```
(S/1
    (GROUP (CAT A T (TO S/2))
           (WRD X T (TO S/3))
           (CAT B T (TO S/4)))))
```

At most, one of the three arcs will be followed. Without GROUPing them together, it is possible that all three might be followed—if the word X had interpretations as both Category A and Category B.

The GROUP arc also provides an efficient means of encoding optional constituents. The normal method of allowing options in ATN is to provide an arc that accepts the optional constituent and a second arc that jumps to the next state without accepting anything. For example, if in State S/2 the word *very* is optional, the following two arcs would be created:

```
(S/2
    (WRD VERY T (TO REST-OF-S/2))
    (JUMP REST-OF-S/2 T))
```

The inefficiency arises when the word *very* does occur. The first arc is taken, but an alternative configuration that will try the second arc must be created, and possibly later explored. When these arcs are embedded in a GROUP, the alternative will not be created, thus saving time and space. As a result, it will not have to be explored, possibly saving more time. A warning should be included here that the GROUP arc can reject sentences that might otherwise be accepted. In our example, *very* may be needed to get out of the state REST-OF-S/2. In this respect, the GROUP arc is a departure from the original ATN philosophy that arcs should be independent. However, for some applications, the increased efficiency can be critical.

The other change to the compiling system (for the semantic grammar application) dealt with the preprocessing operations. The preprocessing facilities described in the last section included (*a*) lexical analysis to extract word endings; (*b*) a substitution mechanism to expand abbreviations, delete noise words, and canonicalize synonyms; (*c*) dictionary retrieval routines; and (*d*) a compound word mechanism to collapse multiword phrases. For the SOPHIE application we added the ability to use the INTERLISP spelling correction routines and the ability to derive word definitions from SOPHIE's semantic net. The extraction of def-

initions from the semantic network for part names and node names
reduces the size of the dictionary and simplifies the operation of changing
circuits. In addition, a mechanism called MULTIPLES was developed
that permits string substitution within the input. This is similar to the
notion of compounding, but differs in that a compound rule creates an
alternative lexical item, whereas the multiple rule creates a different
lexical item. After the application of a compound rule, there is an additional edge in the input chart; after a multiple rule, the effect is the same as
if the user had typed in a different string.

Fuzziness

The one aspect of the LISP implementation that has not been incorporated into the ATN framework is fuzziness, the ability to ignore words in
the input. Although we have not worked out the details, the nondeter-
minism provided by ATNs lends itself to an interesting approach. In a
one-process—recursive descent—implementation, the rule that checks
for a word must decide (with information passed down from higher rules)
whether to try skipping a word, or give up. The critical information that is
not available when this decision has to be made is whether or not there is
another parse that would use that word. In the ATN, it is possible to
suspend a parse and come back to it after all other paths have been tried.
Fuzziness could be implemented so that rather than skip a word and
continue, it can skip a word and suspend, waiting for the other parses to
fail or suspend. The end effect may well be that sentences are allowed to
get fuzzier because there is no danger of missing the correct parse.

Comparison of Results

The original motivation for changing to the ATN was its perspicuity. As
Winograd (1973) has pointed out, simple grammars are perspicuous in
almost any formalism; complex grammars are still complex in any formalism. We found the ATN formalism much easier to think in, write in,
and debug. The examples of redundant processing that were presented
earlier in this section were discovered while converting to ATN. For a
gross comparison on conciseness, the ATN grammar requires 70% fewer
characters to express than the LISP version.

The efficiency results were surprising. Table 10.1 gives comparison
timings between the LISP version and the ATN compiled version. As can
be seen, the ATN version takes less than twice as much time. This was
pleasantly counterintuitive, since we expected the LISP version to be
much faster because of the amount of hand optimization that had been

done while encoding the grammar rules. In presenting the comparison timing, it should be mentioned that there are three differences between the two systems that tended to favor the ATN version. (The exact extent to which each of these differences contributed is difficult to gather statistics on because of the INTERLISP block compiler that gains efficiency by hiding internal workings. The exact contribution of each could certainly be determined but was not deemed worth the effort.) One difference is the lack of fuzziness in the ATN version. The LISP version spent time testing words other than the current word, looking ahead to see whether it was possible to skip this word, which was not done in the ATN version. The second is the creation of categories for words during the preprocessing in the ATN version that reduced the amount of time spent accessing the semantic net and hence reduced the time required to perform a category membership test in the ATN system. The third is the simplification of the grammar and increase in the amount of bottom-up processing that could be done because of the ambiguity allowed in the input chart. In our estimation, the lack of fuzziness is the only difference that may have had a significant effect, and this can be included explicitly in the ATN in places where it is critical, by using TST arcs and suspend actions, without a noticeable increase in processing time. In conclusion, we are very pleased with the results of the compiled semntantic ATN and feel that the ATN compiler makes the ATN formalism computationally efficient enough to be used in real systems.

TABLE 10.1
Comparison of ATN versus LISP Implementation

Times (in seconds) are "prepass" + "parsing."

1. *What is the output voltage?*
   LISP $-$ .024 + .018 = .042
   ATN $-$ .048 + .033 = .081
2. *What is the voltage between there and the base of Q6?*
   LISP $-$ .038 + .039 = .077
   ATN $-$ .090 + .046 = .136
3. *Q5?*
   LISP $-$ .010 + .046 = .056
   ATN $-$ .013 + .060 = .073
4. *What is the output voltage when the voltage control is set to .5?*
   LISP $-$ .045 + .038 = .083
   ATN $-$ .096 + .048 = .144
5. *If Q6 has an open emitter and a shorted base collector junction, what happens to the voltage between its base and the junction of the voltage limiting section and the voltage reference source?*
   LISP $-$ .206 + .188 = .394
   ATN $-$ .259 + .090 = .349

EXPERIENCES WITH SOPHIE AND
TECHNIQUES FOR HANDLING PROBLEMS

When we began developing a natural-language processor for an instructional environment, we knew it had to be (*a*) fast; (*b*) habitable; (*c*) self-tutoring; and (*d*) able to deal with ambiguity. The basic conclusion that has arisen from the work presented here is that it is possible to satisfy these constraints. The notion of semantic grammar presented earlier provides a paradigm for organizing the knowledge required in the understanding process that permits efficient parsing. In addition, semantic grammar aids the habitability by providing insights into a useful class of dialogue constructs, and permits efficient handling of such phenomena as pronominalizations and ellipses. The need for a better formalism for expressing semantic grammars led to the use of augmented transition networks. The ability of the ATN-expressed semantic grammar to satisfy the above stated requirements is demonstrated in the natural language front-end for the SOPHIE system.

A point that needs to be stressed is that the SOPHIE system has been (and is being) used by uninitiated students in experiments to determine the pedagogical effectiveness of its environment. Although much has been learned about the problems of using a natural-language interface, these experiments were not debugging sessions for the natural-language component. The natural-language component has unquestionably reached a state at which it can be conveniently used to facilitate learning about electronics. In this section, we will describe the experiences of students using the natural-language component, and present some ideas on handling erroneous inputs.

Impressions, Experiences, and Observations

As mentioned in the introduction, students are very unskilled at paraphrasing their thoughts. This same inability to perform linguistic paraphrase carried over to the actual interaction with SOPHIE via terminal. Whenever the system did not accept a query, there was a marked delay before the student tried again. Sometimes the student would abandon a line of questioning completely. At the same time, data collected over many sessions indicated that there was no standard—canonical—way to phrase a question. Table 10.2 provides some examples of the range of phrasings used by students to ask for the voltage at a node. As Table 10.2 shows, students are likely to conceive of their questions in many ways and to express each of these conceptions in any of several phrasings. Yet other experiences indicate that they lack the ability to

TABLE 10.2
Sample Student Inputs

The following are some of the input lines typed by students with the intent of discovering the voltage at a node in the circuit.

What is the voltage at node 1?
What is the voltage at the base of Q5?
How much voltage at N10?
And what is the voltage at N1?
N9?
V at the neg side of C6?
V11 is?
What is the voltage from the base of transistor Q5 to ground?
What V at N16?
Coll. of Q5?
Node 16 Voltage?
What is the voltage at Pin 1?
Output?

convert easily to another conceptualization or phrasing. Since the nonacceptance of questions creates a major interruption in the student's thought process, the acceptance of many different paraphrases is critical to maintaining flow in the student's problem solving.

Another interesting phenomenon that occurred during sessions was the change in the linguistic behavior of the students as they used the system. Initially, queries were stated as complete English questions, generally stated in templates created by the students from the written examples of sessions that we had given them. If they needed to ask something that did not exactly fit one of their templates, they would try a minor variant. As they became more familiar with the mode of interaction, they began to use abbreviations, to leave out parts of their questions, and, in general, to assume that the system was following their interaction. After 5 hours of experience with the system, almost all of one student's queries contained abbreviations and one in six depended on the context established by previous statements.

Feedback—When the Grammar Fails

From our experiences with students using SOPHIE, we have been impressed with the importance of providing feedback to unacceptable inputs—doing something constructive when the system does not understand an input. Though it may appear that in a completely habitable system all inputs would be understood, no system has ever attained this goal, and none will in the foreseeable future. To be natural to a naive user, an intelligent system should also act intelligently when it fails. The first step toward having a system fail intelligently is the identification of possible areas of error. In student's use of the SOPHIE system, we have found the following types of errors to be common:

1. Spelling errors and mistypings—*Shortt the CE og Q3 and opwn its base; What is the vbe Q5?*
2. Inadvertent omissions—*What is the BE of Q5?* (The user left out the quantity to measure. Note that in other domains this is a well-formed question.)
3. Slight misconceptions that are predictable—*What is the output of transistor Q3?* (the output of a transistor is not defined); *What is the current thru Node 1?* (nodes are places where voltage is measured and may have numerous wires associated with them); *What is R9?* (R9 is a resistor); *Is Q5 conducting?* (The laboratory section of SOPHIE gives information that is directly available from a real lab such as currents and voltages.)
4. Gross misconceptions whose underlying meaning is well beyond designed system capabilities—*Make the output voltage 30 volts; Turn on the power supply and tell me how the unit functions; What time is it?*

In the remainder of this section, we will discuss the solutions used in the SOPHIE system to provide feedback.

The use of a spelling correction algorithm (borrowed from INTER-LISP) has proven to be a satisfactory solution to typos and misspellings. During one student's session, spelling correction was required on, and resulted in proper understanding of, 10% of the questions. The major failings of the INTERLISP algorithm are the restriction on the size of the target set of correct words (time increases linearly with the number of words) and its failure to correct run-on words. (The time required to determine whether a word may be two—possibly misspelled—words run together increases very quickly with the length of the word and the number of possibly correct words. With no context to restrict the possible list of words, the computation involved is prohibitive.) A potential solution to both shortcomings would be to use the context of the parser to reduce the possibilities when it reaches the unknown word. Because of the nature of the grammar, this would allow semantic context as well as syntactic context to be used.

Of course, the use of any spelling correction procedure has some dangers. A word that is spelled correctly but that the system does not know may be changed through spelling correction to a word the system does know. For example, if the system does not know the word *top* but does know *stop,* a user's command to *top everything* can be disastrously misunderstood. For this reason, words like *stop* are not spelling-corrected.

Our solution to predictable misconceptions is to recognize them and give error messages that are directed at correcting the misconception. We are currently using two different methods of recognition. One is to loosen up the grammar so that it accepts plausible but meaningless sentences. This technique provides the procedural specialists called by the plausible parse enough context to make relevant comments. For example, the concept of current through a node is accepted by the grammar even though it is meaningless. The specialist that performs measurements must then check its arguments and provide feedback if necessary:

```
≫ WHAT IS THE CURRENT THRU NODE 4?
The current thru a node is not meaningful since by Kirchoff's law the
sum of the currents thru any node is zero. Currents can be measured
thru parts (e.g., CURRENT THRU C6) or terminals (e.g., CURRENT THRU
THE COLLECTOR OF Q2).
```

Notice that the response to the question presents some examples of how to measure the currents along wires that lead into the mentioned node. Examples of questions that will be accepted and are relevant to the student's needs are among the best possible feedback.

The second method of recognizing common misconceptions is to "key" feedback off single words or groups of words. In the following examples, the keys are *or* and *turned on.* Notice that the response presents a general characterization of the violated limitations as well as suggestions for alternative lines of attack.

```
≫ COULD Q1 OR Q2 BE SHORTED?
I can handle only one question, hypothesis, etc. at a time. The fact
that you say OR indicates that you may be trying to express two
concepts in the same sentence. Maybe you can break your statement
into two or more simple ones.
≫ IS THE CURRENT LIMITING TRANSISTOR TURNED ON?
The laboratory section of SOPHIE is designed to provide the same
elementary measurements that would be available in a real lab. If
you want to determine the state of a transistor, measure the perti-
nent currents and voltages.
```

These methods of coping with errors have proved to be very helpful. However, they require that all of the misconceptions be predicted and programmed for in advance. This limitation makes them inapplicable to novel situations.

The remaining severe problems a user has stem from omissions and major misconceptions. After a simple omission, the user may not see that he has left anything out and may conclude that the system does not know that concept or phrasing of that concept. For example, when the user types *What is the BE of Q5* instead of *What is the VBE of Q5?*, he may decide that it is unacceptable because the system does not allow *VBE* as an abbreviation of *base emitter voltage*. For conceptual errors, the user may waste a lot of time and energy attempting several rephrasings of his query, none of which can be understood because the system does not know the concept the user is trying to express. For example, no matter how it is phrased, the system will not understand *Make the output voltage 30 volts* because measurements cannot be directly changed; only controls and specifications of parts can be changed.

The feedback necessary to correct both of these classes of errors must identify any concepts in the statement that are understood and suggest the range of things that can be done to–with these concepts. This may help the user see an omission or may suggest alternative conceptualizations that get at the same information (for example, to change the output voltage indirectly by changing one of the controls) or at least provide enough information for the user to decide when to quit.

FUTURE DIRECTIONS

Further Research Areas

The SOPHIE semantic grammar system is designed for a particular context—trouble-shooting—within a particular domain—electronics. It represents the compilation of those pieces of knowledge that are general (linguistic) together with specific domain-dependent knowledge. In its present form, it is unclear which knowledge belongs to which area. The development of semantic grammars for other applications and extensions to the semantic grammar mechanism to include other understood linguistic phenomena will clarify this distinction.

Although the work presented in this chapter has dealt mostly with one area of application, the notion of semantic grammar as a method of integrating knowledge into the parsing process has wider applicability. Two alternative applications of the technique have been completed. One deals with simple sentences in the domain of attribute blocks (Brown & Burton, 1978). Though the sub-language accepted in the attribute-blocks environment is very simple, it is noteworthy that within the semantic grammar paradigm, a simple grammar was quickly developed that greatly improved the flexibility of the input language. The other completed application deals with questions about the editing system NLS (Grignetti *et al.*,

1975). In this application, most questions dealt with editing commands and their arguments, and fit nicely into the case-frame notion mentioned in the fourth section. The case-frame use of semantic grammar is being considered for, and may have its greatest impact on, command languages. Command languages are typically case-centered around the command name that requires additional arguments (its cases). The combination of the semantic classification provided by the semantic grammar and the representation of case rules permitted by ATNs should go a long way toward reducing the rigidity of complex command languages such as those required for message-processing systems. The combination should also be a good representation for natural-language systems in domains where it is possible to develop a strong underlying conceptual space, such as management information systems (Malhotra, 1975).

Conclusions

In the course of this chapter, we have described the evolution of a natural-language processor capable of using complex linguistic knowledge. The guiding strand has been the utilization of semantic information to produce efficient natural-language processors. There were several highlights that represent noteworthy points in the spectrum of useful natural language systems. The procedural encoding technique with fuzziness (third section) allows simple natural-language input to be accepted without introducing the complexity of a new formalism. Encoding the rules as procedures allows flexible control of the fuzziness, and the semantic nature of the rules provides the correct places to take advantage of the flexibility. As the language covered by the system becomes more complex, the additional burden of a grammar formalism will more than pay for itself in terms of ease of development and reduction in complexity. The augmented transition network (ATN) compiling system allows for the consideration of the ATN formalism by reducing its run-time cost, making it comparable to a direct procedural encoding. The natural language front end now used by SOPHIE is constructed by compiling a semantic ATN. As the linguistic complexity of the language accepted by the system increases, the need for more syntactic knowledge in the grammar becomes greater. Unfortunately, this often works at cross-purposes with the semantic character of the grammar. It would be nice to have a general grammar for English syntax that could be used to preprocess sentences; however, one is not forthcoming. A general solution to the problem of incorporating semantics with the current state of incomplete knowledge of syntax remains an open research problem. In the foreseeable future, any system will have to be an engineering trade-off between complexity and generality on one hand and efficiency and habitability on the other. We have presented several techniques that are viable options in this trade-off.

REFERENCES

Bobrow, R. J., & Brown, J. S. Systematic understanding: Synthesis, analysis, and contingent knowledge in specialized understanding systems. In D. Bobrow & A. Collins (Eds.), *Representation and understanding: Studies in cognitive science.* New York: Academic Press, 1975.

Brown, J. S. Uses of artificial intelligence and advanced computer technology in education. In *Computers and communications.* New York: Academic Press, 1977.

Brown, J. S., & Burton, R. R. Multiple representations of knowledge for tutorial reasoning. In D. Bobrow & A. Collins (Eds.), *Representation and understanding: Studies in cognitive science.* New York: Academic Press, 1975.

Brown, J. S., & Burton, R. R. A paradigmatic example of an artificially intelligent instructional system. *International Journal of Man Machine Studies, 1978, 10,* 323–340.

Brown, J. S., Burton, R. R., & Bell, A. G. SOPHIE: A step towards a reactive learning environment. *International Journal of Man Machine Studies, 1975, 7,* 675–696.

Brown, J. S., Rubinstein, R., & Burton, R. R. *Reactive learning environment for computer assisted electronics instruction* (BBN Report No. 3314). Bolt Beranek and Newman Inc., Cambridge, Mass., October 1976.

Bruce, B. C. Case systems for natural language. *Artificial Intelligence,* December 1975, *5,* 327–360.

Burton, R. R. *Semantic grammar: An engineering technique for constructing natural language understanding systems* (BBN Report No. 3453, ICAI Report No. 3). Cambridge, Mass.: Bolt Beranek and Newman Inc., December 1976.

Burton, R. R., & Brown, J. S. A tutoring and student modelling paradigm for gaming environments. *Proceedings for the Symposium on Computer Science and Education,* February 1976,

Burton, R. R., & Brown, J. S. An investigation of computer coaching for informal learning activities. *International Journal of Man Machine Studies,* in press.

Carr, B., & Goldstein, I. *Overlays: A theory of modelling for computer aided instruction* (AI Memo 406). Cambridge: Massachusetts Institute of Technology, February 1977.

Charniak, E. *Toward a model of children's story comprehension* (MIT—TR-266). Cambridge: Artificial Intelligence Laboratory, Massachusetts Institute of Technology, 1972.

Chomsky, N. *Syntactic structures.* The Hague: Mouton and Co., 1957.

Grignetti, M. C., Gould, L., Hausmann, C. L., Bell, A. G., Harris, G., & Passafiume, J. *Mixed-initiative tutorial system to aid users of the on-line system (NLS)* (BBN Report No. 2969). Cambridge, Mass.: Bolt Beranek and Newman Inc., November 1974.

Grignetti, M. C., Hausmann, C. L., & Gould, L. An intelligent on-line assistant and tutor— NLS-SCHOLAR. *National Computer Conference,* 1975, *44,* 775–781.

Malhotra, A. *Design criteria for a knowledge-based English language system for management: An experimental analysis.* Unpublished doctoral dissertation, Sloan School of Management, Massachusetts Institute of Technology, 1975.

Marcus, M. Diagnosis as a notion of grammar. In R. Schank & B. L. Nash-Webber (Eds.), *Proceedings of a Workshop on Theoretical Issues in Natural Language Processing,* 1975, *1,* 6–10.

Miller, R. B. Response time in man–computer conversational transactions. In *AFIPS Conference Proceedings* (Fall Joint Computer Conference). Washington: Thompson Book Company, 1968.

Teitelman, W. Towards a programming laboratory. In D. Walker (Ed.), *Proceedings of the International Joint Conference on Artificial Intelligence,* May 1969.

Teitelman, W. *INTERLISP reference manual.* Palo Alto, Calif.: Xerox Palo Alto Research Center, 1974.

Watt, W. C. Habitability. *American documentation,* 1968, *19,* 338–351.

Winograd, T. *Understanding natural language.* New York: Academic Press, 1973.

Woods, W. A. Transition network grammars for natural language analysis. *Communications of the ACM,* 1970, *13,* 591–606.

Woods, W. A. An experimental parsing system for transition network grammars. In R. Rustin (Ed.), *Natural language processing.* New York: Algorithmics Press, 1973.

Woods, W. A., Kaplan, R. M., & Nash-Webber, B. *The lunar sciences natural language information system: final report* (BBN Report #2378). Cambridge, Mass.: Bolt, Beranek and Newman, Inc., 1972.

Author Index

Numbers in italics refer to the pages on which the complete references are listed.

315

Subject Index

TEXAS A&M UNIVERSITY TEXARKANA